797,885 Books

are available to read at

Forgotten Books

www.ForgottenBooks.com

Forgotten Books' App
Available for mobile, tablet & eReader

ISBN 978-1-331-85131-8
PIBN 10242089

This book is a reproduction of an important historical work. Forgotten Books uses state-of-the-art technology to digitally reconstruct the work, preserving the original format whilst repairing imperfections present in the aged copy. In rare cases, an imperfection in the original, such as a blemish or missing page, may be replicated in our edition. We do, however, repair the vast majority of imperfections successfully; any imperfections that remain are intentionally left to preserve the state of such historical works.

Forgotten Books is a registered trademark of FB &c Ltd.
Copyright © 2017 FB &c Ltd.
FB &c Ltd, Dalton House, 60 Windsor Avenue, London, SW19 2RR.
Company number 08720141. Registered in England and Wales.

For support please visit www.forgottenbooks.com

1 MONTH OF FREE READING

at

www.ForgottenBooks.com

By purchasing this book you are eligible for one month membership to ForgottenBooks.com, giving you unlimited access to our entire collection of over 700,000 titles via our web site and mobile apps.

To claim your free month visit:
www.forgottenbooks.com/free242089

* Offer is valid for 45 days from date of purchase. Terms and conditions apply.

English
Français
Deutsche
Italiano
Español
Português

www.forgottenbooks.com

Mythology Photography **Fiction**
Fishing Christianity **Art** Cooking
Essays Buddhism Freemasonry
Medicine **Biology** Music **Ancient Egypt** Evolution Carpentry Physics
Dance Geology **Mathematics** Fitness
Shakespeare **Folklore** Yoga Marketing
Confidence Immortality Biographies
Poetry **Psychology** Witchcraft
Electronics Chemistry History **Law**
Accounting **Philosophy** Anthropology
Alchemy Drama Quantum Mechanics
Atheism Sexual Health **Ancient History**
Entrepreneurship Languages Sport
Paleontology Needlework Islam
Metaphysics Investment Archaeology
Parenting Statistics Criminology
Motivational

THE
AUTHENTICITY
OF THE
GOSPEL - HISTORY
JUSTIFIED:

AND THE

Truth of the CHRISTIAN Revelation

DEMONSTRATED,

From the Laws and Constitution of Human Nature.

VOLUME II.

By the late *ARCHIBALD CAMPBELL*, D. D.
Regius Professor of Divinity and Ecclesiastical History in the University of St. *Andrew*'s.

EDINBURGH:
Printed by HAMILTON, BALFOUR, and NEILL.
M, DCC, LIX.

CONTENTS.

Pag.

SECT. V.
And, as the Apostles were men governed by the common Principles of human Nature, most certain it is, that, in the Propagation of the Gospel, they were animated by some powerful prevailing Motive, i. e. by the assured Prospect of some Good, either in this or in the other World, thereby to be acquired.   1

SECT. VI.
The Apostles themselves pretend, that the particular Good they had in view was nothing of this World, but a happy Immortality in a future State: And in those their Pretensions, if there is nothing real, they must have been either Impostors or Enthusiasts.   10

SECT. VII.
In the Case of Imposture, all their Views must have terminated in something worldly; but their Doctrines clearly demonstrate, that the Good that served as the prevailing Motive, to support them in the Discharge of their Ministry, had nothing in it of this World.   13

SECT. VIII.
Nor can Dr. Tindal's Objections to the Morality of the Gospel, which are all of them ill founded, afford any the least Ground for a Charge of Imposture against them.   23

SECT. IX.
And not only from their Doctrines, but from every other Branch of their conduct, it is apparent, that the Apostles were no Impostors, were animated by no worldly Motive whatsoever, which is farther made good by demonstrating the following Particulars.   48

VOL. II.   b   SECT.

CONTENTS.

SECT. XXI.
Nor can their Sentiments concerning the Person and Kingdom of Jesus Christ, in any Measure, expose them to the Charge of Enthusiasm. 259

SECT. XXII.
As little can this Imputation be fixed upon them, from what they publish to the World, concerning the Death, and the Resurrection, and the Ascension of Jesus Christ. So that, in all Instances, the Apostles were absolutely free from Enthusiasm. 273

SECT. XXIII.
And, by what Arguments our Free-thinkers can vindicate Socrates *from Enthusiasm; by the same may one justify the Apostles.* 304

SECT. XXIV.
For Deists must know, Socrates *claims a divine Mission: Nor can it greatly hurt those Gentlemen to reflect, that, in the Case of this extraordinary Man, Providence seems to have taught the World, that, to introduce true Religion, and establish it in the World, unassisted Reason is altogether insufficient.* 312

SECT. XXV.
Upon the Whole, the general Conclusion is here deduced and illustrated; shewing, that, in the Propagation of the Gospel, the Apostles were, most certainly, animated from Heaven. 317

SECT. XXVI.
And that the Apostles were commissioned from Heaven to propagate the Gospel among Mankind, is strongly confirmed by the divine Efficacy that appears in the amazing Success of their Ministry. 327

THE TRUTH OF THE CHRISTIAN REVELATION.

SECT. V.

In the Propagation of the Gospel, the Apostles were certainly animated by the assured Prospect of some good thereby to be acquired.

HAVING elsewhere (*a*) made it manifest, I hope, beyond controversy, that mankind, of themselves, are not able to discover the being and perfections of God, nor yet the immortality of human souls, or a future state of rewards and punishments; and therefore, that the knowledge mankind now have of these essential articles of natural religion, must have come originally from supernatural revelation; it seems naturally to follow,

---

(*a*) The Necessity of Revelation.

follow, that, since the Gospel of *Jesus Christ* does expressly teach those particular doctrines, one cannot but apprehend, that this is a strong presumption of its divinity, or that the Authors of it had their informations from heaven.

Certain it is, that, in those days wherein the Gospel first appeared, all the Heathen world were every-where quite destitute of the knowledge of God; nor were their learned men and Philosophers then making any nearer approaches towards a discovery, than they had been doing in former ages. And when, amidst all this darkness and ignorance, a few illiterate men, void of all human improvements, came to strike out a glorious light that clears human understanding, and brings us in view of an infinite mind, and of an after-life and immortality; to what, I say, can one ascribe their having been able to impart this great knowledge to mankind, but to those informations they must have received from heaven?

It is true, the first Publishers of the Gospel were of the *Jewish* nation, and may therefore, perhaps, be understood to have derived their knowledge of those articles from human instruction. But, as the *Jewish* religion seems justly intitled to divinity, from its teaching those religious truths, that no where else were to be found in the world; so the Authors of the Gospel having laid the foundation of their institution in these same principles, and, without confining themselves to their own nation, publishing to the whole world a Catholic religion, a divine system of doctrines, free from all absurdity, idolatry, and superstition, and in its whole structure directly tending to the glory of God, to the present well-being and the future happiness of mankind, one is strongly tempted to think, that the Apostles must

have

have been employed from heaven in this service. And indeed they tell us themselves, that *God who commanded light to shine out of darkness, had shined into their hearts, to give them,* and to enable them to give to others, *the knowledge of God through Christ.* And, say they, *We have this treasure in earthen vessels, that the excellency of the power may appear to be of God, and not of us* (*b*). From whence the Apostles give us to understand, that the power that enabled them to reveal the Gospel, and that supported them in propagating it thro' the world, was none of their own, but came to them from above. And the making this clearly out will demonstrate the truth of the Christian Revelation.

In this argument we look upon the Apostles as the religious Instructors of mankind; And under this character the power to be considered in their case, and which we are to shew, is supernatural, is made up of these two particulars:

In the *first* place, it signifies " that improve-
" ment and comprehension of mind, or that inward
" light and knowledge whereby they discerned
" those glorious truths explained in the Gospel;
" and particularly apprehended the being and per-
" fections of an infinite mind, and a future state of
" rewards and punishments at his direction and ap-
" pointment; together with a noble system of mo-
" ral duties, every way suited to the glory of God,
" and to the perfection of human nature." This was the power with which, in fact, as we learn from their writings, the Apostles were endowed: And from this knowledge they were qualified to teach mankind all the essential articles of natural religion. To have employed *Pythagoras, Aristotle, Cicero,*

(*b*) 2 Cor. iv. 6, 7.

Cicero, any of the antient Philosophers, in this ministry;——so disproportionate and unequal were their abilities, that they could not have been left to their own understanding, but must have been instructed, beyond all the discoveries that ever man, in the exercise of his rational faculties, was found capable of acquiring. What then shall we say of a few Fisher-men, without improvement, void of instruction?—They discover those principles of religion wherein they go beyond the farthest reach of human reason and philosophy, and surpass the highest attainments of the greatest Philosophers! From the *Inquiry*, we have elsewhere made, *into the Extent of human Powers, with respect to Matters of Religion*, one is forced to conclude, that, without question, *God who commanded light to shine out of darkness, hath shined into the minds of the Apostles, and given them the knowledge of the glory of God*; which leads us to apprehend, that the doctrine of the Gospel must be held a divine revelation.

But, not to insist upon this notion of power that consists in the perception of truth, whereby the Apostles were enabled to teach mankind a system of religion, infinitely superior to what all the Philosophers together were able to have collected, and wherein they appear to have been under the immediate influence of heaven; it is to be considered,

In the *next* place, That how well soever a company of men, from their knowledge of things, may be qualified to instruct the rest of the world; 'tis further necessary that some power be applied to their active faculties, that shall be able to excite and support them in propagating their instructions. And indeed such is the temper of the human constitution, that having such particular springs of action laid in our nature, as there would happen an universal

versal stagnation all over our lives, and we should for ever lie quite still and motionless, were not those springs sensibly touched; so, when they come to be affected or struck upon, we are then set a-going and exert ourselves in action, less or more vigorously, in proportion to the force of the impulse they have received (*c*) Now, this impulse that awakens our passions, the great springs of action, or that communicates a motion to our active faculties, is what I call the power that animates and supports a man in the prosecution of that design wherein he is engaged. And whereas this impulse comes to be derived to our passions, or to the active faculties of our nature, from certain views or motives wherein we apprehend the good or evil that shall befal us, as we chuse or refuse to engage in such a particular enterprise, those motives are what we likewise call the power whereby, in any pursuit, we are at first excited, and afterwards all along sustained and fortified.

So that, in order to satisfy ourselves about the pretensions of the Apostles, or whether they were supernaturally employed in the propagation of the Gospel, I shall here examine what that power, or those motives were, that gave a commanding impulse to their active faculties, and that carried them on with firmness and constancy in the discharge of their ministry. And, that the Reader may bring things home to himself, and judge of the conduct of the Apostles, as he is conscious he would act himself in the like circumstances, I shall proceed upon the inward frame, or the essential principles of human nature. And one should think, that a

fairer

(*c*) Quid enim interest, motu animi sublato, non dico inter hominem et pecudem, sed inter hominem et saxum, aut truncum, aut quidvis generis ejusdem? Cic. de Amic. cap. 13.

fairer argument for the truth of Christianity cannot well be proposed, than this which is founded in an appeal to every man's own consciousness.

As I have just now hinted, no man can be excited to action without having an impulse derived to his passions, or without the influence of some motives that awaken his active faculties. And, in every man's experience, I suppose, it is felt, that the great and universal motive that in all instances prevails over us, in some good, either real or imaginary, we have the prospect of attaining to, by means of that course of action wherein we may happen to be engaged. Of this the most disinterested and self-denied, the most rigorous Mystic, must be sensible, how much soever they may pretend the contrary: Nor can the constitution of Beings, capable of pleasure and pain, ever suffer it to be otherwise. For, what is this desire after good whereby all mankind are carried, but the principle of self-preservation putting forth itself? A principle interwoven in our inward make by the first Framer of all things, and so essential to every thinking, sensible nature, that it is much more absurd and impossible in the moral world, for rational Beings to enter into the pursuit of any action or design without being thereto moved or attracted by the prospect of some good, real or apparent, than it is in the natural world for heavy bodies not to move or be attracted towards their centre of gravity (*d*). And,

As the desire of good, of some sort or other, is the great spring of every human enterprize; so, from the enjoyments one foregoes, the hardships he encounters, and the eagerness and steadiness of the pursuit,

---

(*d*) See my *Inquiry into the Original of Moral Virtue*, where this principle of self-preservation is fully explained.

pursuit, we may easily compute what is the value of that particular good, which a man may be supposed to have in view. I confess, we cannot after this manner determine the real value of the good itself: But from hence, I say, it appears clearly, what is the rate which the man himself, who pursues it, must be understood, in his notion of things, to set upon it. Thus, if in the pursuit of such an object, people appear cool and languid, if they do not much care to disturb their present peace and tranquillity, to forfeit any of their enjoyments, or to expose themselves to any hazard for the sake of it; we cannot but reckon that their esteem of that good (however valuable in itself) is very low, and that they judge the price would be too high should they purchase it at the expence of other things they enjoy, or that it would not overbalance the suffering of any great loss or uneasiness.

Whereas, if, for the sake of that good I have in view, I conceive the deepest concern possible, if I make no account of my reputation, of my dearest relatives of my fortune, or life, or of any peace, or pleasure, or advantage, I might otherwise comfortably enjoy, but involve myself in the greatest difficulties, the heaviest reproach and infamy, the hardest poverty, and the cruellest deaths and persecutions; I say, if, for the sake of that good I have in view, I neglect and despise all the pleasures and profits of life, and undergo all sorts of calamities; then is it manifest, that the value I set upon it is greater than that by which I rate all my other present and future comforts, and that, in my estimation, the severest miseries in which it can involve me, do not render it too dear a purchase. So that this good to me evidently out-bids all other enjoyments whatsoever, and powerfully overbears all obstructions how
dreadful

dreadful foever, that can be thought to interrupt my purfuit of it. Upon which it muft be counted, that I regard my attaining to that particular good, as the greateft happinefs I can hope to arrive at; and that, in my judgment, it is more neceffary to my well-being than all other things the moft valuable and agreeable, or that I had better ceafe to be, or not to exift at all, than to continue in being without it. And if, notwithftanding the fierceft oppofitions, and the moft terrible difcouragements I can poffibly meet withal, I ftill go on purfuing after this good with an ardent zeal, an unfhaken refolution and conftancy, and with an open joy and triumph, while I am confcious I am advancing towards it; this, methinks, puts it beyond difpute, that I count all things but *lofs for the excellency thereof*, and but *dung that I may win it* ; or that the value I fet upon it is infinite. From all which it appears,

When we find the Apoftles employed in the propagation of the Gofpel, we muft neceffarily apprehend, they were determined to undertake and purfue this mighty defign, from the profpect of fome good, which, by means of this miniftry, they hoped to attain to. And, when we further confider, what they fo refolutely and cheerfully did forego and fuffer in the profecution of this fervice, we muft likewife neceffarily conclude, that the good they had in view was not mean and inconfiderable, but of the laft confequence, fo far as they were able to judge; and of the greateft moment and importance. In truth, 'tis abfolutely unimaginable, how men could forfeit all the eafe, and ftrip themfelves fo intirely naked of all the comforts they had in life; and look fuch dreadful dangers in the face; and venture upon them, and fuftain them

with

with such bravery and firmness, and still be pushing on their way through the fiercest oppositions with such noble joy and triumph; I say, 'tis beyond imagination, how the Apostles could have acted this part, without being animated and supported by a consciousness they were engaged in the pursuit of a good, which they were fully satisfied was infinitely preferable to all other enjoyments, and which they were well persuaded was worthy to be purchased at the highest expence possible.

Thus the essential principles of human nature oblige us to confess, that, in the propagation of the Gospel, the Apostles had in view a very considerable good, which they must have looked upon as the great reward of their Ministry. And that this good applied to their minds, or exerting its force upon their active faculties, was the great power whereby they were sustained and fortified in the prosecution of their daring attempt, will, I doubt not, be agreed on by every body. So that we shall now inquire, what sort of good, or of power that was, from whence the Apostles had a commanding impulse derived to their passions,' whereby they were all along egged on, in the face of mortal dangers, to propagate the doctrines of Christianity.

SECT. VI.

The particular Good the Apostles pretend to have in in View, is a happy Immortality. And in their Pretensions, if there is nothing real, they must have been either Impostors or Enthusiasts.

WHEN we take into our thoughts the whole compass of those goods whereby human minds can be affected, it cannot but be allowed, that that good which the Apostles had in view must either lie in something present, and to terminate in this world; or it must be situated beyond the grave, and consist in the enjoyments of a future state of existence. Of this I am as certain, as of the truth of any Proposition in *Euclid*. And this being the undoubted case; to justify the character of the Apostles, or to make it appear that they were commissioned from heaven to propagate the Gospel to mankind, it seems only necessary to shew, that in the prosecution of this Ministry, the Apostles were steadily animated by the assured hopes of a glorious immortality, with which, they were persuaded, the Lord God would hereafter reward them, for their faithfully discharging this service, wherein, by his authority, they were employed. In this light the Apostles appear to the world; and the case of each of them is the same with this of the Apostle *Paul* (a). *I have,* (says he) *fought a good fight, I have finished my course, I have kept the faith: Henceforth there is laid up for me a crown of righteousness, which the Lord the righteous Judge shall give me at that day,* the great day of retribution.

(a) 2 Tim. iv. 7, 8.

retribution. And that the Apostles were thus animated from heaven, and uniformly supported in the propagation of the Gospel, I propose to make good in the following *Sections*.

Indeed, if any man will make it appear, that the great power that excited and fortified the Apostles in the prosecution of their grand project, was so far from being *a crown of glory that fadeth not away, eternal in the heavens*, that it was only some worldly consideration, some of the lower gratifications of this present life; and that, in spite of their high pretensions, they had certainly no ambition beyond the riches, or honours, or pleasures of this mortal state; I say, if any thing of this nature can be made out against the Apostles, I will then agree to reckon them so many base designing Impostors, and that the Gospel they taught the world, as the mind and will of God, is a gross imposition on mankind. Or,

If, upon granting that the Apostles seem indeed to be aspiring after a glorious immortality, and to have had no doubt in themselves of arriving, in another world, at a crown of righteousness as the reward of their Ministry; it shall nevertheless be made appear, that all their assurance of this nature was the mere confidence of an over-heated fancy, and that they only took their own warm imaginations, for the powerful impressions of heaven, stirring them up to publish the Gospel to mankind; I say, if it shall be made appear, that these ambitious hopes with which the Apostles seem to have been animated, are all thus vain and groundless, the pure ravings of a visionary brain, I will then agree to reckon them so many poor deluded Enthusiasts, and that the Gospel they taught can be no divine revelation. But,

If

If neither the one nor the other can be possibly made out against the Apostles; I say, if no man has it in his power to make good the charge either of Imposture, or of Enthusiasm, in the character of the Apostles, I would gladly know whether we are not bound to conclude, that those Teachers of mankind were neither dishonest nor mistaken in those assurances they pretended to have had from Heaven, of their coming to future glory, honour, and immortality, as the reward of their ministry; and consequently, that the Gospel, which they were thus animated to propagate to the world, is a divine revelation? For my part, I have not sagacity to comprehend, to what other conclusion one can come in the case of the Apostles. If, in the character they assume, they are neither Impostors nor Enthusiasts, one should think the next step unavoidable, they are Teachers sent of God to instruct mankind. And,

To shew, in the *first* place, that the Apostles were no Impostors, designing some base end under the credit of a pretended commission from Heaven, I shall endeavour to explain, that the great power whereby they were supported in the propagation of the Gospel was no earthly consideration, no impulse derived to their passions from any of this world's allurements. Upon which, as we go along, let the Reader consult his own breast, the principles of human nature, as they necessarily operate, and judge of the conduct of the Apostles from what he feels in his own consciousness, or as he apprehends he would have acted in the like circumstances.

SECT,

SECT. VII.

In order to shew the Apostles were no Impostors, it is made appear from their Doctrines, that the Good that served as the prevailing Motive to excite and support them in the Discharge of their Ministry had nothing in it of this World.

IN alledging that the Apostles, while they pretended a contempt of this world, and to be aspiring after future enjoyments, were secretly animated by some earthly consideration, as the great motive that spurred them on in the service of the Gospel, 'tis to be expected, upon the principles of fair dealing, that no man will content himself with the charge in general, without coming to particulars, or without explaining the special grounds upon which such an imputation can be founded. Very few of mankind are sensible of the powers of another world, or feel themselves engaged in any considerable design, from the influences of a future state of glory. The views of most people are bounded to this present life, and secular regards are the springs that animate the souls of men in almost every undertaking. When we therefore find, that so many persons were zealously employed in the propagation of the Gospel, the common course of the world raises the presumption against them, and we apprehend that they are animated no otherwise in their particular project, than the rest of mankind are in their several pursuits. But, to go upon such a general presumption, or to load the Apostles with so heavy a charge, without bringing forth the particular evidences up-

on

on which, in spite of their most solemn declarations to the contrary, their guilt may be clearly detected, is what every body will own to be highly unjust. At this rate, no man's innocence can be safe, and the best characters may come to be held the most abandoned. Those of our day, who affect to talk so loud of the principles of liberty, and a freedom of thought, cannot but loudly condemn this shameful conduct, and warmly approve the principles of common justice, which forbid the finding a man guilty till a particular charge be laid against him, and that charge be made out by sufficient evidences, that continue to appear so, after all a man has said in his own vindication. Some people, without insisting upon particular proofs, seem disposed to run away with the notion, that the Deists are mere Atheists, men of no virtue, quite abandoned to wickedness. And since the Deists do complain loudly of the manifest injustice done them in thus condemning them upon a general charge without particular proof or evidence, I would fain think they will not be guilty of the like crying iniquity in the case of the Apostles, and go about in a general charge to condemn them as Impostors, without justifying their accusation by particular proofs, that still appear conclusive, after all that can be said to the contrary. Let us therefore despise the shameful way of charging people in general, and have the honesty to examine whether such particular crimes can fairly be made out against them. And,

So far as we can judge of mankind from what is already past in the world, or from attending to the inward springs of our own actions in such particular circumstances, it should seem manifest, that especially in all great and arduous undertakings, that require

quire thought and application, and to have all our powers vigorously exerted, and wherein our views aim at nothing that lies beyond the limits of this present world, men are always determined in their several pursuits from one or more of these motives, namely, pleasures, or riches, or honours. These, I say, are the particular objects that in all ages have actuated the minds of men, and given life to those designs, that only regarded our present state of existence. And, as the nature of things, and the evidence of history, will not suffer us to doubt, that those persons, who, in the pursuit of earthly enjoyments, have made a figure in the world, were all animated by such principles; so, in supposing that the Apostles were pushed on in the propagation of the Gospel, not from the regards of a future state, but from worldly considerations, one must necessarily conceive, that the great power that supported them in the discharge of their Ministry was some one or more of these motives just now mentioned.

Whether the Deists will alledge, that the united force of all these motives together, or only the influence of such a particular one, was the power that animated the Apostles, I know not; but, as I have already hinted, common justice forbids a general charge, and requires the articles to be specified, that one may have access to examine their importance, the particular evidences upon which they are grounded, and what is the weight of what may be said in vindicating the Apostles. And indeed, had the Apostles been put upon their enterprise from any worldly consideration, one may reasonably suspect, that nothing under crowns, and sceptres, or the conquest of kingdoms and nations, or at least the power and splendor that attend the character of prime Ministers of State (things that are wont to
fire

fire noble and elevated minds) could have been the prize for which they were contending: For the bribe certainly muſt have very high, of an exalted and extraordinary nature, that ſo powerfully ſtimulated men of ſuch fine ſpirits and uncommon greatneſs of mind (as one muſt judge them from their writings) to have encountered ſuch frightful dangers, and made their way reſolutely through ſuch fierce and violent oppoſitions. But whether this, or another, or all of the above motives, are alledged to have given the commanding impulſe to the Apoſtles in the propagation of the Goſpel, I would only, I ſay, obſerve, that the charge muſt be particular, and the evidences to ſupport it clear and pointed.

Suppoſing, therefore, that the Apoſtles, as the Deiſts would have it, are liable to the charge of impoſture, for pretending to be inſpired from Heaven, while they are only animated by the power of one or other, or all of thoſe worldly motives; I ſhall endeavour to ſhew, that, in all thoſe ſeveral articles, the accuſation is groundleſs; and that there is no ſort of evidence whereby any one of them can be juſtified. And if, to make good their charge againſt the Apoſtles, the Deiſts have any other ground to inſiſt upon, I ſhall be glad to underſtand it; but, till I ſhall be better informed, I muſt profeſs, that, in my apprehenſion, the doctrines of the Apoſtles, and the courſe of their lives, are the only topics from whence it is poſſible for one to pretend to fetch proofs of their impoſture. Mean while, if from an impartial examination of the Apoſtles, in both theſe particulars, it ſhall be found, that in the proſecution of their Miniſtry, they were abſolutely free of any impulſe derived to their paſſions from the pleaſures, or riches, or honours of this world, I hope

hope we will allow ourselves to be such Free-thinkers, as in common justice to acquit them from imposture, and to declare, that in the propagation of the Gospel they are animated by no worldly consideration.

In the *first* place, As to the doctrines of the Apostles, they are in every body's hands, and in every article they strongly appear so fully consonant to the perfections of God, and to all the principles of reason, that the man who has read them with any degree of attention, would reckon himself affronted, should he be thought to have need to have so manifest a truth made out to him. Can any man be ignorant, that whatever things the Apostles inculcate upon the world, are directly contradictory to all unlawful and criminal passions? No body but knows, that every thing of this nature stands probibited in their writings under such severe penalties, that whosoever indulgeth to himself any one lust or appetite that dishonours God, and is hurtful to mankind, in violating the commands of universal love and righteousness, can look for nothing, upon the Gospel institution, but certain ruin and misery. Are we not expressly taught in the Gospel, that *the friendship of this world is enmity with God? whosoever therefore,* say the Apostles, *will be a friend of the world is the enemy of God* (b). And what stronger can be said in condemnation of every sensual passion, every worldly pursuit, that would carry a man beyond the bounds of reason and religion.

But there is one precept of universal influence, and of such vast consequence in the whole cause of religion and virtue, that it deserves here to be particularly mentioned: The precept is this; *Watch ye*, or *be vigilant* (c), frequently recommended, and urged upon us by

(b) James iv. 4.   (c) 1 Cor. xvi. 13. 1 Pet. v. 8. Mark xiii. 37.

by the most powerful arguments. As the Gospel represents it, the life of a Christian is here a warefare; in our way to the heavenly kingdom we have many enemies to oppose and overcome, and, for securing ourselves and gaining the victory, we are commanded to *put on the whole armour of God* (d). Here therefore, beset with enemies, and in great danger from the instability and treachery, and corrupt propensions and sensual inclinations of our own hearts, from the bad examples and sollicitations of wicked men, from the deceitful insinuations of *false Teachers* (e), and from the snares and temptations of the Devil; nothing can better become our situation than to stand always watching, *keeping our hearts with all diligence,* and guarding against the approaches of every thing base and criminal. And, in truth, if amidst so many enemies that *war against the soul,* we suffer ourselves to live secure and loose, altogether heedless and negligent, the inward bent of our depraved hearts, and the outward allurements of this evil world, must prevail over us, we shall prove an easy prey to every lust and every temptation, nor will the baseness or wickedness of any worldly attempt prevent our being engaged. Whereas, on the other hand, by continually looking about us, and carefully watching what sort of objects court our affections, sollicite our consent, and invite us to action, we will yield to no passion, we will enter into no design, nor will we pursue any measures, but where our duty calls us, and we clearly see our real safety and happiness. Indeed, through inadvertency, or the *deceitfulness of sin,* we may sometimes happen to desert our duty, and to side with our enemies; but by this constant vigilance, and watchful attention to the temper of our hearts, and the actions of our lives,

(d) Eph. vi. 11. (e) Acts xx. 29. et alib.

lives, or how we are engaged; we cannot but soon come to take the alarm, to fly the dreadful ruin threatening us, and to return again to our duty, wherein only we can meet with the mercy of God, and the protection of our Saviour. It is therefore by continual watching, or a constant vigilant care over our hearts and lives, that our minds are kept always open, both to a quick sense of the deformity and baseness, the danger and misery of irreligion and vice, whereby we are made to *renounce the hidden things of dishonesty*, and can *have no fellowship with the unfruitful works of darkness*; and to a clear perception of the beauty and excellency, the safety and happiness of religion and virtue, whereby we are kept steady and resolute in the discharge of our duty, and *stand stedfast, immoveable, always abounding in the work of the Lord*, the work of our salvation. And, as a powerful incitement to this constant care and circumspection, we are told, that *our Lord may come in a day when we look not for him, and in an hour that we are not aware of*; and when he comes, and finds us living loose, and among our enemies, our ruin is inevitable (*f*). So that a continued watching is a strong guard upon our innocence and virtue, our safety and happiness; it discovers the snares laid for us, and all the approaches of irreligion and vice; it warns us of our danger, and prevents our abandoning our duty; and when in any instance we happen to be involved, it rescues and delivers us: Nor, without a shameful neglect of this great extensive duty of watchfulness, can a man suffer himself to engage, or to go along in any wicked infamous pursuits. Such is the nature of this precept, so frequently and warmly recommended in the Gospel, and so mightily does it serve to protect our innocence and secure
our

(*f*) Matth. xxiv. 42. &c. Luke xxi. 34, 35, 36.

our virtue, to cause us *stand fast in the faith, and quit ourselves like men, and be strong* in vigorously defending our souls against the devil, the world, and the flesh, till the coming of our Lord, who will then relieve us, and crown us with glory and immortality. Thus it happened in the case of St. *Paul*; and thus it will happen in the case of all those who continue watchful to the end. *I have fought*, says this Apostle, *a good fight, I have finished my course, I have kept the faith. Henceforth is laid up for me a crown of righteousness, which the Lord the righteous Judge shall give me at that day: And not to me only, but unto all them also that love his appearing* (g). Now, let the Reader reflect——would men in a confederacy to promote any worldly criminal design, have insisted so earnestly on a duty of this nature, which, without bringing themselves into suspicion, they might, one should think, have totally neglected? I have no intention to offend any body, nor will I take upon me to look into people's hearts; but I must observe,

So far in every article are the doctrines of the Gospel from being in any degree favourable to the gratifications of the men of this world, that there are not wanting who alledge, that some, at least, are so much prejudiced against the Christian institution, and ingloriously attempt to overthrow its authority, for no other reason in the world, but a secret aversion to the purity of its doctrines, that would lay them under such uneasy restraints, or because it promises no indulgence to their lusts, but strictly requires that refinement of heart, that piety and virtue, that is pleasing to God, and suits the dignity of human nature. And indeed, besides those things wherein the Christian revelation is infinitely superior

(g) 2 Tim. iv. 7.

or to every other inſtitution that ever was in the world; it contains all thoſe noble precepts of morality that are any where to be found in the writings of the beſt and wiſeſt Heathen Authors, and juſtly deſerves all thoſe high commendations which thoſe great men have beſtowed upon philoſophy, as that which alone purifies the nature of man, and renders us truly good and glorious (*h*). "No-
" thing, ſays Mr. *Toland*, can be wiſer, plainer,
" truer, and conſequently more divine, than what
" *Chriſt* and his Apoſtles have propoſed about the
" means of reconciling God to ſinners; of purify-
" ing the mind and rectifying the manners; of illu-
" minating the underſtanding, guiding the conſcience,
" and directing particular duties; of confirming the
" hopes of recompence to the good, and denouncing
" the dread of puniſhment to the bad; of propogating
" mutual love, forbearance, and peace among all man-
" kind, of cementing, maintaining and ſupporting civil
" ſociety (*i*)." And the ſame Author, in his *Nazarenus*, tells us, " That it is evident to all, but ſuch
" as will not ſee, that one main deſign of Chriſti-
" anity was to improve and perfect the law of na-
" ture, as well as to facilitate and inforce the ob-
" ſervation of the ſame.——And indeed the divine
" wiſdom of the Chriſtian inſtitution is ſo appa-
" rent, enlightening the minds and regulating the
" conduct of men, in procuring their higheſt hap-
" neſs

(*h*) O vitæ philoſophia dux, ô virtutis indagatrix, expultrixque vitiorum; quid non modo nos, ſed omnino vita hominum ſine te eſſe potuiſſet?——Ad te confugimus, a te opem petimus; tibi nos, ut antea magna ex parte, ſic nunc penitus, totoſque tradimus. Eſt autem unus dies bene, & ex præceptis tuis actus, peccanti immortalitati anteponendus. Cujus igitur potius opibus utamur, quam tuis? quæ & vitæ tranquillitatem largita nobis es, & terrorem mortis ſuſtuliſti. Cic. Tuſcul. lib. 5. cap. 2.

(*i*) Conſtitution of the Chriſtian church. chap. 2. § 4.

"ness in all respects; that nothing, I am persua"ded, but a perfect ignorance of what it really is,
"or private interest, a worse enemy to truth than
"ignorance, could keep any from cheerfully em"bracing it (*k*)." In a word, the main drift of
the doctrines of the Apostles, is to disengage the
human mind from this world and all our present
enjoyments, and to raise it to the pursuit of those
immortal glories that are above with God in the
heavenly mansions. And to prove an imposture
against the Apostles, by arguments drawn from an
institution, whose whole contexture is so framed as
to inspire and improve *the life of God in the soul of
man*, is what no man in his right senses will ever
think of undertaking. So that from the doctrines
of the Apostles there is nothing to be alledged that
can at all countenance the smallest suspicion of their
having been determined to propagate the Gospel
from the prospect of thereby making themselves
rich, or great in this world, or of getting a power
into their hands to enjoy their pleasures without
control.

But, tho' it may be granted, that the doctrines of
the Gospel do not afford immediate proofs of imposture against the Apostles; yet are not the Apostles justly liable to this imputation, from their having taught some doctrines, as some people alledge,
unworthy of God, or inconsistent with his moral
perfections, and which, for that reason, can have
no pretension to a divine original? Here therefore it
will not be improper to examine the most considerable of those exceptions that are taken to the morality of the Gospel. And the objections that are
made against it, may be reduced to these three general heads; *viz.* Some of the moral doctrines of the
Gospel

(*k*). Mazaren. chap. 17. p. 67. chap. 18. p. 70.

Gospel are said to be absurd; others to be useless, or of no benefit to mankind; and a third sort to be hurtful and mischievous. Of each of these I shall propose the most plausible instances alledged.

SECT. VIII.

Dr. Tindal's Objections to the Morality of the Gospel are ill founded. And can afford no Ground for a Charge of Imposture against the Apostles.

IN the *first* place, To fasten an absurdity upon the doctrines of the Gospel, 'tis alledged, that, " This " is a general precept, *Sell what you have, and give* " *alms* (a): Nay, the woman that cast into the " treasury her two mites is commended, because *She* " *cast in all she had, even all her living* (b). And, " to shew that none were exempt from this pre- " cept, *Jesus* says to the man, who had observed all " the precepts from his youth, *One thing thou lackest,* " *sell whatsoever thou hast, and give to the poor* (c). " Now, say they, this precept is impracticable in a " Christian state; because there could be no buyers, " where all were sellers (d)." A staring absurdity! But ought not a man to be pretty sure of the premises before he presumes to offer to the world such a conclusion? Most certain it is, that a general precept binding every Christian to sell what he has, and to give it to the poor, stands in direct opposition to the design of the Gospel, and is utterly inconsistent with some of its particular precepts; nor would a man's putting it in practice, ever come of itself to
intitle

(a) Luk. xii. 33.   (b) Mark xii. 44.   (c) Mark x. 21.
(d) Christianity as old as the Creation, chap. xiii. p. 339.

intitle him to any of the bleſſings of the Goſpel: *Though I beſtow all my goods*, ſays the Apoſtle, *to feed the poor, and have not charity, it profiteth me nothing* (e). So that allowing the Writers of the New Teſtament to be men of common ſenſe, the preſumption is ſtrong, there can be no juſt ground for alledging, there is any ſuch general precept. And, indeed, the particular texts here alledged to ſupport it are moſt manifeſtly miſunderſtood.

The firſt text is thus, *Sell what you have, and give alms*; which even taken by itſelf, and without the connection it bears with other things in the ſame paſſage, cannot reaſonably be thought to carry in it any degree of abſurdity. For wherein does it differ from this general precept, *Let every man labour, working with his hands the thing which is good, that he may have to give to him that needeth?* For my part, I ſee nothing abſurd in a man's ſelling his goods, and making gain, and being at the ſame time charitable to the poor. But, to put the determined meaning of this text out of queſtion, we ſhall conſider it as it is a branch of that diſcourſe wherein it ſtands; which is the honeſt way of underſtanding the meaning of any Author whatſoever. And it ſhould appear, that one of the company attending our Saviour, expreſſing an over concern for his worldly affairs; upon this, our Lord takes occaſion to caution his Diſciples: *Take heed*, ſays he, *and beware of covetouſneſs; for a man's life conſiſteth not in the abundance of the things he poſſeſſeth. And he ſpake a parable to them, ſaying, the ground of a certain rich man brought forth plentifully: And he thought within himſelf, ſaying, what ſhall I do, becauſe I have no room where to beſtow my fruits? And he ſaid, this will I do, I will pull down my barns, and build greater; and there will I beſtow all my fruits and my*

(e) 1 Cor. xiii. 3.

my goods. And I will say to my soul; Soul, thou hast much goods laid up for many years; take thine ease, eat, drink, and be merry. Now, in this character, which our Saviour proposes to our aversion, there are three things extremely odious. There is an absolute neglect of a future state; there is the taking up one's rest in present enjoyments, minding only to indulge luxurious and wanton appetites; and there is the hoarding up the good things of this world for one's own personal use and pleasure, neither regarding the wants of those who are able to buy, and to whom, in the way of traffic, we ought to communicate them; nor yet the necessities of those whose poverty disables them to purchase, and to whom therefore we ought to impart them in the way of alms or charity. This, I say, is a most sordid character, void of humanity, and extremely odious. It is from this character that our Saviour would secure his Disciples. And, in order to prevent their acting so infamous a part, he first cautions them against that anxiety of mind about their daily bread, that would expose them to that covetous, unsocial, inhuman disposition; and by the most beautiful arguments (which I am surprised how any man of discernment can suffer himself to ridicule (*f*),) he warmly presses them to put their steady trust in the bountiful Providence of our heavenly Father. Upon which he proceeds to recommend to them a conduct of life quite the reverse of that described in the parable: *Rather seek ye*, says our Lord, *the kingdom of God, a treasure in the heavens that faileth not, where no thief approacheth, nor moth corrupteth*: And when Providence blesseth you with the good things of this world, hoard them not up, but *sell that ye have*, communicate of them to those that want and are able to purchase,

Vol. II. D

(*f*) Vid. Christianity as old as the Creation, p. 344.

purchase them ; and to those who cannot buy, *give alms.* A precept otherwise expressed by *Solomon*, when he says, *The liberal soul shall be made fat, and he that watereth shall be watered also himself; he that withholdeth corn, the people shall curse him; but blessing shall be upon the head of him that selleth it* (g). This is the real meaning of this text; so far from absurdity, that nothing can be more humane and generous, nothing can more effectually tend to private and public happiness. And, as this text gives not the least hint of selling all we have, and giving it to the poor; so neither does the next text here alledged, in the least commend such a practice. The whole passage is thus:

And Jesus *sat over against the treasury, and beheld how the people cast money into the treasury; and many that were rich, cast in much. And there came a certain poor widow, and she threw in two mites which make a farthing. And he called unto him his Disciples, and sayeth unto them, verily, I say unto you, that this poor widow hath cast more in than all they which have cast into the treasury. For all they did cast in of their abundance: but she of her want did cast in all that she had, even all her living.* I say, what our Saviour here observes concerning this poor widow, can, at no rate, be understood to intimate his approbation of her conduct, so as to make every man regard it as an example which he ought to imitate. The matter is; the Apostles seem to have set an excessive value on riches, and to have been carried away by an opinion that the rich were the great favourites of Heaven, and the persons who had the best title to the happiness of the *Messiah*'s kingdom (*h*). Now, as our Saviour, upon all occasions, was careful

(*g*) Proverbs, xi. 25, 26.
(*h*) Vid. Mark, x. 23.—27.

careful to rectify the notions of his Apostles, so he takes this opportunity to set them right in their apprehensions about riches; and lets them know, that, was God to favour men according to their external actions, this poor widow would be preferred before those rich persons: For, judging of the merit of external actions, as they are proportioned to the abilities of the Agent, which is most reasonable, and is judging of men according to what they have, and not according to what they have not, this poor woman must be understood to have contributed more; and consequently, by this way of reckoning, ought to be intitled to higher favour. From whence the Apostles are given to understand, how foolish they were in setting so great a value on riches, as if only the rich, or the rich especially, were to be preferred in the kingdom of the *Messiah*. And let any man judge : If, upon some extraordinary occasion that seems to require people to enlarge their charity, I chuse to make a fast-day of it, and contribute a shilling, the whole of my daily subsistence, while my rich neighbours, whose daily income is sixty shillings a-piece, only contribute each of them a guinea, could it be counted any commendation of me, if to persons mightily taken with outward appearances, and admiring the shew of rich men's contributions, and how happy they are in their riches that enable them to make such a figure, it should be observed, that *I had contributed more than all they which have cast in of their abundance?* One would think, that such an observation only serves to put people in a just way of thinking, and to lead them to reflect that in religious or moral judgment, the Giver ought to be regarded not from the greatness of the gift, or even the proportion it bears to his abilities, but from the disposition or intention with

which

which he gives it (*i*): In which case, it is possible, that even the All, the two mites of the widow, may intitle her to no commendation, but quite the contrary. So that as our Saviour does by no means condemn (as he must have done, had there been such a general precept as is pretended) those rich men, for contributing only a part; so neither does he commend this poor widow, for contributing the whole of her living. He only, I say, means, in this comparison of things, to instruct his Disciples, that they had no reason so much to admire riches, or to esteem the possessors so very happy. However, if this reflection of our Saviour must needs be understood to commend the conduct of this poor widow, whose pious and beneficent dispositions, might, indeed, derive a greatness to her two mites that made them more than all the offerings of the rich (*k*); I am not able to conceive how this commendation can be brought in proof of a general precept, to *sell all that we have, and to give it to the poor.* It should seem, or one may reasonably suppose, that this widow had a certain fund that afforded her two mites a day, (judged sufficient for the daily subsistence of a poor man:) Now, it is not the fund itself that the widow disposes of, and casts into the treasury, but only the produce of it for one day; chusing for that day either to fast, or to go dine with a friend or neighbour. So that if this passage insinuates any command

---

(*i*) Donavit aliquis magnam pecuniam: sed dives, sed non sensurus impendium. Donavit alius: sed toto patrimonio cessurus. Summa eadem est: beneficium idem non est.—Eadem licet sint, aliter data non idem pendent. Senec. de Benef. lib. iii. cap. 8.

(*k*) Si ad calculos revocetur, parvum.—Si animo erogantis, omni pecunia majus:—eo quidem majore cum commendatione, quo promti studii certius indicium est supra vires niti, quam viribus ex facili uti. Alter enim quod præstat, potest; alter etiam plus quam potest. Valer. Max. lib. iv. cap. 8.

mand whatsoever, it can only be this, that, on some particular occasions, people ought to contribute towards pious uses, one day's produce of their estates; which is a thing common enough in the world; nay, in their charitable contributions, people go frequently beyond it. At no rate therefore can this text justify the notion of there being in the Gospel a general precept requiring all Christians to sell their estates and to give them to the poor: Understanding it as a commendation of the widow's practice, and therefore proposed to other people for their imitation, it plainly intimates the clean contrary. But, the next text is thought to be conclusive:

In this we are told, that a certain young man having, by an ingenuous account of his virtuous course of life, very much recommended himself to our Saviour, *Then* Jesus *beholding him, loved him, and said unto him, one thing thou lackest; go thy way, sell whatsoever thou hast, and give to the poor, and thou shalt have treasure in heaven; and come, take up the cross and follow me.* Here, indeed, there is an express precept for this young man, (whom from this epithet, as well as the command, one may judge to have been without wife or children, which he was bound to provide for) to sell his whole estate, and to give it to the poor: But how to make a general precept of it, affecting all Christians whatsoever, is far beyond my comprehension. Nothing can be more manifest, than that this precept, as to the design of it, is precisely of the same nature with those, wherein, at different times, our Saviour calls his twelve Apostles to follow him; which never mortal man took to be general. And, considering the nature of *Christ*'s kingdom, and what was the most likely and unexceptionable method to promote it in the world, it seems necessary that our Saviour
should

should particularly direct this young man, whom he called to be one of his Apostles, to sell whatsoever he had, and to give it to the poor. For, had any of our Lord's immediate followers been men of plentiful fortunes, as was this young man, *who had great possessions*; this, no doubt, would have tempted the world to suspect a confederacy of a secular nature, and, by that means, have greatly obstructed the propagation of the Gospel. So that, I say, to prevent all suspicion of a worldly design, and to remove every thing that might prejudice the world against the Christian institution, our Saviour, offering to employ this young man as one of his Apostles, proposes to him to part with his estate in a manner that would put it out of his power to resume it, and to follow him in his glorious design of reforming mankind; wherein it is impossible for the wit of man to find out a general precept. Upon whom therefore the ridicule must fall, which Dr. *Tindal* here employs in laughing at an absurdity of his own making, the world may judge.

Nor is this Gentleman less to be blamed for insinuating from those texts, that the Gospel would teach us to maintain the poor in idleness (*l*). What ground they afford, in their plain and obvious meaning, for so heavy an imputation, is easily seen from what I have said. And I cannot but here remark, that so far is the Christian institution from encouraging idleness in any set of men whatsoever, that therein this infamous vice is most expressly condemned; and every man is commanded to pursue some useful business. *When we were with you,* says the Apostle, *this we commanded you, that if any would not work, neither should he eat. For we hear that there are some which walk among you disorderly,*
working

(*l*) Vid. Christianity as old as the Creation, p. 344.

SECT. VIII. *Christian Revelation.* 31

working not at all, but are busy bodies. Now them that are such we command and exhort, by our Lord Jesus Christ, *that with quietness they work, and eat their own bread. And if any man obey not our word by this Epistle, note that man, and have no company with him, that he may be ashamed* (m). *For if any provide not for his own, and especially for those of his own house, he hath denied the faith, and is worse than an Infidel.* Nay, the giving alms to those, whom it would make or keep idle, is prohibited : *The younger widows refuse, let them not be maintained by the Church ; for—they learn to be idle, wandering about from house to house ; and not only idle, but tatlers also, and busy bodies, speaking things which they ought not* (n). So that, according to the Gospel, our alms can only be laid out upon those poor, who are either not able to work, or who cannot carry on their work, without our charitable assistance. And how reasonable this is, how beneficial to society, I need not observe.

In the next place : Against the moral doctrines of the Gospel, it is objected, That they are useless or of no benefit to mankind. " Should not rules con-
" cerning morality be suited to men's particular
" circumstances, plainly describing that conduct
" which they require ? Is not this the design of mu-
" nicipal laws in every country ? What benefit
" could subjects have from laws written in such a
" loose, general, and undetermined manner ; as,
Lend,

(m) 2 Thess. iii. 10.—14.
(n) 1 Tim. v. 8. 11.—13. The sentiments of the Apostles concerning charity, are thus explained :

Εἰ γὰρ χήρα τις ὑπάρχουσα ἡ δυναμένη ἐπαρκεῖν ἐν τῷ βίῳ τὰ χρηστήρια, ἑτέρα δὲ ἢ χήρα, ἀλλ' ἐνδεὴς ὑπάρχει διὰ νόσον ἢ τεκνοτροφίαν, ἢ δι' ἀσθένειαν χειρῶν, ἐπὶ ταύτην μᾶλλον ἐκτεινάτω τὴν χεῖρα. Εἰ δέ τις ὡς καταφαγὰς, ἢ μέθυσος, ἢ ἀργὸς, ἐν τοῖς βιωτικοῖς θλίβεται, οὐκ ἔστιν ἄξιος ἐπικουρίας, οὔτε μὴν ἐκκλησίας Θεοῦ. Constitut. Apost. lib. ii. cap. 4.

" *Lend, hoping for nothing again*; *if any man will sue*
" *thee at law, and take away thy coat, let him have*
" *thy cloak alſo: Of him who takes away thy goods,*
" *aſk them not again.*—the ſame may be ſaid of all
" general and undetermined rules in the New
" Teſtament, tho' more plainly delivered. As for
" inſtance, tho' it is ſaid, *Servants obey your maſters*
" *in all things*; *and pleaſe them well in all things*; yet
" is the meaſure of obedience due from ſervants to
" maſters, any otherwiſe to be learnt, than from the
" agreement of the parties, or the cuſtom of the coun-
" try? It is ſaid, *we are to render to* Cæſar, *the things*
" *that are* Cæſar's; but muſt we not learn from the
" laws in every nation, who is *Cæſar*; and what is
" his due?" (*o*)

In this objection, what particular ideas the Author has in his mind, I confeſs, I am at a loſs to
underſtand. He ſeems to me to conceive, that ſuch
precepts of the Goſpel muſt be counted looſe, general, and undetermined, and conſequently of no benefit to mankind, becauſe they do not deſcribe to
us the particular cuſtoms, the conſtitutions and laws
of the ſeveral ſtates and kingdoms in the world:
Otherwiſe, why does he tell us, that it is not from
ſuch precepts of the Goſpel, *Servants obey your ma-*
ſters in all things; *and render to* Cæſar, *the things*
that are Cæſar's; but from the cuſtom of the country and the laws in every nation, that we muſt
learn the meaſure of obedience due from ſervants to
maſters; and who is *Cæſar*, and what is his due?
But if all ſuch precepts of the Goſpel muſt be held
uſeleſs, and of no benefit to mankind, becauſe
from thence we cannot learn the particular cuſtom
of the country, or the arbitrary laws of every nation; I wonder what ſhall become of the law of nature,

(*o*) Chriſtianity as old as the creation, p. 344.

ture, a law of absolute perfection? Sure I am, that the law or religion of nature, does as little as the Gospel, explain to us any articles of that nature; and yet Dr. *Tindal* is infinitely far from alledging, that this absolutely perfect law contains no precepts concerning servants and subjects, or that its precepts in those instances are useless and of no benefit to mankind. And why he refuses to do the same justice to the Gospel, which he reckons a republication of the religion of nature, I am not able to conjecture. In a word, the very quality which this Gentleman seems to judge necessary in every system of laws, to render them useful and of consequence, is most apparent in the christian institution. " Should not rules, " (says he,) concerning morality, be suited to men's " particular circumstances, plainly describing that " conduct which they require?" Now this, I say, is the very thing that is particularly remarkable in the rules of the Gospel.

As the religion of nature, so the Gospel of *Jesus Christ*, does not consider men as of this or of that nation, but it regards them as rational creatures, in society with God and with one another: It is the same in *Britain*, that it is in *France*; *Nec erit alia lex Romæ, alia Athenis, alia nunc, alia posthac, sed et omneis gentes, et omni tempore una lex, et sempiterna, et immortalis continebit.* And it especially respects the motions of the mind, without regarding the actions of the body, any farther than as they proceed from the inward judgment and affections (p). And this blessed Gospel, a law of universal extent, and of a spiritual nature, so well is it suited to men's particular circumstances, that it plainly describes that inward conduct, those affections and dispositions, which it requires every man in such particular

VOL. II.   E   circumstances

(p) Vid. Matth. xv. 19.

circumstances to pursue and cherish. This, beyond question, is the nature and design of the municipal laws, as one may call them, of the kingdom of the *Messiah.*

Nor can I imagine any situation of life a man can be in, wherein the Gospel does not plainly prescribe to him his inward deportment, the only thing that constitutes a moral character, and which in all instances must regulate a man's outward behaviour. Let the Reader reflect on these particulars mentioned in the above quotation transcribed on the margin from *Plutarch*: In all those circumstances, in many more, in every thing else, the Gospel pointedly settles our inward conduct. As for the duty of subjects, I shall have occasion to explain it afterwards.

And here, as to servants; what can be more plain and pointed in describing their inward deportment, as it ought to be, not in this or that country only, but all over the world, than these rules of the Gospel? *Servants be obedient to them that are your masters, according to the flesh, with fear and trembling, in singleness of your heart, as unto Christ: Not with eye-service, as men-pleasers, but as the servants of Christ, doing the will of God from the heart, with good-will, doing service, as to the Lord, not to men. Knowing that whatsoever good thing any man doth, the same shall he receive of the Lord, whether he be bond or free* (*q*). *Again, Servants, obey in all things your masters according to the flesh; not with eye-service, as men-pleasers, but in singleness of heart, fearing God, And whatsoever you do, do it heartily as to the Lord, and not unto men: Knowing that of the Lord ye shall receive the reward of the inheritance; for ye serve the Lord Christ. But he that doth wrong, shall receive*

for

(*q*) Eph. vi. 5, 8.

for the wrong that he hath done: And there is no respect of persons (r): I say, in these Texts the inward deportment of the mind suited to the circumstances of the body (let the agreement of the parties and the custom of the country be what they will) is most exactly described; nor is there any thing, necessary to form the moral character in such a particular situation of life, left loose or undetermined. Indeed, the *all things*, i. e. the outward services which servants are bound to pay to their masters, are not mentioned. Those of necessity must be left to be determined by the agreement of the parties, and the custom of the country. And how ridiculous would it be to talk of those moral precepts of the Gospel, that they are loose and undetermined, and therefore useless, and of no benefit to mankind, because, for instance, they do not plainly describe, whether such a man in the station of a servant, shall plough in the fields, or dig in the garden? Or for how many hours he must every day be at work, &c? And what else can be made of this objection, I really know not.

Much after the same manner may the same Texts, here charged with being useless and to no purpose, be clearly vindicated. I shall only now explain these two: *Of him who takes away thy goods, ask them not again; and lend, hoping for nothing again* (*f*). And, as the meaning of no Author, in any passage of his writings, ought to be determined, without considering the connection which that passage bears with the other branches of the discourse, whereof it is a part; so we must here examine into the meaning and drift of that particular discourse, wherein our Saviour gives out these precepts.

(r) Coloss. iii. 22—25. (*f*) Luke vi. 30—35.

cepts. And, beginning at *ver.* 20. it is apparent, that our Lord having before him the diftreffed perfecuted condition of his Difciples in propagating the Gofpel among mankind, (for this is no part of that difcourfe in *Matth.* v.) he comes in the 27. *ver.* to prefcribe to them their inward conduct, together with fome inftances of outward behaviour, in thofe circumftances of perfecution wherein they are hated, and curfed, and defpitefully ufed, and are bereaved of their worldly enjoyments. *But I fay unto you, which hear, love your enemies; do good to them which hate you; blefs them that curfe you; and pray for them which defpitefully ufe you.* Thus, their inward conduct is no loofe and undetermined character, but is plainly defcribed in fuch particular affections of mind, which they are commanded to maintain towards their perfecutors. But, as the exercife of charity, of patience, and meeknefs towards our oppreffors, is far from being inconfiftent with our endeavouring to recover thofe goods they have robbed us of; to prevent his Difciples from attempting any thing of that nature, which, in thofe days of perfecution, could not well fucceed, and might rather involve them in greater hardfhips, and befides, divert them from attending the propagation of the Gofpel, our Saviour fets this rule to our outward behaviour, *of him that taketh away thy goods, afk them not again;* fpend no thought or time in demanding reftitution, but take joyfully the fpoiling of your goods for the fake of the Gofpel, and fteadily purfue its propagation. Upon which he again renews his charge in reference to their inward conduct, and giving them to underftand, that they muft act a more generous and divine part than finners, who, in fome fort obferved an intercourfe of kind offices, such as *lending to them of whom they hoped to receive;* he requires them,

SECT. VIII.   *Christian Revelation.*   37

them; when their enemies should be so modest as to pretend only to borrow, not to refuse, but to lend *hoping for nothing again*; a disposition of mind necessary to prevent all entanglements, and to keep them wholly devoted to the service of the Gospel. Nor indeed, as the world was then affected, had they any good reason to expect their loan would be returned: Besides, that their refusing to lend any one thing, might, in those days, have exposed them to the loss of all. Thus, it plainly appears, that these two passages of the Gospel, taken in their obvious and literal meaning, as they stand in that discourse of our Saviour, contain no loose and undetermined rules, but do pointedly settle even the external behaviour of Christians, towards those who persecute and oppress them, for the sake of their religion; in which circumstances, when neither life nor fortune can be in any great safety, people had much need to be *wise as serpents, and harmless as doves* (*t*).

I come, in the *last* place, to consider, whether the morality of the Gospel, in any instance, can be counted hurtful, or mischievous. To make it out, 'tis alledged, that the Gospel, in some of its doctrines, discourages industry, the want of which directly ruins trade, and the prosperity of a nation. " Should we not (says Dr. *Tindal*) taking things " merely as they stand in the Gospel, be apt to think, " that the poor, as such, were the only favourites " of Heaven : *Blessed are ye poor ; for yours is the " kingdom of God. Blessed are ye that hunger; for " ye shall be filled ?* And should we not be apt to " imagine, that the Gospel was an enemy to the " rich, as such ; and consequently to all those me- " thods which make a nation rich : As, *Wo unto*
" *you*

(*t*) Matth. x. 16.

" you rich ; for you have received your consolation (u)?
" It is easier for a camel to pass through the eye of a
" needle, than for a rich man to enter into the kingdom
" of God (x)?" How any man, who has read the Gospel, can give himself leave to insinuate, that, as things are there represented, one may be apt to think, that such an outward condition of life will recommend people to the favour of God, and the contrary expose them to his displeasure, is not a little surprising. The Gospel of *Jesus Christ*, in the whole strain of its doctrines, and in many express declarations, is utterly repugnant to every thing of that nature. But we shall examine the particular passages, upon which they pretend this imputation is grounded.

In the Text in St. *Luke*, here referred to, our Saviour represents his Disciples not only poor, but in hunger, and grief, hated, under reproach, persecuted for the sake of the Gospel. And thus, conceiving them in circumstances of distress and misery, for their comfort, he gives them the prospect of better treatment: And, in pronouncing them blessed, he sets forth their future spiritual enjoyments in a variety of borrowed ideas, opposed to the various sorts of their present bodily calamities. *And he lifted up his eyes on his Disciples, and said, Blessed be ye poor ; for yours is the kingdom of God. Blessed are ye that hunger now ; for ye shall be filled. Blessed are ye that weep now ; for ye shall laugh. Blessed are ye when men shall hate you, and when they shall separate you from their company, and shall reproach you, and cast out your name as evil, for the Son of man's sake.* Thus our Saviour addresses himself to his Disciples then present; and apprehending them in a distressed situation

(*u*) Luke vi. 20. 21—24. (*x*) Christianity as old, &c. p. 339.

tion for the sake of his Gospel, he pronounces them blessed, not merely because of their poverty, their hunger, or grief, or persecution; but in consideration of their patiently suffering those calamities *for the Son of man's sake*, whilst they resolutely adhered to his Gospel, and were zealous in propagating its doctrines to the world. No man, therefore, capable of reading an Author with any understanding, can be apt to think, that this Text in any degree insinuates that the poor, as such, are the favourites of Heaven. Nor, from the following words, can it any more be imagined that the Gospel is an enemy to the rich, as such.

Our Saviour having assured his Disciples of happiness, in exchange for that misery to which they were reduced for the sake of his Gospel, he turns his mind towards those persons who acted the contradictory part; and well knowing, that the love of riches, of ease, and pleasure, and other worldly enjoyments, made them reject his Gospel, and persecute his Disciples, he denominates them from those outward bodily things, that betrayed them into so guilty a conduct, and plainly sets forth the folly and misery of their choice. *But, wo unto you that are rich; for ye have received your consolation. Wo unto you that are full; for ye shall hunger. Wo unto you that laugh now; for ye shall mourn and weep. Wo unto you when all men shall speak well of you; for so did their Fathers to the false Prophets.* This, I say, is a character set in direct opposition to that of the Apostles; it represents men in the condition of false Prophets that oppose the sincere doctrines of God, and would prevent their being regarded in the world. And therefore, as the Apostles are pronounced happy in preferring the Gospel before every earthly

earthly pleasure whatsoever.; so those other persons are pronounced miserable in preferring their worldly enjoyments. So that the Gospel of *Jesus Christ* is no enemy to the rich, as such; but only to those rich men, who, rather than part with their riches, will act the part of false Prophets, reject the Gospel, and persecute its professors.

As for the other Text here mentioned; *It is easier for a camel to pass through the eye of a needle, than for a rich man to enter into the kingdom of God*; it shews the folly of the imputation which it is brought to support. The case, as it stands in St. *Mark*, is thus: Upon a rich man's refusing to part with his large possessions, to take up the cross, and to follow *Christ* in the service of the Gospel, we are told, that " *Jesus* looked round about, and said " to his Disciples, *How hardly shall they that have* " *riches enter into the kingdom of God!* And the Dis- " ciples were astonished at his words. But *Jesus* " answereth again, and saith unto them, *Children,* " *how hard is it for them that trust in riches to enter* " *into the kingdom of God! It is easier, &c.*" And if a man comprehends the meaning of one's trusting in riches, he will observe some dispositions of mind, not very fit for the profession of the Gospel here (frequently, and perhaps in this Text, understood by one's entering into the kingdom of God) or for the enjoyment of the happiness of heaven hereafter. But,

How in the name of wonder! can any man pretend to say, that the Gospel of *Jesus Christ* is an enemy to those methods which make a nation rich, and to which the religion of nature is a friend? Sure, nothing of this nature can be charged upon an institution, that makes industry a necessary ingredient into the character of its professors; that expressly prefsly forbids our being flothful in business; and, under the severest penalties, commands every man to work, to be useful in the world; and allows of no objects of charity, but such poor only as are either not able to work, or not capable of carrying on their work without our assistance. In the mean while, one may wonder we are not likewise told, that the Gospel makes our enjoying the favour of God to depend, not on our own, but on the dispositions and actions of other people that are not in our power: For our Saviour likewise says, *Blessed are ye when men shall hate you, and shall separate you from their company:* And, *Wo unto you when all men shall speak well of you!*

But, in further proof of the mischievous nature of the doctrines of the Gospel, 'tis alledged, that the Gospel ties up our hands, deprives us of self-defence, and lays us open to the insults and injuries of every bold and wicked invader. " From this Text, *Resist* " *not evil ; but whoever shall smite thee on thy right* " *cheek, turn to him the other also* (y), and some " others of the like nature; not only the primitive " Fathers, but a considerable sect, even now a-" mong the Protestants, think all self-defence un-" lawful (z)." How unfair would it be to impose upon the religion of nature any one of those absurdities, which many Philosophers pretend to hold as its dictates ? And, is it not equally unreasonable to insinuate, that some people misunderstand the words of an Author, and therefore they must be taken in that sense which the Author never meant they should express ? Without regarding what either antient or modern have understood by these propositions, 'tis incumbent on us, in order to apprehend

Vol. II,   F   their

(y) Matth. v. 39.   (z) Christianity as old, &c. p. 340.

their true meaning, honeftly to confider what there is in the context to determine and fix it.

From *ver.* 21. of this fifth *chap.* of *Matthew*, to the 26. our Saviour having inftructed his difciples in the part they ought to act upon their having been injurious to other people; he comes in the 38. *ver.* to the 42. to teach them after what manner they muft behave when other people happen to be injurious to them. *Ye have heard,* says our Lord, *that it hath been said, an eye for an eye, and a tooth for a tooth. But I say unto you, that ye refift not evil, but whofoever shall smite thee on the right cheek, turn to him the other also. And if any man will sue thee at the law, and take away thy coat, let him have thy cloak also. And whofoever shall compel thee to go a mile, go with him twain.* Here our Saviour has in view what was practifed among the *Jews*, under the law of retaliation. And, no doubt, as it is here infinuated, under the credit of this law, fome people took occafion to gratify a malicious and revengeful fpirit, either violently refenting injuries themfelves, or with rigour profecuting before the Judge even the flighest injuries that might be done them. So that in the cafe of injuries received, our Lord forming the conduct of his Difciples, in oppofition to that of the *Jews*, as they acted under the law of retaliation, we are led directly to apprehend, that by this precept, *refift not evil,* we are commanded to fupprefs all malicious and revengeful paffions, that may be apt to rife in our minds againft thofe who have done us an injury. And indeed the word ἀντιστῆναι, here rendered *refift*, frequently fignifies only that refiftance or oppofition that refts in the inward powers of the mind, without employing the body, or ufing any fort of external force whatfoever. And taking it in this fenfe, as the context and the nature of the evangelical

tical inftitution determine it, the oppofition or refiftance made to injuries received, here prohibited,
muft confift in wrath, malice, and revenge, the
paffions that fet our mind in enmity to another.
So that, I fay, the non-refiftance of evil or of injuries received, here plainly fignifies, the non-indul-
gence of malicious and revengeful paffions. And as
our Saviour, in this article, informs his Difciples
what particular paffions they muft avoid; fo, in the
other articles, he lets them know, what particular
affections or difpofitions they muft entertain; which
he defcribes in a form of fpeech, that intimates a
readinefs of mind to fubmit to a repetition of the
like injuries, without being provoked to any malicious refentment. *Whofoever*, fays he, *fhall fmite
thee on thy right cheek, turn to him the other alfo*, &c.
I fay, in thefe articles, as every man of common
reflection and fair dealing muft underftand them,
we are commanded to bear what affronts and injuries are done us, with compofure of mind, with
patience and meeknefs, without either avenging ourfelves, or *giving place unto wrath* and rigorous law-
fuits and profecutions, for doing ourfelf juftice, or
repairing the hurt we have received. And thefe moral precepts being thus underftood, in a plain and eafy
meaning, as they are oppofed to the conduct of the
Jews under the law of retaliation, it feems very
manifeft, that we are in no degree deprived of that
felf-defence, which a good man would wifh to have
in his power.

There are *three* cafes that here feem to be put by
our Saviour; the *firft* is, That of a fudden affront,
when a man fmites us on the right cheek; the *fe-
cond* is, That of a man's injurioufly fuing us at law,
and taking away our coat; and the *third* is, That
of a man's ufing main force and violence, invading
our

our liberty, and compelling us to go a mile. Now, in all these several cases, we are commanded to be so void of passion and revenge, to be masters of so much greatness and composure, that undisturbed, and regardless of the impotent malice of our enemies, we could even turn to our smiter the other cheek, and receive a second indignity; we could even let the man who at law has found means to take away our coat, have our cloak also; and with the man who has forced us to go a mile, we could even go twain. By all which, it is clearly intimated, that in case of injuries received, of whatever sort, our inward composure, patience, and meekness, must never fail, so as to give place to wrath, malice, and revenge. Nor, I say, do these precepts tie up a man's hands, or restrain him from defending himself. On the contrary, as all such precepts set us above our enemies, and derive a dignity to our conduct; so they preserve a constant calm and serenity within, and, when it is in our power, enable us to vindicate our just rights, without disturbing the laws of reason or of society. In short, in one of the cases here mentioned, we have our Saviour's example teaching us to justify and defend ourselves; and in the other two, we see the principle of self-preservation is exerted. Thus we are told, that when our Saviour stood before the High-priest, *one of the officers struck Jesus with the palm of his hand:* Upon which, our Lord, not *turning* literally *his other cheek* to the smiter, but receiving the affront with an unshaken greatness and composure of mind, which shews him superior to all insults and injuries, and is all that is understood by the phrase, exerts the principle of self-defence, and without any degree of malice, or revenge, severely checks the insolence of the man : *If I have spoken evil,* says our Lord,

bear

Sect. VIII.   *Christian Revelation.*   45

bear witness of the evil; but if well, why smitest thou me (*a*) ? And if a man may use his tongue in suppressing the insolence of his enemy, why may he not, to the same purpose, when his safety requires it, make use of any other member of his body? In the second case, a man is represented to be sued at law, and, in the issue, to have lost his coat, which supposes he made defences. And in the third case, a man is compelled to go a mile ; which plainly intimates, that what opposition he thought proper to make, did not prove effectual. From all which, it seems extremely manifest, that those precepts of the Gospel do by no means tie up a man's hands, and restrain the principle of self-defence, so as to expose us to the insults and injuries of every bold, wicked invader.

The great design of the Gospel of *Jesus Christ* is to adjust the inward conduct of mankind ; and when people keep their minds under the steady influence of those spiritual precepts it prescribes to us, they may be trusted with the outward motions of their body, and will not fail, in all circumstances, particularly in the matter of self defence, to act a just, a generous, and a noble part, the part of a great mind, animated with divine sentiments, above being shaken with the tumults of wrath and revenge (*b*).

Let

(*a*) Joh. xviii. 22, 23.

(*b*) Nec vero audiendi, qui graviter irascendum inimicis putant, idque magnanimi et fortis viri esse, censent. Nihil enim laudabilius. nihil magno et præclaro viro dignius, placabilitate atque clementia. Cic. de Offic. lib. i. cap. 25.

Illud non venit in dubium, quin se exemerit turbæ, et altius steterit, quisquis despexit lacessentes. Proprium est magnitudinis veræ, non se sentire percussum. Sic immanis fera ad latratum canem lenta respexit. Sic irritus ingenti scopulo fluctus assultat. Qui non irascitur, inconcussus injuria perstitit: Qui irascitur, motus est. Senec. de Ira lib. iii. cap. 25.

Dum

46 *The Truth of the* SECT. VIII.

Let it now be remarked, that the moral doctrines of the Antients, renowned for wisdom, may, in the same instances, with as good reason, be accused of depriving people of self-defence, and exposing them to every invader. The sentiments just now transcribed, in the margin, from *Seneca*, one might pretend, are liable to this imputation : But I shall only instance in *Socrates:* This divine man, not only expressly declares it a base and wicked thing to be, in any degree, injurious to another ; but he warmly professes, that what injuries soever we may happen to suffer at the hands of other people, we ought, by no means, to avenge ourselves, or *to render to any man evil for evil (c).* This indeed he confesses is a doctrine that few people will agree to. But he is positive in asserting it ; nor does he fail to put it in practice, whilst he *turned the other cheek to him that smote him,* that is, patiently bore such indignities, and exerted no passion of wrath or resentment *(d)* ; even going the length, as *Plato* represents the matter, in

---

'Dum inter homines sumus, colamus humanitatem : non timori cuiquam, non periculo simus : detrimenta, injurias, convicia, vellicationes contemnamus, et magno animo brevia feramus incommoda. Id. ibid. cap. 43.

Sed adversus hostes, inquit, necessaria est ira. Nusquam minus : ubi non effusos esse oportet impetus, sed temperatos et obedientes.——Deinde quid opus est ira, cum idem perficiat ratio ? Id. ibid lib. i. cap. 11.

At sapiens colaphis percussus, quid faciat ? Quod Cato, cum illi os percussum esset : non excanduit, non vindicavit injuriam : ne remisit quidem, sed factam negavit. Majore animo non agnovit, quam ignovisset. Id. de Constant. Sapient. cap. 14.

(*c*) Οὔτε ἄρα ἀνταδικεῖν δεῖ, ὄτε κακῶς ποιεῖν ὀδένα ἀνθρώπων, ὀδ᾽ ἂν ὁτιῶν πάσχη ὑπ᾽ αὐτῶν. Plat. in Crit. p. 49. vol. i.

(*d*) Socratem aiunt colapho percussum, nihil amplius dixisse, quam molestum esse, quod nescirent homines cum galea prodire deberent. Senec. de Ira. lib. iii. cap. 11. Vid. cap. 38. D. Laert. in Socrat. Plutarch. de Liber. educand. p. 10. c.

in his *Crito*, to let those that had taken away his liberty, *have his life also*; rather than prove injurious to the laws of society, or civil government, which, he apprehended, forbid a prisoner to make his escape out of custody. Thus, I say, the doctrines and practice of *Socrates* may be counted hurtful or mischievous, as they seem to render men pusillanimous, to restrain the principle of self-defence, and to expose people to the insults and injuries of every aggressor. But what man of common understanding ever took it in his head, to charge the doctrines of *Socrates* with so senseless an imputation? And why the writings of *Plato* should meet with more candid treatment than those of the Apostles, I am not able to understand. *Celsus* himself acts a much fairer part; for those very Texts which Dr. *Tindal* would have to be so absurd and mischievous, do, in his opinion, contain such excellent doctrines, that, to lessen the reputation of the Apostles, he tells us, " They were taught by antient Philosophers, men " greatly famed for their wisdom (*e*)." The conduct of some people seems really very unaccountable, nor am I able to reconcile it to the character of scholars, or of honest men: They shew a great deal of art in clearing up the sentiments of antient moral Philosophers, and, in several instances, would set them in a better light than they are able to bear; but, as to the doctrines of the Gospel, all their art is employed to expose and ridicule them. For my part, I cannot but rest satisfied, that if with the same good dispositions, wherewith people read, and endeavour to understand *Plato*, *Cicero*, &c. they would read and study the writings of the Apostles; so far would they be from finding them, in any article, absurd, or useless, or mischievous, that they
would

(*e*) Vid. Orig. contra Celf. lib. vi. p. 286. lib. vii. p. 370.

would honestly confess, they are altogether consistent with the purest informations of reason, and serve effectually to promote the order of the world, the peace and happiness of human kind, in every situation of life, in every stage of existence.

Thus it appears, that the doctrines of the Gospel, those doctrines taught by the Apostles, can afford no ground for a charge of imposture against them.

SECT. IX.

From their general Conduct it appears, that the Apostles were no Impostors.

AND, therefore, in the next place, if there is ground to suspect the Apostles of having been animated in the service of the Gospel, from any worldly consideration, this must certainly appear from their other actions of life. And if the Apostles shall be found, in any one instance of their conduct, ever to have betrayed an inclination to make an attempt towards compassing any carnal or worldly enjoyment, as that which they were mainly driving at; as this is utterly inconsistent with the whole scheme of their doctrines, so it must necessarily expose them to our deepest abhorrence, as men of the most atheistical principles, who, under the strongest shews of religion, believed nothing concerning the Deity, and secretly made a jest of a future state of rewards and punishments. So black a charge cannot easily be admitted against any man; but in the case of the Apostles, how can it possibly be admitted without the most overbearing evidence?

SECT. IX. *Christian Revelation.*

No doubt, mankind have, in all ages, been capable of acting very wickedly; but, in spite of all those villainies that are far too common in the world, one should think, that by how much a crime is shocking to human nature, by so much ought the evidences to be clear and strong, that would prove a man guilty of it. And must not these evidences be yet so much the clearer and stronger, as the crime alledged happens to be more contradictory to a man's avowed principles, and the common course of his life? And still a great deal clearer and stronger must not those evidences be, when the crime alledged is not a transient act, but a constant course of horrid violence to the common sentiments of humanity, and to one's own avowed principles and profession? Thus it is that common justice would dictate to us. So that how the Deists will find it possible to make out against the Apostles the charge of imposture, that would involve them in the guilt of obstinate atheism, or of a settled contempt of God, and a future world, I will not pretend to determine: Only, besides the common impressions of human nature, the divine doctrines they published, and taught, the fervent zeal with which, at the hazard of their lives, they propagated through the world those heavenly instructions; and the spotless integrity that always appeared in the whole course of their Ministry, are strong, very strong presumptions of their innocence, and that so hainous a charge, that would involve them in such shocking guilt, cannot possibly be justified.

"*Socrates*, the greatest of Philosophers, the very "founder of philosophy itself (*a*)," is the man, whose character, in several instances, comes nearest to that of the Apostles: A noble Author is of opinion, that his

---

(*a*) Characterist. vol. iii. p. 244.

his presenting himself openly in the Theatre when the Comedy was acting which *Aristophanes* wrote, on purpose to expose him, is " a demonstration that " there was no imposture either in his character or " opinions (*b*)." And I do believe, that the Deists would count it a very extravagant attempt, should any one undertake to make out such a crime against this man of *invincible goodness* (*c*). But how is such an attempt against the Apostles, in any measure less absurd or extravagant? I dare venture to say, that by what arguments the Deists shall vindicate *Socrates*, by the same and stronger arguments may any one justify the Apostles. And if the Deists find good reason to acquit *Socrates* from the imputation of imposture, it is impossible they can judge consistently when they compare characters together, without finding far better reason to acquit the Apostles.

I have just now explained, that the doctrines of the Apostles can afford us not the least ground to suspect them of imposture; and I am now to endeavour to show, that the other actions of their lives can as little expose them to any such imputation. But, before I proceed to clear them from the particulars of the charge brought against them, I shall propose some general reflections that make it strongly evident, that, in the service of the Gospel, the Apostles could not possibly have been animated by any worldly consideration whatsoever. And,

First of all, it must be observed, that the Apostles were certainly men of good sense; that, especially in moral matters, they were very capable of understanding the nature of things, and of foreseeing what might be their consequences. As to all this, every body will rest satisfied, who, in any sort, has attended

(*b*) Characterist. vol. i. p. 31. (*c*) Ibid.

attended to those excellent writings they have left behind them, wherein we see that, in fact they have proposed to the world a noble system of doctrines for the government of human life ; and that from their knowledge of the humours and passions of mankind, they foresaw what they should certainly meet withal in prosecuting their grand undertaking. And as a man of sense, when he proposes to himself such a particular end, must be understood to make choice of those means that are adapted to the compassing his design, and cannot be thought to have pitched upon those that have no tendency but to baffle all his intentions ; so, when it is supposed that the main end the Apostles were driving at in the propagation of the Gospel, was some carnal or worldly enjoyment, it cannot possibly be imagined, that the means they employed were utterly repugnant to their principal design ; but we must expect, that the measures they framed shall be found to suit with their intentions. Some people indeed may have the skill to lay their design so deep, or to cover it over so artfully, that it shall not be easy to penetrate into it. But when a man sits down, and having his main end in his eye, is composing a scheme of things, as the certain or probable means whereby he can gain the accomplishment, let him be master of ever so much artifice, it seems quite impossible but his main end must betray itself, either in the contexture of the whole, or in some particular branch of that plan he lays down to be pursued : For one should think, that the mind, always filled with the principal plot, and being at all times under its commanding influence, of necessity, in a train of things, or a course of time, it will make some steps, or bring forth some actions, of the same nature and complection with that which it is chiefly
aiming

aiming at. — Thus it plainly happened in the case of that grand impostor *Mahomet* (*d*); thus it likewise happened in the church of *Rome*; and no instance can be given to the contrary. So that in the case of the Apostles, the Gospel being the only means which they can be thought to have employed in the pursuit of the end they intended, if they were indeed animated only by some secular regards, it is impossible but we must find the Gospel, in some particular instance, at least, clearly pointing towards that which they were mainly projecting. But let us consider,

What is there in the whole contexture, or in any particular branch of the Gospel published by the Apostles, that can seem adapted to any secular design, or upon which a supposition can be grounded, that, in the prosecution of their purpose, the Apostles were under the prevailing power of some worldly consideration? They do not introduce into their system of religion, or set at the head of the moral world, a god whose nature would protect them in the gratification of sensual passions; nor do we find them teaching the lawfulness of wars undertaken for the sake of empire, or giving out the extent of dominion as a glorious proof of one's love of one's country;

(*d*) La verité est que Mahomed merite toutes ces railleries, '& quand il n'y auroit dans son Alcoran que ces ordures perpetuelles sur les plaisirs des sens, qu'il ose placer dans le Paradis, comme sur le trône, qui leur convient, elles suffiroient pour nous le rendre meprisable. On voit qu'il s'est prevalu du climat & des chaleurs de l'Arabie, pour s'insinuer dans les bonnes graces de ses compatriotes, qui, ne connoissant gueres que ces sortes de voluptez, ont donné là dedans avec beaucoup d'appétit. C'est dans le même esprit qu'il a permis à ses sectateurs & la polygamie & le divorse, & la jouissance même des esclaves que l'on possede. La relig. des Mahomet. tiré du Latin de M. Reland. p. 156.

try; there is not any thing like a community of wives that they would recommend to mankind; nor do they pretend to promise in a future state any of the gross enjoyments of sense, that would engage people to indulge them here in this world. Such doctrines were maintained in the Heathen world, even by some of their best Philosophers; they were, some of them, acceptable to the *Jews* (*e*); and they might have served the purpose of the Apostles, had their end in the propagation of the Gospel been any sensual gratification. But so far are the Apostles from giving any the least turn to their doctrines, that would seem to favour the designs of worldly men, that no system of things can be framed that shall bear in it a stronger contradiction to worldly pursuits and to worldly ends.

In the Gospel, we are given to understand, that mankind in this world are mere strangers passing on to another life, and that all our present enjoyments must therefore be regarded only as so many accommodations prepared for us by kind Providence, for the conveniency of our journey. And thus letting us know that here we are only strangers, the Gospel sets before us a future state of immortal happiness, and strongly sollicites our ambition while it invites us to aspire to the heavenly mansions, to the presence of God, and an innumerable company of blessed spirits, among whom there is joy unspeakable and full of glory. And that we may not mistake our way, or wander in pursuits that would carry us quite off from that future life and immortality, the Gospel clearly explains to us the nature and perfections of an infinite mind, as the pattern upon which, so far as we are able, we must necessarily form ourselves;

or

(*e*) Vid. Selden. de J. Nat. et Gent. secund. Hebr. lib. 6. cap. 3 et 12.

or it reveals to us a system of laws, in observing of which we shall escape the pollutions of this world, and acquire all those endowments that will qualify us for the enjoyment of God, and the society of the heavenly inhabitants. So that in the Gospel which they taught, the Apostles call off our hearts from all worldly gratifications, wherein should we rest, we are undone for ever; and they direct us to set our effections on those things that are above; *in the first place to seek the kingdom of God and his righteousness,* assuring us, that while we are thus employed in aspiring after future glory, honour, and immortality, the Providence of God will take care of us with respect to our present accommodations, and favour our honest endeavours to procure them, as in his infinite wisdom he shall see it most consistent with our supreme good and felicity.

This, in general, is the scheme of things which the Apostles propose to us in the Gospel, and which they inculcate upon mankind with the greatest zeal and the most pressing arguments. *Dearly beloved,* say they, *we beseech you as strangers and pilgrims, abstain from fleshly lusts which war against the soul (f). We beseech you by the mercies of God, that ye present your bodies a living sacrifice holy, acceptable unto God, which is your reasonable service: And be not conformed to this world; but be ye transformed by the renewing of your mind (g). Take heed that you lay not up for yourselves treasures upon earth, where moth and rust doth corrupt, and where thieves break through and steal. But lay up for yourselves treasures in heaven, where neither moth nor rust doth corrupt, and where thieves do not break through nor steal. For where your treasure is, there will your heart be also (h).* And, upon

---

(f) 1 Pet. 2; ii. 11.   (g) Rom. xii. 1, 2.
(h) Matth. vi. 19, 20, 21.

upon thus setting your affections on things above, and not on things on the earth, you may rest assured, that *when Christ-who is our life shall appear, then shall ye also appear with him in glory* (i). *For we must all appear before the judgment-seat of Christ, that every one may receive the things done in his body, according to that he hath done, whether it be good or bad* (k). Upon which mankind are left to reflect, *What is a man profited, if he shall gain the whole world and lose his own soul ? or what shall a man give in exchange for his soul ?* And when the Apostles, with the utmost earnestness, do thus recommend to mankind a course of life that prevents our taking up our rest in this world, and elevates our souls above all earthly things, to the pursuit of a glorious immortality, in imitating the perfections of God, and in a steady observance of the laws of his heavenly kingdom; where is the means fitted to a secular design? What sort of doctrines could they teach more contradictory to worldly purposes? Or what measures could they take more effectually to confound their plot, had it been of a secular nature?

It must be owned, that in the execution of their intentions, the Apostles could have no prospect of assistance but from their own Disciples. But what assistance could they possibly expect from those persons, in whose minds they made it their business to establish those principles that make it necessary for mankind to regard all that is in the world, *the lust of the flesh, and the lust of the eyes, and the pride of life*, as things highly criminal (m), and that inspire us with an ardour of soul in the pursuit of piety and virtue, as the great accomplishments that fit us for the heavenly mansions? One should think, that
to

(i) Colos. iii. 4. (k) 1 Cor. v. 10, (l) Matth.
xvi. 26, (m) 1 Joh. ii. 16.

to purify human minds from all wordly paſſions, and to poſſeſs them with the love of God and of mankind, with univerſal goodneſs and righteouſneſs, is ſo far from preparing people to ſerve us in accompliſhing any unlawful ſecular deſign, that we are thereby arming them againſt us, and doing the beſt we can to render their oppoſition ſteady and reſolute. And does not this lead us to apprehend, that the doctrines propagated by the Apoſtles were the moſt effectual means they could employ, to diſappoint the ſucceſs of any worldly purpoſe that could poſſibly be intended? Upon the ſuppoſition of their having been animated in the ſervice of the Goſpel, from ſome worldly conſideration, let us imagine, that the Apoſtles have at length come to pull off the maſk, and to ſhow themſelves in their real character; would they not, in this event, have found the whole world their moſt implacable enemies, furiouſly inraged, and fiercely bent on their ruin? Moſt certainly, ſuch as hitherto had oppoſed them, would now with juſtice openly, on their ſide, exert their revenge with greater heat and violence; and thoſe very perſons whom they had perſuaded to declare for the Goſpel, and from whom alone they could hope to be ſupported, would, to the higheſt pitch, be now exaſperated againſt them, and by the force of thoſe very principles which they had been at pains to inculcate upon them, would find themſelves powerfully determined to join the reſt of the world in purſuing them to death, as the moſt impious and abandoned Impoſtors. And indeed what could have been more provoking, what could have more inflamed people's indignation, than their finding, that the Apoſtles, while they pretended, under the greateſt ſhew of piety, to lead them on to future glory and immortality, only meant to employ them as inſtruments

struments to compass some base worldly purposes? Thus, I say, had the Apostles made use of the Gospel as an engine, whereby to make a party in the world, that should sustain and protect them in any secular design they had formed; nothing can be more manifest, than that this could have only served to oblige those very persons, on whom alone they could rely, to abandon their interest, to withstand them to the utmost of their power, and to join vigorously in their total overthrow, when ever they should come to understand what they were aiming at.

So that the open contradiction which the doctrines of the Gospel, the only means employed by the Apostles for compassing the end they intended, I say, the violent contradiction which the Gospel bears to every secular view, to all worldly purposes, puts it beyond all possible doubt, that the Gospel was never framed with any the least intention thereby to procure earthly enjoyments; and that the Apostles were neither put upon their enterprise, nor supported in prosecuting it, from any worldly power or motive whatsoever. And if a man of common understanding will consult the sentiments of his own heart, or how he himself would act in such particular circumstances, I dare venture to say, he will find, that this is so clear a demonstration upon the principles of human nature, that the Apostles, in the propagation of the Gospel, were no Impostors; that, to propose any thing further in their justification upon this article, may be thought altogether needless. However, I shall go on to another general reflection. And,

Had the Apostles, in the propagation of the Gospel, designed to have promoted any worldly plot, they would certainly have found themselves necessitated to take most of their Disciples into the concert. Such a conduct, I confess, seems contrary to the rules of prudence: But the doctrines they taught being naturally all calculated to train people up, and to support them, only in the pursuit of spritual and heavenly objects; to prevent the influence of those doctrines, or to bring it about that they should not engage the world to defeat the plot, when it should be ripe for execution, must it not have been strongly inculcated, that by those doctrines it was only meant to cover a design of gaining some worldly purpose? Upon which one cannot but observe, that not only the Apostles must have given up themselves to the most abandoned principles, but they must likewise have brought the world about them into the same state of atheism. But how extravagant such an imputation is in the case of the Apostles, and how impossible such an event must be reckoned with respect to the rest of mankind, while the doctrines of the Gospel are openly pressed on their attention, I leave to every man to judge. I would only, I say, observe, that in the service of the Gospel, had the Apostles had in view any secular design, they must of necessity have discovered it to most of their Disciples.

Now, the case being thus situated, great numbers of people being taken in as accomplices, how was it possible to prevent the whole from being made public? To trust a plot in but a few hands, every body knows, is very dangerous; but to commit the secret to many, is to multiply the dangers in proportion to the numbers that are admitted; and if those many come to suffer for it, is it not then absolutely impossible but among thousands, especially of common people, who in all ages have been every where very unfit confidents, the design must very soon
come

come fully to be detected? All this seems to lie obvious to one who reflects on the principles of human nature, on the several weaknesses and passions of mankind, and on what has never yet failed to happen in the world. And what was to hinder this from coming to pass in the case of the Apostles, had they employed the Gospel as an engine whereby to compass any carnal or worldly interest? One should think it unavoidable. But so far was any thing of this nature from happening, that the Apostles and their Disciples always resolutely persisted in the clean contrary declarations. And is it not surprising how this plot, which must have been intrusted to infinite numbers of people, every where through the world, never came to be discovered, neither from the horror of the thing itself, (and full of horror it must have been, when carried on under the the most sacred appearances of religion, the most awful representations of God and another world); nor from any one single imprudent word or action, nor from any sort of futility, nor discontent, nor bribes, nor tortures, nor from any other temptation, to which people in such circumstances are obnoxious?

The Disciples of the Apostles did not all of them continue in their profession; some of them renounced the doctrines of the Gospel, and took up again with their former principles. And it is to be thought, that, instead of justifying the change they had made, by exposing the cabal wherein they had been engaged, they would chuse to give an account of things, that directly vindicates the Apostles, and proclaims the sacredness of the scheme they had formed? Is it not amazing, that among all the Apostates from Christianity, who returned again to Idolatry, and, as a proof of their being in good earnest, cursed curfed and blafphemed *Chrift Jefus*, there was not one of them that difclofed the grand fecret; but to their own lafting reproach, gave a quite contrary account of the nature and defign of the Chriftian inftitution, and did really reprefent it in that light, that fhews it not only to be altogether harmlefs and innocent, but to be wifely framed to derive infinite benefit to mankind?

The Apoftles were perfecuted themfelves, they neither promifed, nor were they able to protect their Difciples from the cruelleft fufferings. And, is it to be thought, that, every-where through the world, vaft numbers of people, in oppofition to their own countrymen, their beft acquaintances, and neareft relations, would obftinately keep the fecret, and lay down their lives in a caufe, from which they could then hope to reap no advantage, and which, by the principles of the Gofpel they profeffed, would certainly involve them in eternal mifery; and all this for the fake of a few obfcure perfons, mere ftrangers of no character? Did it ever happen among mankind, that multitudes of poor-fpirited, fickle and needy creatures, through all parts of the world, efpecially weak timorous women, (who particularly were put to the rack, as being far more apt, becaufe of the delicacy of their conftitution, to be frightened, or tortured into a confeffion) I fay, was it ever known among mankind, that vaft numbers of fuch fort of people, did all keep miraculoufly firm to one another in the moft fteady and uniform manner, notwithftanding the feveral weakneffes, and all the ftrongeft paffions of human nature, triumphantly rejecting bribes, and defpifing tortures, rather than betray a few abject Impoftors, whereby they might be bettered, at leaft,

least, secured all their own most valuable enjoyments?

That thus it actually happened, in the case of the primitive Christians, is attested by a very considerable man, *Pliny*, a *Roman* Senator and Consul, who himself took cognizance of the matter, and made inquisition by torture, to bring the plot to light, but found none (*n*). And must not this be reckoned another clear demonstration, that the Apostles, in the discharge of their office, were far from being Impostors? One should think, that, in the moral world, it as impossible for the Apostles to have been animated

---

(*n*) Propositus est libellus sine Auctore, multorum nomina continens, qui negarent se esse Christianos, aut fuisse quum, præeunte me, deos appellarent, et imagini tuæ, quam propter hoc jussorum cum simulacris numinum afferri, thure ac vino supplicarent, præterea maledicerent Christo: quorum nihil cogi posse dicuntur, qui sunt revera Christiani. Ergo dimittendos putavi. Alii ab indice nominati, esse se Christianos dixerunt, et mox negaverunt: fuisse quidem, sed desisse, quidam ante triennium, quidam ante plures annos, non nemo viginti quoque. Omnes et imaginem tuam, deorumque simulacra venerati sunt, ii et Christo maledixerunt. Affirmabant autem hanc fuisse summam vel culpæ suæ, vel erroris, quod essent soliti stato die ante lucem convenire, carmenque Christo, quasi Deo dicere secum invicem; seque sacramento non in scelus aliquod obstringere, sed ne furta, ne latrocinia, ne adulteria committerent, ne fidem fallerent, ne depositum appellati abnegarent. Quibus peractis morem sibi discedendi fuisse, rursusque coeundi ad capiendum cibum, promiscuum tamen et innoxium: quod ipsum facere desisse post edictum meum, quo secundum mandata tua hetærias esse vetueram. Quo magis necessarium credidi, ex duabus ancillis, quæ ministræ dicebantur, quid esset veri et per tormenta quærere. Sed nihil aliud inveni quam superstitionem pravam et immodicam, ideoque dilata cognitione, ad consulendum te decurri. Visa est enim mihi res digna consultatione, maxime propter periclitantium numerum; multi enim omnis ætatis, omnis ordinis, utriusque sexus etiam, vocatur in periculum, et vocabuntur. Neque enim civitates tantum, sed vicos etiam atque agros superstitionis istius contagio pervagata est. Plin. Epist. 97. lib. x.

animated in the propagation of the Gospel, from the influence of a traiterous conspiracy against God and mankind, as it is in the natural world for this stupenduous fabric of the universe to have taken its rise from the jumbling together of atoms.

And indeed the Apostles themselves, far from the condition of those persons that are secretly carrying on any traiterous design, were so little concerned about what any man in the world had in his power to make public against them, that they dealt by their own Disciples in such a manner, as could not but have provoked them to disclose all their villainies, had they been privy to any conspiracy of a secular nature. Such, I say, was the conduct of the Apostles, that while the managers of a plot, against the interests of other people, must be extremely cautious not to disoblige any of their associates, and find it necessary to be always very indulgent, they, by no means, go about, in any degree to caress or humour such as they had engaged to embrace their interest; nor do they suffer them to commit, without severely checking them, any whatever action inconsistent with the doctrines of the Gospel; but, while they openly appeal to God, and call upon the world, upon all that had been most intimately acquainted with them, to bear witness to the uprightness of their hearts, and the integrity of their lives, they never fail to exercise all proper severities against such of their followers as, in any instance, did not walk answerably to those principles of universal righteousness, which they had been taught, and whereof they had made public profession. And from this conduct of the Apostles, what can be plainer, than that they were in no concert for promoting any worldly design? To check people for every act of unrighteousness, and not

not to bear with them in the neglect of any inſtance of goodneſs, is but very bad diſcipline for thoſe who are to be employed in the executing a plot full of wickedneſs. One ſhould think that, in the proſpect of ſuch an event, the Apoſtles would have been a little more indulgent to their Diſciples, and rather have choſen to have overlooked their failings, which not hurting the main deſign, might afford them ſurer hopes of having their aſſiſtance. Nor do the Apoſtles ſo contrive it, that the cenſures inflicted upon offenders, ſhall be the leaſt provoking, or ſuch as may be confiſtent with their ſtill retaining an intereſt in the main thing intended; whereby their exerting themſelves in carrying it on might ſtill be ſecured. So far were the Apoſtles above the fear of being diſcovered, and ſo little did they mind people's contributing their aſſiſtance in campaſſing any worldly deſign, that it was their common way to command their Diſciples, in the moſt ſolemn manner, to *withdraw themſelves from every brother that walked diſorderly, and not after the tradition,* or the inſtructions of the Goſpel, *he had received of them*; and when the offence required it, they did not ſcruple to ſingle out particular perſons, and to proceed againſt them with the utmoſt ſeverity, in *excommunicating them the Chriſtian ſociety*. And when people came to be thus publicly branded with ſo much infamy, that they were held too ſcandalous to be converſed with, and were at the ſame time cut off from all proſpect of reaping any benefit from the confederacy wherein they had been embarked; is it to be thought, that ſuch perſons, who were thus publicly affronted, and totally deprived of all their expectations, would not have expoſed the Apoſtles had it been in their power,

power, and laid open the whole train of their wickedness?

There is nothing more certain, than that, in all ages of the world, men have been always strongly affected with a quick sense of infamy, and would have rather chose to submit to any thing, than to be every where pointed at as the hateful spectacles of contempt and aversion. And indeed, what comfort can a man have in life, when he comes to be shunned by every body, as a worthless ignominious wretch, too infamous with whom to have any intercourse? A man, in such circumstances, cannot but have his passions mightily inflamed against those who have done worse than banished him human society, have laid him under all the agonies of public reproach and ignominy. And, as it has always raised abhorrence in human nature, for one man to accuse or reproach another with those crimes whereof he himself is known to be guilty; so one's indignation and revenge must be exasperated to the highest pitch, when one reflects that all his disgrace has come upon him, from those very men, who, at the bottom, are as wicked and infamous as himself. And, when a man has suffered thus much, will he refuse to make reprisals, when he has it in his power to do himself justice? No, his enraged passions, and the malicious pleasure he wants to have indulged, in seeing his enemies made equally odious, will violently push him on to lay open their character, and to discover all their secret villainies. And, without question, this he will do the more unmercifully, for his being disappointed of all those advantages which he had promised himself by engaging in their interest, and keeping their crimes secret in the pursuit of that conspiracy wherein they were embarked.

Such

Such persons, therefore, as the Apostles cut off from the body of Christians, as too scandalous to be owned by that society, and who, by that means, were given up to public disgrace and infamy, and to suffer the disappointment of all their hopes, would most certainly have disclosed all their secret plottings, had there been any worldly concert devised amongst them. And when not the least shadow of any thing of this nature ever did appear to the prejudice of the Apostles, is not this a most convincing proof, that, in the service of the Gospel, the Apostles were animated by no secular design of any sort? Those holy men, strongly fortified by a consciousness of the innocence, the excellency of their intentions, and the uprightness, and integrity of their lives, are not afraid of being discovered, how much soever any one may be provoked against them; but dare be bold publicly to chastise their own Disciples with the utmost severities. And yet, I say, every body knows how exceeding dangerous it is for an Impostor to give the least discontent to any one of his cabal, tho' the meanest and most inconsiderable; and that nothing in the world is more inconstant, or less to be depended on, even amidst the most indulgent treatment, than the minds and affections of the multitude, whereof the Apostles followers mostly consisted.

But supposing, what never possibly could have happened, That the plot was only intrusted with the public Ministers of the Gospel; yet even in this case, one cannot imagine but it must have been detected. Among the Twelve whom our Saviour in his life-time made choice of for his constant attendants, there was one so treacherous as to betray innocent blood, and another so timorous as to deny his Master.

ster. And as for those whom the Apostles employed as their assistants in the propagation of the Gospel; as they must have been all of a villainous conduct towards the rest of mankind, so there is not the least doubt but many of them were disposed to prove perfidious to the Apostles.

There was a set of men who had got to be Teachers in the Christian church, who *transforming themselves into the Apostles of Christ,* or pretending in all instances to be equal to the Twelve themselves, were in reality only *false Apostles, and deceitful workers* (*o*). Now, this set of men, who seem to have been of the *Jewish* nation, and obstinately zealous to introduce *Jewish* rites into the Christian institution, did every where, with great heat and violence, oppose themselves to the Apostle *Paul* in particular, using all means in their power to ruin his credit in the world, and to expose him to universal contempt and hatred. Nay, so far did those false brethren suffer themselves to go in their malice against this Apostle, and so eager were they to have him out of the way, that they put him in frequent danger of his life (*p*). And is it to be thought, that men of such dispositions, had they been conscious of any design, the discovering of which was certain ruin to St. *Paul,* would have kept the secret, and thereby saved the man whom they mortally hated, and whose destruction they had conspired? For no other reason, but his altering his resolution of coming from *Macedonia* to *Corinth,* occasioned from his understanding that the *Jews* laid wait for him by the way (*q*), they accuse him of lightness or inconstancy, of *walking according to the flesh,* or of consulting his own carnal ease and safety, more than the interest of the Gospel; thereby insinuating he could be no faithful Apostle of *Jesus*

(*o*) 2 Cor. xi. 13. (*p*) Ibid. ver. 26. (*q*) Acts xx. 3.

sus Christ, but would frame his doctrines as they might be consistent with his own preservation (*r*). Nor do these miseries wherein this Apostle comes to be involved move their pity, or in any degree extenuate their malice; on the contrary, his afflictions heightened their revenge, and rendered them more active totally to oppress him. Thus, while he was in bonds at *Rome* those *false brethren* become mighty zealous and bold in preaching the Gospel; not that they valued the success of its doctrines, or had any hearty concern for its prosperity; but that they might thereby incense the civil magistrate, and hasten the ruin of the prisoner, to whose influence the whole would be imputed, as he was counted *a main support of this new religion* (*s*). After this manner did the impotent malice of those false Apostles exert itself. And had those men, who laid hold of such opportunities to gratify their malice, had it in their power to have discovered any criminal design, wherein they were conscious this Apostle was concerned, against any branch of the liberties of mankind, is it, I say, to be thought they would have concealed it? Would *Alexander*, exasperated as he was, and who had otherwise done the Apostle much evil (*t*), would this man have faithfully kept the secret? Beyond all question, they would have brought it out against him, with all its aggravations.

In short, the Apostles themselves were sometimes upon such terms with one another, that the supposed plot must have either been betrayed or quite disappointed. For it must be observed, that how divine soever their doctrines, and however holy their lives, yet in every instance of their conduct
the

(*r*) 1 Cor. i. 16, 17. x. 2.   (*s*) Philip. i. 14, 15, 16.
(*t*) 1 Tim. i. 20. and 2 Tim. iv. 14.

the Apostles were not totally exempt from all the frailties of human nature. We are told that *Paul withstood Peter to the face, because he was to be blamed*; and that, in relation to the Evangelist *Mark*, there happened a contention betwixt *Paul* and *Barnabas*, which *became so sharp, that they departed asunder one from the other*, and took with them each his own companion. And how dangerous it is, how fatal it always proves to men confederated together in any criminal design, thus to oppose one another, and upon their opposition to break up and fly asunder, going off in different parties, the world is very sensible. So that, I say, had the plot been entrusted only with the public Ministers of the Gospel; even in this case it is impossible but it must have been detected. And there being on all hands, even among those *false brethren*, who, altogether regardless of the success of the Gospel, only wanted an opportunity to ruin the Apostles; there being, I say, even among such persons, an absolute silence as to any thing of this nature, this must afford to every impartial man, who attends to human nature, full conviction of the innocence of the Apostles.

To all this, let me now add, There is a sincere undisguised honesty, a native plainness and simplicity that appear conspicuous all over the apostolical conduct. Such is the human constitution, that if it be not absolutely perverted, no man can engage in any criminal pursuit, without exposing his mind to uneasiness. To prevent therefore the inward reproaches of a guilty conscience, and to bring about our being easy and undisturbed in prosecuting the wicked design in which we are resolute, it is our constant way to extenuate and lessen the crime, or to set it in such a light that it may appear innocent, and perhaps laudable. Nor can any thing be more

artful

SECT. IX. *Christian Revelation.* 69

artful or ingenious than the human mind frequently seems to be, in impoſing upon itſelf in ſuch inſtances. So that had the Apoſtles been ſo many cheats and Impoſtors, one might expect to find deceit and falſehood, the reigning vice they were guilty of, repreſented in ſuch a manner, as, in ſome circumſtances, at leaſt, not to prove too troubleſome to one's conſcience. But how very contrary to every thing of this nature, is the whole conduct of the Apoſtles? Like ſincere honeſt men, who have no temptation to diſguiſe the enormity of lying, or to ſet it in a falſe light for the eaſe of a guilty conſcience, they not only expreſsly forbid lying (*u*); but they repreſent it as the moſt odious and dangerous thing poſſible. Not content with giving it out as an effect of the corruption of human nature; to heighten the horror of the crime, they ſet it forth as the work of the *devil, who is a liar and the Father of lyes*, that evil Spirit in whom there is no truth, and whoſe nature is directly oppoſite to the nature of *God* (*x*). No wonder therefore that ſo hainous and black a crime brings along with it the ſevereſt puniſhment: *All liars*, ſays the Apoſtles, *ſhall have their part in the lake that burneth with fire and brimſtone, which is the ſecond death* (*y*).

And as the Apoſtles had more honeſty than in any degree to colour the odious and pernicious nature of lying; ſo on all occaſions they expreſs a particular regard for truth. They tell us, that truth is an eſſential attribute of the divine nature, whoſe moral perfections we are bound, in all inſtances, to imitate: That they had a promiſe of having the *Spirit of God* imparted to them from heaven, in order *to lead them into all truth*: That in the mind of every real Chriſtian truth is the genuine, native

(*u*) Coloſſ iii. 9.   (*x*) John viii. 44.   (*y*) Rev. xxii 8.

native *fruit of the Holy Ghost*; and they strictly enjoin all their Disciples, that *putting away lying, they should speak every man truth with his neighbour*: For, say they, *we are members one of another*; and *by speaking the truth in love we grow up into him in all things, which is the head, even Christ* (z); who is likewise *the way, the truth and the life*; and *by him alone we can come unto the Father* (a). Thus truth, as the Apostles represent it, is the foundation of our union with *Christ*, and with one another; and upon truth we are built up, till we acquire a meetness to be united with the God of truth to eternity. So that a greater regard for truth can no where be met withal than is expressed by the Apostles in their instructions to mankind. Nor is truth less regarded in every other part of their conduct.

I confess one of the Apostles came to be guilty of a most infamous piece of falsehood in denying his Master. But how inconsistent this was with the settled principles of his nature, one may judge from the deep concern into which it very soon threw him: For his conscience quickly recovering its force, so severely did it reproach him, that the thoughts of what he had done, made him weep bitterly. And so far was *Peter*, in his after-conduct, from ever falling into the like enormity, that, amidst the greatest hardships and dangers, he boldly professed his adherence to his Master, and in his service suffered death chearfully. I say, the Apostles, not only in their doctrines, but in every step of their conduct, shew an intire regard for truth and honesty.

The resurrection of *Jesus Christ* is so essential an article in the Christian institution, that without it, the Gospel can have no subsistence: And how very
cautious

(z) Eph. iv. 15, 25.   (a) John xiv. 6.

cautious were the Apoſtles in admitting this matter of fact? So far were they from being raſh and precipitate, from going headlong into the belief of this article, that however well they might think of one another's honeſty, yet by no means would they truſt to each other's relations about the certainty of the reſurrection, but every one of them, deſpiſing the ſtrongeſt aſſurances he could have from the teſtimony of any of his companions, obſtinately witheld his aſſent, till he had all the evidence which his own ſenſes were capable of affording him. And as the Apoſtles openly ſhew a ſtrong attachment to truth, in guarding ſo ſcrupulouſly againſt being impoſed upon in the matter of the reſurrection; ſo they expreſs the ſame honeſty of heart, in recommending the belief of this article to the reſt of mankind. They aſſured the world, that this extraordinary event, the truth of which they reported, is of ſuch conſequence, that *if it be not true, ſhould they believe in Chriſt, their faith is abſolutely vain,* and they can reap no benefit from the Goſpel. And thus impreſſing the minds of men with a ſenſe of the high importance of this article, and thereby giving ſufficient warning to every man, not to be over-haſty in receiving it, but carefully to inquire into the evidence upon which it is ſupported; they are very exact and particular in relating the place, and time of the reſurrection, the witneſſes, what objections were made againſt it, and all other circumſtances with which it was attended, that may ſerve to clear the matter of fact. So that people's faith is not ſollicited by deluding appearances, but they are put upon a true ſcent, and without any artifice to biaſs them, are fairly left to the conviction of a rational inquiry. Nay, with ſo much ſimplicity do the Apoſtles act, that, in their account of things, they

they take notice of some circumstances that may be apt to induce unthinking people to suspect the whole.

The Rulers of the *Jews* were mightily concerned to have the article of the resurrection to pass for a forgery; and other people, even the Apostles themselves, were with great difficulty brought to confess the truth of it. Supposing therefore an Impostor to have once got the better of people's infidelity in this article, would he not ever after be very cautious to avoid hinting the least circumstance that might revive people's scruples, and give advantage to those who were still endeavouring to expose it? Conscious however of their own innocence, and beyond all doubt, as to the truth of every fact they reported, the Apostles, far otherwise than an Impostor would have done, who has every thing of his own framing, honestly tell us, that *the Disciples having met together in* Galilee, at a mountain where *Jesus* had appointed them, *when they saw him they worshipped him; but some doubted whether it was* Jesus (*b*). Some doubted! What occasion to mention any thing of this nature? Does not such an insinuation seem to countenance the enemies of the resurrection in their prejudices, or to give a handle to half-witted people to object? This single circumstance, which, I must still think, an Impostor, in his account of things, would most carefully have avoided, seems to me to be a powerful proof of the innocence and integrity of the Apostles, and to proclaim them plain honest men, void of all guile and artifice. Nay, their honest hearts are so little apprehensive of being suspected, that they do not so much as inform us, whether those doubts were removed, and only leave us to conjecture it, from what

---

(*b*) Matth. xviii. 17, 18.

what they immediately subjoin ; *And* Jesus *came and spake unto them, saying, all power is given unto me in heaven and in earth, &c.* And let it be here remarked, that these marvellous events, the resurrection and ascension of *Jesus Christ*, had they been in the hands of men not daring to trust their accounts to the force of truth, or to a rational inquiry, no doubt, they would have been set off in a strong glare of pompous images, and with all their circumstances of wonder and amazement, that might strike the imagination, and carry away the passions of mankind. But, under the direction of the Apostles, in how plain and simple a manner are they related? Without all dress, without any sort of ornament that can deceive the mind, or impose upon the judgment, they are sent abroad, and, in order to make their way in the world, are wholly committed to the pure influence of naked truth, or to the bare weight of undisguised honesty, in a plain and simple narration.

At the same time, the Apostles are far from giving it out, as if their doctrines had been universally counted rational, or had gone on smoothly and without opposition. On the contrary, they honestly tell the world, that they were excepted against, not only by the *Jews* and Heathens, but, in several articles, by some who professed themselves Christians: What those objections were, they explain ; and having made their answers, they leave the world to judge. Nor do they go about to palliate the matter, by insinuating that only the ignorant part of mankind took exception ; but they fairly own they were learned men and Philosophers who judged their doctrines foolishness, and themselves bablers. This indeed appears threatening. But so far were the Apostles from dreading the penetration and wit of the moſt learned Rabbi, or the acuteſt Philoſopher, that, without offering to perplex the argument concerning the truth of the Goſpel, by abſtruſe, metaphyſical reaſoning, they put it upon a very ſhort iſſue, they refer the whole to a plain matter of a fact, which had lately happened, which, in all its circumſtances, they deſcribe in the exacteſt and moſt pointed manner, and for the truth of which they appeal to hundreds of living witneſſes. What can be fairer? Or what can ſooner put an end to the controverſy? *If Chriſt, ſay they, be not riſen, then is our preaching vain, and the faith of Chriſtians is alſo vain; yea, and we are found falſe witneſſes of God; becauſe we teſtified of God, that he raiſed up* Chriſt (c).

In a word, there is no ingredient that can enter into the character of an honeſt man, but is to be found in the Apoſtles. In all their accounts of doctrines and facts, if we interpret them with the common candour, which every Writer has an unqueſtionable title to, they are conſiſtent with themſelves and with one another. So impartial are they, that, finding it neceſſary to mix their own hiſtory with that of their Maſter and of the Goſpel, however much it may leſſen their character, they honeſtly relate their own and each others miſtakes and prejudices, and other faults and failings wherewith they were chargeable, both before and after the death and reſurrection of *Jeſus Chriſt*. Nay, ſo little do they think of diſguiſing matters for the ſeeming benefit of their cauſe, that they publiſh abroad thoſe imputations that were laid upon their Maſter: And, what may be thought rather too much ſimplicity, ſo great is their confidence in the

mere

(c) 1 Cor. xv. 14, 15.

mere force of naked truth, that, in several instances, they make no reflections in justifying their Master's character, or in censuring his Accusers, but, contenting themselves with barely relating things, they leave the world to find out the iniquity of the charge from the whole tenor of his conduct.

Thus honest and impartial in what concerned their Master and themselves, they are no less so in their treatment of other people. Being sensible how extremely dangerous it was to oppose the superstition and idolatry then universally prevalent in the world; as they were willing themselves, in the cause of religion, to suffer the greatest hardships, so they honestly told the world around them, they could promise them in this life no better treatment; and therefore left it to their own choice, whether, in such circumstances, they would undertake the profession of the Gospel, whose rewards are of another world. Nor were they more zealous to gain proselytes, than they were careful, as I hinted before, by using proper severities upon delinquents, to keep them constant and regular in the steady pursuit of all godliness and righteousness, which is all along the avowed design of their Ministry.

But what is there wanting in the character of the Apostles, that is needful to assure us of their honesty? Even amidst the severest persecutions and the cruellest sufferings, they retract nothing, as to any point of doctrine, or any article of fact, but still persist in the same declarations. In face of their Judges, when the impending evil must alarm the guilty, and reduce them to all their art in covering their crime, or in suing for favour, the Apostles, who might have saved themselves, only at the expence of quitting their cause, openly avow the charge of preaching the doctrine of the resurrection, and,

and, in all their defences, uniformly express that manly composure and sedateness of mind, that resolute boldness and intrepidity of conduct, that can arise from nothing but an honest heart supported by the steady conscioufness of a righteous cause of the last importance (*d*). In short, when a guilty mind, not hardened in Atheism, cannot but tremble and be confounded, the Apostles deliberately venture upon death for the cause they maintained, and with solemn protestations in their mouth, of its being *the cause of God and religion*, they fearlessly go into another world, professing a full assurance, that there, as *the reward of their Ministry*, they shall attain to a blessed life and immortality. Thus, I say, there is a strong lively air of honesty, without any the least symptom of imposture, that appears conspicuous upon the whole face of the Apostolical conduct.

When we therefore consider that the Gospel, the only means employed by the Apostles for compassing the end they intended, was so far from being calculated for any worldly purpose, that, on the contrary, it trains people up in a direct opposition to every thing of a secular nature, in those principles that must prevent the execution of any earthly design whatsoever:—When we consider the principles, the several weaknesses and passions of human nature; and particularly,—that vast numbers of naturally poor-spirited, fickle, and needy creatures, through all parts of the world, were under the strongest and the most violent temptations, that man can be under, to betray a secret:—That such as renounced Christianity, and returned again to Idolatry, were powerfully sollicited for their own credit and safety, to make all the discoveries, that could blacken and discredit

(*d*) Acts iv. 8 &c. v. 28, &c. vii.

discredit the Gospel:—That many who had embraced the interest of the Apostles, had the greatest provocations imaginable, even from the Apostles themselves, to lay open whatever can be supposed to have been the conspiracy:—That among the first Publishers of the Gospel, there happened such differences, as could not fail to bring about a detection:—That the enemies of the Christian institution were engaged in the most passionate manner to prevent its propagation; and being under no restraint, but having every thing in their power, employed all possible means to discover a plot, whereby they might have exposed the Apostles and their followers, and rendered them infamous to all mankind: In a word,—That a bright, vigorous air of honesty appears conspicuously all over the Apostolical conduct; I say, when we consider all these particulars laid together, it appears utterly impossible, but the Apostles must have been sincere, honest men, or must infallibly have been detected, had there been any thing secular or carnal in their design or conduct. And no discovery having ever been made, notwithstanding all those things that concurred to render a discovery absolutely inevitable, is not this a full demonstration, that the great Power that sustained and animated the Apostles in the propagation of the Gospel, was no worldly motive whatsoever; and consequently, that the Apostles were no Impostors? In my apprehension, these general reflections do strongly justify the Apostles from all suspicion of imposture.

But, to show the world what great store of invincible proof we have, of the integrity of the first Publishers of the Gospel, I shall proceed to consider those particular articles upon which the charge against them must be founded; and endeavour to demonstrate,

monstrate, that in none of those articles they can justly be held liable. And this I the more gladly undertake, because therein I shall have an opportunity, not only further to explain the conduct of the Apostles, but to lay before the Reader a more particular account of the nature of their doctrines.

SECT. X.

In particular, the Apostles, in propagating the Gospel, were in no Degree animated by the Love of Money, or a Passion for worldly Riches. Their Conduct compared with that of Socrates.

I HAVE already hinted, that in any particular pursuit, especially of a dangerous nature, the riches, pleasures, or honours here below, are the great motives whereby the men of this world are stimulated. So that in reducing the charge against the Apostles to particulars, we must conceive that in the service of the Gospel, they were carried on by a power derived to their active faculties, from some one or more of those worldly considerations. And, as I said before, if the Deists know of any other worldly motive, whereby they apprehend, they have ground to alledge the Apostles were animated, I shall be glad to understand it. I am now to make it appear, that in the prosecution of their Ministry, none of those just now mentioned had any degree of influence over them. And,

In the *first* place; As for covetousness or the love of money, the Apostles take particular notice of this crime, and do not fail to inform the world of its hainous nature, and its mischievous consequences. They

SECT. X. *Christian Revelation.*

They tell us, that *the covetous man is an idolater* (a), one who, in reality, has renounced the worship of the true God as the only spring of all life and felicity, and who having placed his main happiness in riches, is absolutely devoted to the service of *Mammon.* And as the love of money is thus set forth to be totally inconsistent with the love of God, it being altogether contrary to the nature of things *to serve both God and Mammon* (b). So we are told, that *it is the root of all evil; that they that will be rich fall into temptation, and a snare, and into many foolish and hurtful lusts, that drown men in destruction and perdition* (c). And indeed in this world, the covetous man is hard-hearted, insensible to the miseries of his fellow-creatures, he is guilty of all the meannesses and violences of fraud and oppression; every thing is prostituted and becomes a prey to his devouring passion; and in another world, he has no inheritance in the kingdom of God, but receives his portion with the children of disobedience, amidst all the agonies of despair and a guilty conscience (d). And while the Apostles do in this manner set before us the hainous nature and the mischievous consequences of a covetous mind, they use at the same time the most pressing instances, and all the most powerful arguments to prevent their Disciples from giving up themselves to this destructive passion. *Take heed,* say they, *and beware of covetousness; for a man's life consisteth not in the abundance of the things that he possesseth* (e). Such is our condition, that *we brought nothing into this world, and it is certain*

(a) Eph. v. 5.   (b) Matth. vi. 24.

Οὐκοῦν δῆλον ἤδη τοῦτο ἐν πόλει, ὅτι πλοῦτον τιμᾶν ᾗ σωφροσύνην ἅμα ἱκανῶς κτᾶσθαι ἐν τοῖς πολίταις, ἀδύνατον, ἀλλ' ἀνάγκη ἢ τοῦ ἑτέρου ἀμελεῖν ἢ τοῦ ἑτέρου.   Plat. de Republ. lib. viii.

(c) 1 Tim. vi. 9.   (d) Eph. v. 5, 6.   (e) Luk. xii. 15.

tain we can carry nothing out. So that *having food and raiment, let us be therewith content* (*f*). And this we may well agree to, when we have such assurances of the care of God's Providence over us; for he hath said, *I will never leave thee, nor forsake thee* (*g*). And that such admonitions may have the stronger influence upon our hearts, they are enforced by the parable of a rich man whose ground brought forth plentifully: It should seem that while this man was blessing himself in the increase of his wealth, and promising his soul much happiness for many years, his latter end overtakes him; *God said unto him, Thou Fool, this night thy soul shall be required of thee, then whose shall those things be which thou hast provided?* What an instance of desperate folly! *So is he that layeth up treasure for himself on earth, and is not rich towards God* (*h*).

It is true, people are not to throw away that substance, with which God in his Providence hath been pleased to bless them; but as riches are very apt to prove a hindrance to our pursuit after future happiness, the Apostles are at pains to guard their Disciples against the bad effects of their earthly treasures; and to lay down rules whereby they may improve them to the best advantage, so as to render them the means of their attaining to the treasures of heaven. Thus they *charge them that are rich in this world, that they be not high-minded nor trust in uncertain riches, but in the living God, who giveth us all things richly to enjoy: That they do good, that they be rich in good works, ready to distribute, willing to communicate* to others of their wealth; *laying up in store for themselves,* by their constancy in a thankful and moderate, a charitable and beneficent use of their riches,

a good

(*f*) 1 Tim. vi. 7, 8. (*g*) Heb. xiii. 5. Matth. vi. 25, &c.
(*h*) Luk. xii. 16.—21.

SECT. X.   *Christian Revelation.*   81

a good foundation against the time to come, that, when these things fail, *they may lay hold on eternal life* (*i*). And so careful were the Apostles to preserve their Disciples from the infection of this ruining vice, that they command them to withdraw themselves from all such as supposed, that *gain is godliness*, who were covetous, and valued every thing according to the present profit they were able to make of it (*k*). In short, among the qualifications necessary to those who are to be employed in preaching the Gospel to the world, it is expressly required, that *they be not greedy of filthy lucre, nor covetous,* but, on the contrary, that *they be given to hospitality* (*l*). Nor do they load men with burthens grievous to be borne, while they themselves will not touch them; this qualification they solemnly claim, while they call God to witness, that *they never used a cloak of covetousness* (*m*). And as it is observed of false Teachers, that *an heart they have exercised with covetous practices, while through covetousness, they with feigned words make merchandise of other people,* so the Apostle warmly declares, that *they are cursed children, whose judgment now of a long time lingereth not, and whose damnation slumbereth not, to whom the mist of darkness is reserved for ever* (*n*).

Now, when we thus find that the Apostles represented covetousness in the most odious light, hateful to God, in both worlds mischievous to mankind, and used all possible means to guard their Disciples against it, themselves appealing to God for their own innocence; can it ever be imagined, that those

Vol. II.   L   very

(*i*) 1 Tim. vi. 17, 18, 19. Luk. xvi. 9.
(*k*) 1 Tim. vi. 5.   1 Cor. v. 11.
(*l*) 1 Tim. iii. 2, 3.
(*m*) 1 Thess. ii. 5.
(*n*) 2 Pet. xi. 3. 14. 17.

very men had no other motive to excite and support them in the propagation of the Gospel? One cannot possibly enter into this thought, without holding the Apostles daring Atheists of the blackest character; which, as I hinted before, is an imputation not easily to be admitted against any man. But what is the evidence, or the shadow of evidence, upon which this charge of covetousness can be made out, or at all conceived against them?

Had the love of money been the commanding motive that animated the Apostles in the propagation of the Gospel, considering they went on resolutely through the fiercest oppositions, and exposed themselves to the greatest dangers, and ventured their lives to have it gratified, it is impossible but their lust after riches must have been insatiable. But under the violence of this passion raging in the souls of the Apostles, where are the mischievous consequences that must have necessarily broken out in the heat of their pursuit? The infamous love of money that prevailed in the church of *Rome*, is most visible; and the mischiefs it occasions have been felt most sensibly. And is it not surprising, or rather inconsistent with the nature of things, that none of those foolish and hurtful lusts, none of those mischiefs that arise from avarice, and drown men in destruction and perdition, did in any measure, ever shew themselves in so much as one single instance of the conduct of the Apostles? *Out of the abundance of the heart the mouth speaketh:* And to alledge against a man, a prevailing passion lodged in his breast, of which in his whole course of life, there is no one symptom appearing, is certainly the most groundless, the very absurdest thing in nature. *A tree is known by its fruit:* And so far were the Apostles from being men of a greedy covetous

tous heart, that their temper and conduct proclaim their character to be quite the contrary. It is needless to explain the whole wretched offspring of the love of money, and to make it appear that nothing of that nature can be fathered upon the Apostles; I I shall only observe,

Where the love of money prevails, it contracts a man's mind, and locks him up within the narrow bounds of his own false interest; it makes him quite regardless of his fellow-creatures, and renders him wholly insensible to human miseries, leaving him neither heart nor hand to relieve them; but on the contrary, prompting him to all the acts of fraud, violence and oppression. That this is the effect of the love of money, is obvious to the world. And I take upon me to say, that whoever examines into the character of the Apostles, will find it equally obvious, that they were men of a noble greatness of soul, generous beyond expression, and inspired with an uncommon munificent love towards mankind; and could not therefore be under the power of this mean sordid passion.

So far indeed were the Apostles from having it in their power, out of their own treasures, to exercise any acts of beneficence in relieving the necessities of the distressed and indigent, that being possessed of no personal estates, and employing all their time and labour in the propagation of the Gospel, they must themselves have been subsisted by the charity of other people. But as their provision this way was so very scanty, that they were frequently made to suffer hunger, and thirst, and cold, and nakedness; so when they had reason to suspect, that their living upon other people's bounty might come to obstruct the success of the Gospel, or hinder some people from embracing their doctrines that

naturally

naturally lead to univerſal piety and righteouſneſs, and train us up for the ſervice and happineſs of heaven; ſo diſintereſted were their hearts with reſpect to any thing merely perſonal, ſo generous, ſo prevalent was their concern for the real good and proſperity of mankind, that they refuſed all charitable contributions for their own uſe, and choſe rather to ſubſiſt themſelves and *them that were with them by working with their own hands* (*o*): *So that in thoſe circumſtances, labouring night and day, becauſe they would not be chargeable to any man, they preached unto them freely the Goſpel of God* (*p*). This in particular was the conduct of the Apoſtle *Paul* among the *Corinthians*, the *Theſſalonians*, and ſeveral others. In an open aſſembly of the Elders of the church at *Epheſus*, and all the Diſciples at *Miletus*, thus does that great man, in a ſublime and pathetic manner, expreſs himſelf; *I have coveted*, ſays he, *no man's ſilver, or gold, or apparel: Yea you yourſelves know that theſe hands have miniſtred to my neceſſities, and to them that were with me* (*q*). Such was the openheartedneſs, ſuch the noble generoſity of the Apoſtles! And can we have the conſcience to ſay, that theſe were the men of whom it may be thought, they intended to make themſelves rich by the propagation of the Goſpel?

The ſame nobleneſs of mind that determined the Apoſtles, when neceſſary to the good of mankind, to refuſe charitable contributions for their own ſubſiſtence, made them exert themſelves in providing relief for the neceſſities of other people. Every man muſt acknowledge, that the whole plan of the Goſpel ſeems to be formed to inſpire human minds with the love of God, and the love of mankind; that

(*o*) Act. xx. 34.   (*p*) 1 Theſſ. ii. 9.   (*q*) Act. xx. 33, 34.

that with hearts full of adoration towards God, we may come, at the same time, so to be united to our fellow-men, as mutually to feel each other's pains and pleasures, which will naturally dispose us to use our best endeavours to lessen the one, and increase the other. Nor can we fail in this, when by a mutual sympathy, we are made to *rejoice with them that do rejoice*, and to *weep with them that weep* (r). But the Apostles, not content with recommending to the world universal benevolence, explain its particular branches, and warmly insist that every man, according to his abilities, or as God has blessed him with worldly substance, should contribute to supply the wants of the needy and indigent, *whoso hath this world's good*, say they, *and seeth his brother have need, and shutteth up his bowels of compassion from him, how dwelleth the love of God in him? My little children, let us not love in word, neither in tongue, but in deed and in truth; and hereby we know that we are of the truth, and shall assure our hearts before him* (s). Thus brotherly charity is strongly inculcated. And many are the powerful motives, whereby the Apostles, in a beautiful and engaging manner, excite their Disciples to be *rich in good works, to be ready to distribute, willing to communicate* of their wealth to their distressed brethren. Nor do they confine their care to those of their own partnership, but they open the views of their Disciples, and direct them in their kind affections, to bear a sympathy, in all instances, with human nature, so as to extend their charitable offices to their enemies, to all mankind of what denomination soever. *As we have therefore,* say they, *opportunity, let us do good unto all men, especially unto*

(r) Rom. xii. 15.   (s) Joh. iii. 17, 18, 19.

to them who are of the houshold of faith (*t*); feeding our enemies if they hunger, and giving them drink if they thirst (*u*). And not only do the Apostles, in their excellent rules for the conduct of life, and the mighty motives whereby they encourage our obedience, make the best provision possible for the necessitous part of mankind; but as the circumstances of their poor brethren, and the situation of affairs required it, they chearfully exposed themselves to the greatest fatigues, while they undertook long journeys in order to make charitable contributions, or to distribute them to those for whom they were made (*x*). And, I say, all this generous concern did the Apostles express for other people, while they were wholly regardless how they subsisted themselves; which is a disinterestedness, a greatness of soul, too great to enter into the thoughts of a covetous man. How then can the love of money be counted the motive that supported the Apostles in the prosecution of their ministry? Nay, so far were they from being animated by a prevailing lust after riches, that all the favourable conjunctures which they had, and which the men of this world would have improved to the purposes of avarice, were by them absolutely neglected, and they followed a quite contrary course.

While the Gospel, in the hands of the Apostles, was just appearing, and as yet had made but a very small progress, so powerfully did the principles of benevolence and brotherly love prevail in the hearts and affections of the first Disciples, that, in order to relieve the necessities of their brethren, *as many as were possessors*

(*t*) 1 Gal. vi 10.   (*u*) Rom. xii. 20.   (*x*) Rom. xv. 25, 26. 1 Cor. xvi 1. &c. 2 Cor. ix.

possessors of lands or houses, sold them, and brought the prices of the things that were sold, and laid them down at the Apostles feet, with full power to dispose of them among the needy, as they shall judge it most equitable and fitting (*y*). This, one would think, was a fair opportunity for a covetous mind to have its passion gratified. But an impregnable honesty in the contempt of riches, shews itself in the conduct of the Apostles. According to the design of the generous donors, they faithfully distributed those sums of money among their needy followers, in proportion to their wants, and as each man's necessities required. Nor can it be suspected, that those distributions were made in order to gain a party, or to secure an interest for the pursuit of some worldly design that was formed. As those persons who sold their possessions, were persuaded to it on religious considerations, and expected thereby to approve themselves to the favour and mercy of God, who, as the Apostles taught them, would reward their charity to the poor, in providing for them eternal treasures in another world; so, beyond question, they had good reason to rest assured, that the Apostles distributed those sums of money, no otherwise than according to the views and intentions they had, when they first put them wholly in their power. For, as I observed formerly, had the Disciples had any the least ground, from any one instance of their conduct, to suspect the Apostles of aiming at any secular interest of their own, as the great end they intended to compass; so far would they have been from thus contributing their assistance, or, after they had done it, from bearing their misfortunes patiently, that, on the contrary, upon

the

(*y*) Acts iv. 34, &c.

the first discovery they made of the cheat, they would doubtless have pursued them with implacable hatred, as the most abandoned and impious Impostors. And this the Apostles themselves, in the case of a secular attempt, could not possibly but foresee.

In short, when the number of Disciples being multiplied, there arose a murmuring of the *Hellenists*, or *Jews of the dispersion*, against the *Hebrews*, because their *widows were neglected in the daily administration*; and the Apostles came to find that their attending to those distributions, so as to prevent all such murmurings, would take up too much of their time, and by that means interrupt their preaching of the Gospel, or hinder them from the constant pursuit of the main design of their office; *they proposed to the multitude of the Disciples, that they would make choice of seven men of their own number, and of known honesty and integrity, whom they might set over this business; while they, in the mean time, would give themselves continually to prayer, and the ministry of the word* (z). Now this proposition, and leaving the choice to the whole body of the Disciples, without offering to assume the power of this election to themselves, afford us, in my apprehension, an incontestable evidence of the disinterestedness of the Apostles in this matter, and a full demonstration, that, in propagating the Gospel, they were neither minding nor pursuing any secular interest of their own, such as the amassing of riches, or getting money into their hands. For, had they combined together in any confederacy of this nature, 'tis impossible they could have concerted or followed those measures, which they must have known, would, in the

(z) Acts vi. 1, &c.

the most effectual manner, have confounded their design, and absolutely disappointed them.

But the integrity of the Apostles hearts, the innocence of their design, their freedom from imposture, may yet more strongly appear, from considering the free and gratuitous manner in which they communicated that most valuable stock of knowledge they were possessed of, and those other extraordinary blessings they had in their power to impart to mankind. And since *Socrates* is a character highly valued by the Deists, and among all good men; hoping that, by equal reason, in both cases, the Deists will, at least, be equally affected, I shall, in this article, consider his conduct along with that of the Apostles.

This great man, whilst other Philosophers were vainly employed in the study of nature, wherein they were so far from being useful, that they were of mischievous consequence to mankind; I say, *Socrates* coming to be sensible of the folly of such speculations, applied himself wholly to the study of moral philosophy; and having acquired the knowledge of some moral truths, that direct mankind in the conduct of life, and are the great means of private and public happiness, he does not reserve that knowledge to himself, but he imparts it to other people, and makes it the sole business of his life, within the bounds of *Athens*, to recommend to every man, citizen and stranger, the study and pursuit of virtue and goodness. Nor does he follow the example of other Philosophers and Sophists, who, as one may say, traded with their knowledge, and made gain of their instructions; but he employs all his time and labour in teaching the world *gratis*, and will receive no money, no reward; rich and poor being equally welcome to his inſtructions, equally the objects of his tender generous concern. Nay, ſo far was *Socrates* from making his philoſophy ſubſervient to any worldly intereſt, that, for the ſake thereof, he ſuffers poverty, he bears calumny and ridicule, and comes at length to lay down his life (*a*). Thus, there is a glory ſhining forth in *Socrates*'s character, that renders it mighty illuſtrious, and which every Deiſt will confeſs puts it out of the reach of an imputation of covetouſneſs. And, I ſay, may I not hope, that all our Free-thinkers, who value themſelves upon an impartiality in judging, will be ready to do the ſame juſtice to the character of the Apoſtles?

Theſe were men, who, in ſpite of their own education, had got above the ſuperſtition of the *Jews*; who expoſed the idolatry of the Heathen; and had acquired, or were rather endowed with a moſt extenſive knowledge of moral truths, of infinite conſequence to mankind. Neither do thoſe men retain thoſe truths, ſo as to keep them ſecret among themſelves, but they publiſh them abroad to the world, and make choice of it for their buſineſs of life, their only employment, to recommend true religion and univerſal righteouſneſs, to *Jews* and *Heathens*, to all mankind. Nor do the Apoſtles rate their inſtructions at any worldly price, ſo as to turn their doctrines to their ſecular advantage; but all their time and labour are laid out freely, and it coſts the world nothing to be trained up in the knowledge of thoſe valuable truths, that derive happineſs to mankind in all circumſtances of life, and in all their different ſtages of exiſtence. Nay, inſtead of expecting to reap any worldly gain from the Goſpel, the Apoſtles entered upon

---

(*a*) Vid. Apolog. Socrat. apud Plat. & Xenoph.

SECT. X. *Christian Revelation.* 91

upon their miniſtry with the certain proſpect of thereby forfeiting all their earthly comforts, of being involved in the deepeſt afflictions, and of loſing their lives in that ſervice. Of all this, in the caſe of the Apoſtles, we have, at leaſt, full as good evidence, as of what we obſerved in relation to *Socrates*. So that ſuch articles, being deſervedly counted by the Deiſts noble ingredients in *Socrates*'s character, do they not render the character of the Apoſtles equally illuſtrious, and as much above an imputation of covetouſneſs? One ſhould think that a little attention would ſhew us the character of the Apoſtles infinitely ſuperior, as in ſome few particulars I ſhall explain afterwards; but far beyond any thing *Socrates* could pretend to.

The Apoſtles having a power to heal diſeaſes, to relieve mankind from their bodily infirmities; and, being capable to derive the ſame power to other people, had they been ſubject to the love of money, or aimed at riches in the ſervice of the Goſpel, they were certainly in a ſituation more favourable than man could hope for, to gratify an avaritious paſſion. To open the eyes of the blind, to make the dumb to ſpeak, and the lame to walk, to recover people from their pains and ſickneſs, and to reſtore them to health and vigour, theſe are ſervices that juſtly intitle one to very liberal rewards; no man would be aſhamed to make a fortune from ſuch good offices; without doubt, a covetous man would fill his coffers very plentifully. But to every thing of a worldly nature, the Apoſtles are quite inſenſible. *Silver and gold* (ſays one of them to a lame man aſking his alms) *have I none, but ſuch as I have give I thee: In the name of* Jeſus Chriſt *of* Nazareth, *riſe up and walk* (*b*).

After

(*b*) Acts iii. 6.

After this manner, in all instances, they performed their cures freely. As they had set out in the world, so did they always steadily proceed, upon the most generous principles possible; *freely they had received,* and *freely they gave* to all ranks of men without distinction, to the rich as well as to the poor (*c*).

And not only do the Apostles freely, without any earthly reward, employ their power in relieving mankind from all sorts of diseases; but they communicate the same power to others to be employed after the same free gratuitous manner. Some people, indeed, had the assurance to offer them money, if they would impart to them the faculty of deriving to others this wonderful power of healing diseases. But how much they were above every sordid temptation of avarice, may be learned from their conduct in the case of one *Simon* at *Samaria, who, by his sorceries,* had acquired so extraordinary a reputation, that *all the people, from the least to the greatest, gave heed to him,* and in a manner adored him, *saying, this man is the great power of God.* It should seem that this man, having quitted his former way of sorcery, and made profession of the Christian faith, when he came to observe, that the Apostles, by laying on of hands, conferred the miraculous gifts of the Holy Ghost, judging, we may believe, that, were he likewise made capable of deriving the same gifts to other people, it would greatly promote his interest, and prove a fine source of worldly gain; did therefore take upon him to propose a bargain to the Apostles, and to offer them money, provided they would give him also this power, that, *on whomsoever he laid hands, he should receive the Holy Ghost.*

(*c*) Matth. x. 8.

Ghost. But this offer, irresistible to men under the power of an insatiable thirst after riches, with a noble indignation the Apostles reject as most impious, and openly show, without fearing to be contradicted, that, in preaching the Gospel of *Jesus Christ*, and in communicating those miraculous gifts of the Holy Ghost, they had in their power to convey to others, they were infinitely above all mercenary views whatsoever. Peter *said unto him, thy money perish with thee, because thou hast thought, that the gift of God may be purchased with money. Thou hast neither part nor lot in this matter, for thy heart is not right in the sight of God. Repent therefore of thy wickedness, and pray God if, perhaps, the thought of thine heart may be forgiven thee. For, I perceive that thou art in the gall of bitterness, and in the bond of iniquity* (*d*). Thus the Apostles dare be bold to represent the disinterested nature of their enterprise; and that all the blessings they were enabled to impart to mankind, were designed to be free and gratuitous. In every article they look like honest men, that are strongly fortified with a good conscience; they express a noble greatness of soul, that disdains all sordid views, and that shews them fired with motives more than human. As the Deists cannot, therefore, but here observe, that the Apostles had it in their power to make themselves masters of vast treasures, so, at the same time, it cannot but be confessed, that they absolutely contemned all such base and ignoble pursuits.

Thus, from many unquestionable truths, more than can be had in the case of *Socrates*, or any other man whatsoever, it evidently appears, that the love of money was by no means the great power or motive

(*d*) Acts viii. 9, &c.

tive that animated the Apoſtles, in the propagation of the Goſpel. And, if nothing of this nature can at all be laid againſt them, one ſhould think it impoſſible, in reaſon, to charge them with any other earthly conſideration, as the commanding paſſion that engaged and ſupported them in their grand undertaking.

For, as to the other motives, the pleaſures, and honours of this world, every body knows, that no man can maintain himſelf, or his followers, in thoſe enjoyments, without conſiderable ſums of money. The frequent ruin that comes upon people's fortunes, makes it manifeſt, that, to indulge one's pleaſures without control, is not a little expenſive. And, does not every man that is ſtimulated by the luſt of power, and who has actually entered into a plot to gratify his ambition, and aggrandize himſelf in the world, find money abſolutely neceſſary to give life and ſucceſs to the deſign he has formed? So that, from this neglect and contempt of riches, which the Apoſtles had fair opportunities to get into their hands, and which they abhorred to improve, as a thing moſt impious and abominable; I ſay, from this neglect and contempt of riches, which the Apoſtles openly expreſſed upon all occaſions, it ſeems to be put beyond diſpute, that they never intended to attempt the pleaſures, or to attain to the honours of this world: And this might prevent my proceeding any further. But that the world may ſee what accumulated proofs we have of the integrity of the firſt Publiſhers of the Goſpel, I ſhall make it appear, from particular conſiderations, that, in the ſervice of the Goſpel, the Apoſtles were as little animated by any of thoſe other motives, and are therein as little liable to the charge of impoſture.

S E C T.

SECT. XI.

None of the base Pleasures of this World, no lewd or intemperate Passions, supported the Apostles in the Ministry of the Gospel.

AS it is an undoubted truth, that no man can preserve the dignity of his nature, be easy in himself, or useful to his fellow-creatures, or happy in the enjoyment of God, without bridling his bodily appetites, and keeping them within the bounds of moderation; so the Gospel being framed with a view to exalt human nature, and to render mankind in themselves, and in one another, really happy in both worlds, it prescribes to us certain rules that direct us in the government of those passions inlaid in our nature for the support of the individual, and the preservation of the species. Thus we are commanded to *take heed to ourselves, lest at any time our hearts be overcharged with surfeiting and drunkenness* (a). And having informed us, that *incontinency* does not wholly lie in bodily acts, but that *whosoever looketh on a woman to lust after her, hath committed adultery with her already in his heart* (b); *this* (say the Apostles) *is the will of God, this your sanctification, that ye should abstain from fornication, that every one of you should know how to possess his vessel in purity and honour; not in the lust of concupiscence, even as the Gentiles do which know not God* (c). And not only do the Apostles enjoin their

---

(a) Luke xxi. 34.
(b) Matth. v. 28. Vid. Ælian. Var. Hist. lib. 14. cap. 42.
(c) 1 Thess. iv. 3, 4.

their Disciples to be careful to avoid all lewdness and intemperance, but they represent to them the danger of indulging such appetites. They tell them, that, as these vicious practices arise from the depravity of human nature, and are wholly repugnant to the Spirit of God, with whose influences every true Christian is animated (*d*); so, as well as other evil works, they exclude people from the kingdom of heaven. *Be not deceived,* (say the Apostles) *neither fornicators, nor adulterers, nor effeminate, nor abusers of themselves with mankind, nor drunkards, shall inherit the kingdom of God* (*e*). So that *their end is destruction, whose god is their belly, and whose glory is in their shame, who mind earthly things* (*f*). And the man who is not governed by the dictates of chastity, who, in particular, goes beyond the bounds of matrimony, and defrauds his brother in this matter; *the Lord is the avenger of all such. For God hath not called us unto uncleanness, but unto holiness* (*g*). Such are the considerations from whence the Apostles go about to persuade their Disciples to keep themselves unspotted from the pollutions of this world, to be in all instances temperate and chaste. But,

Not contenting themselves with arguments, that work upon people's fears, the Apostles endeavour to engage their Disciples in the pursuit of these virtues, from the decency of the thing, or its being a conduct of life highly becoming their circumstances, from the folly of their acting otherwise; and its inconsistency with the relation they bear to God and to *Jesus Christ*. The Heathen world being in darkness, ignorant of God, of the compass of their duty, and
of

(*d*) Gal. v. 17, &c.   (*e*) 1 Cor. vi. 9, 10.
(*f*) Phil. iii. 19.   (*g*) 1 Thess. iv. 6, 7.

of an after-life and immortality, might be tempted to indulge their criminal appetites, and to take up with the present gratifications of sense: But such as profess the Gospel, being enlightened in the knowledge of an infinite mind of spotless purity and holiness, having the beauty of virtue in all its several branches set before them, and being assured of a future state of refined rational enjoyments, in the society of God and happy spirits, such persons, in the view of so much excellency, cannot prostitute themselves to intemperance and incontinency, without profaning their light or disgracing their knowledge, without rendering themselves base and unworthy. *The night is far spent*, say the Apostles, *the day is at hand: let us therefore cast off the works of darkness, and let us put on the armour of light. Let us walk honestly as in the day; not in rioting and drunkenness, not in chambering and wantonness, not in strife and envying. But put ye on the Lord Jesus, and make not provision for the flesh, to fulfil the lusts thereof* (*h*). And herein indeed we would escape the folly of placing our rest in things that perish, that will leave us miserable. *For meats*, say the Apostles, *are for the belly, and the belly for meats*; neither of them have any other use; nor can they answer this use any longer than this present life; *the time will come when God will destroy both it and them* (*i*). Nor in any instance can we give up ourselves to lasciviousness, without basely dishonouring the *body of Christ*, and impiously polluting the *temple of God*. In the Gospel, Christians are set forth as *the members of that body whereof Christ is the head*; or *they are a building fitly framed together, that groweth unto an holy temple in the Lord, for an habitation of God through the Spirit* (*k*). And in this view of things, the argument proceeds with

Vol. II.   N   great

(*h*) Rom. xiii. 12, 13, 14.   (*i*) 1 Cor vi. 13.
(*k*) 1 Cor. xii. 12, 27. Eph. ii. 21, 22. and iv. 15, 16.

great strength and beauty: *Know ye not, that your bodies are the members of Christ? Shall I then take the members of Christ, and make them the members of an harlot? God forbid. What, know ye not, that he which is joined to an harlot is one body? For two, saith he, shall be one flesh. But he that is joined unto the Lord, is one spirit. Fly fornication. Every sin that a man doth, is without the body; but he that committeth fornication, sinneth against his own body. What, know ye not that your body is the temple of the Holy-Ghost which is in you, which ye have of God? And ye are not your own; for ye are bought with a price: Therefore glorify God in your body, and in your spirit, which are Gods* (l); and which, for that reason, cannot be employed in any acts of intemperance, or lewdness, without the height of injustice, and basest ingratitude, without lying exposed to the utmost danger. *For if any man defile the temple of God, him shall God destroy; for the temple of God is holy, which temple ye are* (m).

Thus, in a variety of arguments, with great elegancy and force, the Apostles recommend to their Disciples the love and practice of temperance and chastity. They show a generous concern, that every individual should preserve his constitution in good order, with all his faculties duly balanced, that he may be in a constant fitness for the offices of society, and the service of God: And they express a noble zeal for the regular propagation of human kind, that no misery may befal any of the species from loose pleasures, or lewd enjoyments; but that every production may be safely reared up, and rightly formed to social life, under the notice and care of the tender parents. So ardently do they desire that mankind should pursue this amiable course, that it grieves them to the heart,

(l) 1 Cor. vi. 15.——20.   (m) 1 Cor. iii. 17.

heart, and brings tears from their eyes, when people act otherwise. *Brethren*, says the Apostle, *be ye followers together of me, and mark them which walk so, as ye have us for an ensample, for many walk, of whom I have told you often, and now tell you even weeping, that they are the enemies of the cross of Christ: Whose end is destruction, whose god is their belly, and whose glory is in their shame, who mind earthly things. For our conversation is in heaven, from whence also we look for the Saviour, the Lord Jesus Christ: Who shall change our vile body, that it may be fashioned like unto his glorious body; according to the working whereby he is able to subdue even all things unto himself*, (*n*).

And while the Apostles are so extremely sollicitous to inspire mankind with all temperate and chaste affections, and thereby to establish in the world universal order and happiness, is it to be imagined, that in all this, they had nothing in view, but to raise themselves into such a situation, wherein they might safely gratify the clean contrary passions, that bring forth only confusion and misery? To press upon people temperance and chastity, by arguments taken from the nature of God and another world, to represent the danger of riot and luxury in the case of a rich man, here clothed in purple and fine linen, and faring sumptuously every day; but hereafter consigned over to the fire of hell (*o*); and openly to profess, that *marriage is honourable in all, and the bed undefiled, but that whoremongers and adulterers God will judge* (*p*); I say, to go about to awaken people's minds to a lasting sense of the deformity and danger of intemperance and lewdness, under the impressions of God and another world, and at the same time, to be themselves secretly pursuing
the

(*n*) Phil. iii. 17, &c.   (*o*) Luke xvi. 19. &c.
(*p*) Heb. xiii. 4.

the same wicked passions as the main end of their enterprise, would render them, beyond example, impious and athieftical, and upon the discovery of what they were aiming at, have exposed them to universal hatred; so that, instead of carrying their design, together with the indignation of almighty God, they would have fallen under the just revenge of mankind. But that the Apostles were such silly ridiculous Athiefts, so void of sense, so stupid in projecting measures, as this would make them, is beyond all possibility of suspicion.

It is alledged, in the case of *Mahomet*, that one of the great motives that supported that grand Impostor in the prosecution of his enterprize, was the love of women, or that he might have it in his power, without restraint, to enjoy his lascivious appetites. And indeed the *Alcoran* allowing not only a certain number of wives, but the use of any number of women slaves, seems to be framed with a view to gratify a leacherous passion (*q*); and the scandalous provision that is therein made for *Mahomet* himself, makes it manifest, that as that Impostor's lust must have been unbounded and furious, so his conduct was certainly most brutal and infamous (*r*). But
where

(*q*) Il faut convenir de bonne foi, qu'il y a quelque chose de vrai dans ce qu'on dit, que les Mahometans ont la permission d'en entretenir autant qu'ils peuvent. C'est qu'en effect, outre les 4 legitimes, qui leur sont allouées par la loi civile & religieuse (qui est presque la même chose dans les pais Mahometans) il y a parmi eux des particuliers, qui ont jusqu'à 10 ou 12 servantes concubines qu'on ne distingue des autres femmes qu'à certains égards, & nullement à l'egard de la lignée. With respect to their women-slaves, their maxim is, Quand on a acheté quelque chose legalement, rien n'est plus légitime que d'en user. La relig. des Mahomet. tiré du Latin de M. Reland. p. 233, 234.

(*r*) There are certain things, says Mr. Roland, in the Alcoran, which might convince the Mahometans of the imposture.
Comme,

SECT. XI. *Christian Revelation.* 101

where is there the faintest shadow of any thing of this nature to be observed in the character of the Apostles? They declare against polygamy and divorce, and revive the primitive institution, whereby one woman and one man were joined together for life. Upon which with great justice, they affirm, that *the wife hath not power over her own body, but the husband*; *and likewise the husband hath not power over his own body, but the wife.* So that husband and wife must continue mutually faithful to one another, and cannot be beyond the bounds of chastity, without exposing themselves to the judgments of God. Nay, so far were the Apostles from being disposed to make provision for the gratifying of a lascivious passion, that St. *Paul*, in particular, professes, *It is good for a man not to touch a woman: Nevertheless*, says he, *if people have not the gift of continency; to avoid fornication, let every man have his own wife, and let every woman have her own husband* (s). And what rules of chastity they prescribe to their Disciples, the same do they religiously observe in their own conduct. Their history informs us, that some of the Apostles were married; that others lived in a single state; that all of them, in their different circumstances, were constantly faithful to all the dictates of purity; and among the qualifications necessary to those who should be employed, or succeed them in the work of the Ministry, it is expressly required,

Comme, par exemple, ce que Mahomed y donne à entendre, que Dieu, en revelation, lui accorda, par grace spéciale, savoir, la satisfaction de ses desirs impurs & adulteres, par l'appropriation qu'il lui adjugea, dit-il, de quelques femmes, qui appartenoient à d'autres; en quoi impudemment & blasphematoirement il fait la divinité complice de ses passions & de ses voluptez infames. ibid. p. cxxxix.
(s) 1 Cor. vii. 1. 2. 4.

required, that they be *the husbands of one wife, sober, not given to wine* (*t*).

But had any intemperate or lascivious passion been the motive that carried on the Apostles in the propagation of the Gospel, must not this passion have shown itself in some instances of their behaviour? If we reflect upon the many difficulties and hardships through which the Apostles pushed their way towards the enjoyment of the riotous or lewd passion, with which, it is supposed, they were animated; it must be confessed, that the force of that passion was certainly extremely imperious. But that the fury of a passion raging to that degree in a man's breast, that it hurries him on to encounter the greatest dangers, shall yet in the whole course of his life, produce none of its own proper natural effects, in any one instance whatsoever, is an event absolutely impossible, quite inconsistent with the nature of things. And as it is impossible but the Apostles, in some instance or other, must have betrayed their intemperance or lewdness, had they been under the commanding power of any such passions; so their enemies, glad of the opportunity, would have taken the advantage, laid open their crimes, and exposed them to public infamy. I say, the Heathen world was violently set to obstruct the progress of the Gospel; and had the immoralities of the Apostles put it in their power to discredit their ministry, or to blacken their reputation, what was to hinder them from employing those successful means in gaining their purpose? The Apostles boldly charge the Heathen, and publish it abroad, that *being past feeling, they have given themselves over to lasciviousness, to work all uncleanness with*

(*t*) 1 Tim. iii. 2, 3.

SECT. XI.   *Christian Revelation.*   103

with greediness (*u*). And one should think so heavy a charge would have awakened the resentment of the Heathen world, and made them fiercely recriminate, had they been able to have discovered any thing of the like nature in the conduct of the Apostles, Indeed,

When one considers the different interests and humours of mankind, or after what manner people's passions operate when they are eager to prevent the success of their rivals or enemies, one might have suspected the credit of the Gospel-history, had they represented the great Author of our religion, or his Apostles, to have met with better treatment in the world, than *Socrates*, that is, to have escaped all censure, or not to have been loaded with reproaches. But as it was impossible for men not to be reproached, who went about to set up a religion intirely opposite to what was then held sacred in the world; so we learn from the history of the Gospel, that *Jesus Christ* and his Apostles had several heavy imputations laid upon them. Besides the general charge of their being impious, founded on their attempting to overthrow the religions then established; the Author of our religion is called a *man gluttonous, and a wine-bibber, a friend of publicans and sinners,* one who *deceived the people,* a man in confederacy with *Beelzebub* the prince of devils; and his Apostles are reported to have said, *let us do evil, that good may come,* &c. But all such accusations do so manifestly arise from malice or ignorance, and to every sober man must appear so extremely incredible, so intirely void of all appearance of truth, that the Apostles do little more than barely relate them, despising such things themselves, and
having

(*u*) Eph. iv. 19.

having no apprehension that the world could ever think they need a confutation. Only the charge of a secret correspondence with *Beelzebub*, being a thing without the compass of human observation, this by an invincible argument is demonstrated to be absolutely groundless and absurd. *Every kingdom*, says our Saviour, *divided against itself, is brought to desolation: And every city and house divided against itself, shall not stand, and if Satan cast out Satan, he is divided against himself; how then shall his kingdom stand* (x)? So that every thinking impartial man has infinitely better reason to assert the innocence of our Lord and his Apostles, than any Infidel can have to justify *Socrates*, or to declare him innocent when he is accused of being impious, of corrupting the youth, *&c.* But tho' the Heathen had nothing criminal, which with any shadow of reason, they could fasten upon the Apostles, and all their accusations were mere calumny; yet the Apostles had a great deal in their power to object to the Heathen, and the particular enormities with which they charge them, seem to be too well grounded. Not only was fornication notorious in their practice; but the example and worship of their deities (y), their public laws and customs, and the doctrines of their best Philosophers, patronized it; nor are they less favourable to drunkenness, while they represent it, as an act of worship in the service of their gods (z)

And

(x) Matth. xii. 24. &c.

(y) Siccæ enim fanum est Veneris, in quod se matronæ conferebant; atque inde procedentes ad quæstum, dotes, corporis injuria, contrahebant, honesta nimirum tam inhonesta vinculo conjugia juncturæ. Valer. Max. lib. 2. cap. 6. Locrenses—voverant—ut die festo Veneris virgines suas prostituerent. Justin. lib. 21. cap. 3.

(z) Si quis est, (says Cicero pro M. Caelio, cap. 20.) qui etiam meretriciis,

SECT. XI.   *Christian Revelation.*   105

And as the Apostles dare be bold, without dreading a discovery of any thing criminal in their own conduct, openly to accuse the Heathen world of such enormities; so they testify a high displeasure at those of their own followers, who prostitute themselves to lewdness or intemperance, and they mark them out as persons with whom their other Disciples must not keep company; *If any man,* says the Apostle, *that is called a brother, be a fornicator or a drunkard, I have written unto you not to keep company with such an one, no not to eat* (a). And not only to prevent the influence of so bad an example, but to vindicate the purity of the Gospel, as meretriciis amoribus interdictum juventuti putet; est ille quidem valde severus, negare non possum : Sed abhorret non modo ab hujus sæculi licentia, verum etiam a majorum consuetudine, atque concessis. Quando enim hoc non factum est? Quando reprehensum? Quando non permissum? Quando denique fuit, ut, quod licet, non liceret? Accordingly Epictetus (Enchir. cap. 47.) directs people to use those entertainments as the law prescribes: Περὶ ἀφροδίσια, εἰς δύναμιν, πρὸ γάμε καθαρευτέον. ἁπλομένῳ δὲ, ὡς νόμιμόν ἐςι, μεταληπτέον. And Plato tells us (Conviv. p. 181. E. et de Leg. lib. 8. p. 841. D.) that the law prohibited only the corresponding with free women, τῶν ἐλευθέρων γυναικῶν ἐρᾶν. So that, as to all others, people had no sort of scruple: Τὰς μὲν ἑταίρας ἡδονῆς ἕνεκα ἔχομεν, τὰς δὲ παλλακὰς τῆς καθ᾽ ἡμέραν παλλακείας, τὰς δὲ γυναῖκας τε παιδοποιεῖσθαι γνησίως, ᾗ τῶν ἔνδον φύλακα πιςὴν ἔχειν. (Demost. cont. Neræam, apud Athen. l. 18. p. 573. Vid. p. 569. D.) which is a course of life suitable enough to the sentiments of the Stoics. Καὶ τὸς Στωϊκὸς δὲ ὁρῶμεν, ἐκ ἄτοπον εἶναι λέγοντας τὸ ἑταίρᾳ συνοικεῖν, ἢ τὸ ἐξ ἑταίρας ἐργαζίας διαζῆν. (Sext. Emp. Pyr. Hypot. lib. 3 cap. 24.) While Plato justifies excess in wine, after this manner: Πίνειν δὲ εἰς μέθην, ὅτε ἀλλοθί πε πρέπει, πλὴν ἐν ταῖς τε τὸν οἶνον δόντος θεῦ ἑορταῖς, ὅτ᾽ ἀσφαλὲς. (De legib. lib. 6. p. 775. B) Μὴ θαύμαζε, ὦ ξένε, νόμος ἐσθ᾽ ἡμῖν ὅτος. Ibid. lib. i. p. 637. C. Vid. Athenæ, lib. 2. p. 40. C.

(a) 1 Cor. v. 11.

as utterly irreconcileable to such lewd practices, they command, in particular, that the incestuous person among the *Corinthians* be excommunicated and solemnly cut off from the Christian society. And can it be thought, that those persons who were thus publicly affronted, and turned out to the world as objects of infamy, to be shunned by every body, and who could not but understand the whole of the Apostles deportment; had they been conscious of any lust prevailing among them, would have checked their just indignation, their resentment of being so severely chastised by those equally guilty, and not have gratified a natural passion to extenuate their own guilt, to ward off the public infamy, or to keep themselves in countenance, by showing, that their accusers were no less involved, or rather more criminal? Had such a thing happened, human nature, in those persons whom the Apostles had to deal with, must have been quite another thing than it now it is, than it has been in all the rest of mankind, since the first of our species. *Physician cure thyself,* never fails to be objected to those who set up to be Reformers, while they are known to be themselves fully as obnoxious. But so little liable are the Apostles to have the accusation returned upon them, that while their enemies, and those they gave up to public censure, were reduced to silence, and to bear the shame of their evil deeds, they triumph in their own innocence, *this is their rejoicing, the testimony of their conscience, that in simplicity and godly sincerity, not in fleshly wisdom, but by the grace of God, they have had their conversation in the world:* And for this they appeal to those very persons, among whom they had used their discipline in chastising riot and incontinency (*b*). The truth

---

(*b*) 2 Cor. i. 12.

truth of it is, had it been possible for any riotous or wanton lust to have at first engaged the Apostles, the *hunger*, and *cold*, and *nakedness*, the great fatigues they suffered in propagating the Gospel, would very soon have cooled the heat of their passion, and by that means made them wholly desist, totally abandon their enterprise.

When we therefore consider, that the Apostles prescribe rules that strictly require temperance and chastity: —That with the warmest zeal they recommend the practice of these amiable virtues, and urge them upon their Disciples by the most prevailing arguments:—That their training the world to a settled aversion to all lewdness and intemperance, was the most effectual means to arm mankind against them, and to ruin the design of putting themselves in a condition to indulge, without restraint, these infamous passions:—That they could not project a plot of so black a nature, without being in their hearts consummate Atheists:—That in their institution of religion, so far are they from therein providing for the gratifying of an inordinate passion of any sort, that the whole is visibly framed with a view to promote the clean contrary:—That whatever purity they injoined their Disciples, the same they observed themselves in their own conduct, and expressly required it in all their fellow-labourers and successors in office:——That had the Apostles been under the power of any lewd or intemperate passion, it must necessarily have appeared in some of its effects in the course of their lives:——That none of their Heathen enemies, whom they publicly charged as highly criminal in such instances; none of those persons among themselves, whom they severely punished for their riot and incontinency,

nency, were able to discern any the least blemish of this nature in any one step of their conduct: In short, that the distressed indigent situation of the Apostles, of necessity, breaking the force of every wanton riotous passion, would have put a speedy end to the whole of their project: I say, when we consider all these several particulars laid together, one cannot but profess, that the Apostles, in the propagation of the Gospel, were no Impostors, supported by the power of lewd or intemperate passions, while they gave out they were animated from Heaven. So that we come to examine,

In the last place, whether it might not be their passion for worldly honours that carried them on in the course of their Ministry. And to set this article in its full light, I shall consider it as consisting of these two particulars, namely, popular applause, and worldly power, authority, or dominion.

SECT. XII.

The powerful Passion of Fame or popular Applause had no Influence over the Apostles in the Service of the Gospel. Here the Deists justify themselves, and, at the same rate, must they justify the Apostles.

AS for people's passion after popular applause, this, we know from experience, is able to animate and support men in the most dangerous undertakings. But that the Apostles were under the prevailing influence of this narrow, contracted passion, or that this was the spring whereby they were actuated in the execution of their office, is in no man's power to render in the least degree probable.

Indeed,

Indeed, the desire of honour is an essential ingredient in the human constitution: And when this passion comes to be so enlarged, as to exert itself in seeking after the lasting esteem and commendation of all those beings, God and man, to whom we are naturally associated, it is certainly the noblest ambition, with which the soul of man can be fired. Under its influence, our minds are opened to the prospect of the universal good of that rational system whereof we are a part; and we resolutely exert ourselves in the pursuit of those actions that glorify God, and promote the happiness of mankind (*a*). And as the desire of universal esteem for ever to be enjoyed, is a divine ardour of soul, arising from the love of God and rational beings, inciting us to recommend ourselves to their favour, and by that means proving the steady spring of every worthy and laudable action; so the Gospel of *Jesus Christ*, that neglects not to cultivate and improve every human passion, of consequence to private or public happiness, makes a powerful address to this passion in particular, by offering to our pursuit, glory, honour, and immortality. So that the Apostles, in the Ministry of the Gospel, animated, as doubtless they were, by a commanding desire after universal and eternal esteem, arising from the whole rational system, must be counted men nobly ambitious, acting upon a principle highly pleasing to God, and most productive of good to human kind. Mr. *Woolston* indeed insinuates, that the desire of mere worldly fame was the principle that put the Apostles upon their enterprize, and that supported them in all their sufferings, in the utmost extremity of death itself. " Many cheats (says he) and cri-
" minals,

(*a*) See my *Inquiry into the Original of Moral Virtue*, where this natural passion after esteem is fully explained.

"minals, besides them, have asserted their inno-
"cency, and denied their guilt in the utmost extre-
"mity of death, without the like views of honour
"and fame (*b*)." And the Reader may here reflect, that this is the only passion, from whence, as
the great spring of action, Mr. *Woolston* pretends to
account for the conduct of the Apostles. But that,
laying aside all regard to the approbation of God,
the Apostles only meant to catch at worldly fame,
the vain applauses of their fellow-creatures, or to
gain the esteem of any particular party of men;
this, I say, is an opinion that can be justified by no
shadow of argument. On the contrary,

In the writings of the Apostles, this passion for
popular applause, in religious matters, is most expressly condemned; and the great folly of indulging
it is set before us, sufficient to prevent any thinking
man from yielding to its influence. *Let us not*, say
the Apostles, *be desirous of vain glory* (*c*). It greatly
concerns us to *take heed that we do not our righteousness before men, to be seen of them:* For those who are
devoted to this poor ambition, and only mean to
feed their vanity by their religion, *have their reward*, they carry the pitiful point they have in
view, they attain to the dying praises of frail mortals; but *they have no reward of their heavenly Father*,
they forfeit all share in the lasting approbation of an
eternal munificent God, whose favour is better than
life (*d*). So far are such hypocrites from recommending themselves to the Father of lights, the
great Fountain of all honour, and the prime Author
of all happiness, that by prostituting the glorious
name, and all the sacred institutions of God, to their
own pride and vanity, or as an engine to accomplish
some

(*b*) Sixth Discourse, p. 27.   (*c*) Gal. v. 26.
(*d*) Matth. vi. 1, &*c*.

SECT. XII.   *Christian Revelation.*   111

some base and wicked purposes, they incur his highest displeasure, and, as their enormous impiety deserves, have alloted to them the severest punishments to which criminals can be condemned in another world (*e*). *Know ye not*, says the Apostle, *that the friendship of the world, the love of vain glory, is enmity with God? Whosoever therefore will be a friend of the world,* and court its empty praises, that man, profess what he will, *is the enemy of God,* and can never possibly escape the judgments of the Almighty (*f*).

This is the light wherein the Apostles set our desire after popular applause. It is a vain deluding passion, that leaves us overwhelmed in everlasting contempt and misery. So that those people who put on their religion only as an outward dress to gain them the esteem of the world about them, cannot but be counted acting a part all over folly and madness. This the Apostles declare. And every man must observe, that the whole frame of the Gospel is calculated to guard our minds against the influence of so mischievous a passion, and to engage us in the love and practice of those virtues that naturally lift us up to true glory. Lowliness of mind, meekness, humility, are the graces with which the Gospel requires our souls to be adorned, and wherein we cannot but *be kindly affectioned one to another, with brotherly love, in honour preferring one another* (*g*). And while we are thus pursuing those shining virtues, *providing things honest in the sight of all men, things that are lovely, of good report, and praise worthy,* that naturally tend to gain us real esteem among our fellow-creatures (*h*), we are, at the same time, commanded particularly to eye the approbation of
God,

(*e*) Matth. xxiv. 51.   (*f*) Jam. iv. 4.
(*g*) Rom. xii. 10.   (*h*) Rom. xii. 17. Phil. iv. 8.

God, and to be looking forward beyond all the reputation of this life, to *that blessed hope, and the glorious appearing of the great God, and our Saviour* Jesus Christ (*i*), when by the grace and bounty of the Father of mercies, amidst the applauses of the heavenly hosts, we shall be crowned with *glory that fadeth not away* (*k*).

Thus, with great reason, the Apostles condemn the pursuit of popular applause; and addressing themselves to the leading powers of our nature, offer to our ambition the enjoyment of solid esteem, of eternal fame and glory. And while the Apostles with great zeal insisted upon such doctrines, and recommended such principles to the world, what shadow of presumption can any man pretend to have, upon which he may alledge, that they themselves, in their hearts, hated and despised those noble pursuits, and were only seeking after worldly fame, the fleeting praises of their fellow-mortals? One should think, that not only their doctrines, but every instance of their conduct is a strong proof of the contrary.

Among the many different ways whereby people rise above the common level, and attract the notice and admiration of mankind, that of discovering or establishing useful truths, especially moral truths, that tend to the improvement and perfection of human nature in religion and virtue, is one of the most considerable. Thus it was that *Socrates* distinguished himself at *Athens*; that he prevented his dying in obscurity, and still lives in a name great and illustrious. And indeed, when one considers that all the learning of those days lay quite another way, and that *Socrates* himself had all the prejudices of education to secure his attachment to the then philosophy,

---

(*i*) 1 Cor. x. 31. Tit. ii. 13. (*k*) 1 Cor. ix. 25.
1 Pet. v. 4.

losophy, wherein only a man could hope to gain a reputation; one cannot but admire that extraordinary force of genius, that made him see the folly of the learned disquisitions then in vogue, and enabled him to discover a most important collection of moral truths. Nor can one deny him the glory of a manly courage, a noble generosity of soul, that engaged him, at all hazards, to teach those truths to mankind. Now, after the same manner, but upon infinitely better grounds, the Apostles might have acquired and established their fame in the world.

In opposition to the superstition of their own nation, wherein they had themselves been educated, and to the idolatry and superstition of the rest of mankind, to which the Heathen world had been long accustomed; I say, in opposition to the absurd, the false, and mischievous doctrines, which then universally prevailed among *Jews* and *Gentiles*, the Apostles openly appear, and with great firmness and resolution propose to the world a divine system of doctrines, wherein the being and perfections of God, are fully vindicated; the assurance of a future state of rewards and punishments, is strongly inculcated; and the moral duties that exalt human nature, that glorify God, and bring happiness to mankind, are clearly explained, and powerfully recommended. And upon the discovery of such important truths, of the last consequence to rational beings, which they propagated to all nations with the utmost zeal and steadiness, might not the Apostles have promised themselves, among their fellow creatures, an unrivaled reputation? But so far were those honest men from aiming at popular applause, or vain glory, that in the accounts they afford us concerning themselves, they quite sink their own character, and let us know how very little is owing to them. They

Vol. II.   P   give

give us to underſtand, that, before they entered upon the Miniſtry of the Goſpel, as their education was mean and illiterate ; ſo, in their judgment and inclinations, they were abſolutely devoted to the ſuperſtition, to the prejudices and falſe doctrines then prevailing in the *Jewiſh* nation. This, indeed, would have added to their fame, had they overcome their prejudices, conquered their ignorance, and diſcovered thoſe truths which they imparted to the world, by the ſtrength of their own genius. But, to prevent our being deceived into ſo favourable an opinion of them, which would have recommended them to our higheſt eſteem, as men of an uncommon greatneſs of mind, and the deepeſt penetration, they honeſtly tell us, that their ignorance and their prejudices never left them, till they came to be illuminated from Heaven, had their minds ſupernaturally opened to conceive the truths of the Goſpel; and their hearts inſpired with a divine courage to publiſh them abroad to the world. So that they lead us quite off, from attributing any thing to their own abilities, and direct us to regard them only as Meſſengers, mean, and contemptible in themſelves, qualified and ſupported by the ſpirit and hand of God, to reveal to all nations the great principles of religion, the ſure means of ſocial, of rational life and happineſs. *For God* (ſay they) *who commanded the light to ſhine out of darkneſs, hath ſhined in our hearts,* to enable us to give to the reſt of mankind *the light of the knowledge of the glory of God in the face of Jeſus Chriſt. And we have this treaſure in earthen veſſels, that the excellency of the power may be of God, and not of us.* And when the Apoſtles do thus openly declare, that none of thoſe endowments, wherein they were viſibly ſuperior to all others in the world, were the effect of a better

uſe

use and improvement of their rational faculties, and *they had nothing but what they had received*, may not this be counted an ample demonstration, that the love of vain glory did in no degree predominate in their minds? Renouncing all foundation of merit in their own persons, as they do themselves acknowledge their being indebted to the immediate grace of God, for the wonderful discoveries they were enabled to make (*l*); so they enjoined the world about them, to ascribe the praise and glory of all to God alone. In a word, as I have just now hinted, the plain history they give us of themselves, before they were employed in their public Ministry, must effectually hinder us from honouring them any farther, than as they were men immediately fitted of God to propagate his Gospel to the world. And,

As the Apostles claim no praise, no degree of honour from the glorious doctrines they taught, or the great hardships they every where endured in promoting them; so as little do they claim from the extraordinary works they performed, in relieving people from their bodily miseries. To open the eyes of the blind, to loose the tongue of the dumb, to make the lame to walk, to rebuke the violence of fevers, and to heal all manner of diseases; these things done without any external applications, only by a word; without any earthly reward, in a free and gratuitous manner; are works that must recommend the Authors to the highest veneration, much more effectually among the bulk of mankind, than any thing else whatsoever. Indeed, the discovery of moral truths, as I have already observed, is a noble ground upon which to raise a reputation; but to perceive the beauty and excellency of these truths, requires a mind of a

particular

(*l*) Eph. vii. &c.

particular caſt, not altogether ſo common in the world: Whereas the happineſs ariſing from people's being delivered from any ſort of illneſs or diſtemper, is univerſally felt, is very ſenſible in every man's own experience. So that, I ſay, a company of men travelling thro' the world, and generouſly relieving mankind from all their ſeveral ailments; by a word, without any money, giving health to the ſick, eyes to the blind, ſpeech to the dumb, feet to the lame, cannot poſſibly fail to have their name every where celebrated. The novelty of the thing, and the miraculous manner of performing the works, their being done freely, without reward, and the happineſs they derive to mankind, muſt render the diſpenſers of ſuch ſenſible bleſſings extremely popular, and procure them every man's eſteem and admiration. Let any man imagine, ſhould a dozen of perſons divide this iſland among them, and in their ſeveral diſtricts, after ſo extraordinary manner, reſtore health and vigour to all ſort of ſick and diſtreſſed people, would not every heart confeſs their uncommon merit, and every mouth be full of their loudeſt praiſes? Since, therefore, nothing is more pleaſing than the free uſe of all our natural members, and health is the foundation of all our enjoyments, without which we can reliſh nothing, it is eaſy to conceive, that the recovering of theſe by a word, and without the ſmalleſt expence to the patient, muſt be one of the moſt effectual ways whereby a man can raiſe himſelf to popular fame and glory. Upon conſiderations infinitely meaner in the matter of curing diſeaſes, have ſome perſons been counted deities, and had temples and altars dedicated to their ſervice. Nor in the caſe of the Apoſtles were there wanting fair opportunities of acquiring and enjoying ſuch blaſphemous honours. But,

So

SECT. XII.   *Christian Revelation.*   117

So far were the Apostles from employing their power of working miracles, in courting the applauses of the world, that they distributed those blessings to mankind, without the least ostentation, or vanity, and openly professed, that as this power was none of their own, so they freely exerted it, as God had commanded them; particularly with a design to confirm the Christian institution, or to assure the world, that the same Being, who was the Author of those beneficent works for the health of human bodies, did by their Ministry reveal to mankind the salutary truths of the Gospel, for the life of human souls. I say, the Apostles tell us expresly, that the wonderful works they did were not done by their own power, but by a power they had received from *Jesus Christ* (m): that the same power was imparted to them, not in consideration of their superior merit or distinguished holiness, but by the good pleasure of Almighty God; that their exerting that power freely, and without reward, in healing all manner of sickness, and all manner of disease, was not owing to the overflowing of their humanity, or to the superior force of their beneficent dispositions, but was done, in obedience to the command of their Master (n); and that all the good they did to the bodies of men, they only did it, as the witnesses of God, attesting the truth of his Gospel, to advance its credit, or to recommend it to the belief and practice of the world (o). All these particulars seem to be expressed in this account of a notable miracle, which I shall here transcribe at large from the *Acts* of the Apostles.

" Now

(m) Matth. x. 1.   *(n)* Matth. x. 8.
(o) Acts i. 8.

"Now *Peter* and *John* went up together into the temple at the hour of prayer, being the ninth hour. And a certain man lame from his mother's womb was carried, whom they laid daily at the gate of the temple which is called Beautiful, to afk alms of them that entered into the temple: Who feeing *Peter* and *John* about to go into the temple, afked an alms. And *Peter* faftening his eyes upon him; faid, look on us. And he gave heed unto them, expecting to receive fomething of them. Then *Peter* faid, Silver and gold have I none, but fuch as I have give I thee: *In the name of* Jefus Chrift *of* Nazareth, *rife up and walk.* And he took him by the right-hand, and lift him up! And immediately his feet and ankle bones received ftrength: And, he leaping up, ftood, and walked, and entered with them into the temple, walking, and leaping, and praifing God. And they knew that it was he which fat for alms at the beautiful gate of the temple, and they were filled with wonder and amazement at that which had happened unto him. And as the lame man, which was healed, held *Peter* and *John*, all the people ran together unto them, in the porch which is called *Solomon*'s, greatly wondering. And when *Peter* faw it, he anfwered unto the people, Ye men of *Ifrael*, why marvel ye at this? Or, why look ye fo earneftly on us, *as though by our own power or holinefs we had made this man to walk?* The God of *Abraham*, and of *Ifaac*, and of *Jacob*, the God of our Fathers, hath glorified his Son *Jefus*; whom ye delivered up, and denied him in the prefence of *Pilate*, when he was determined to let him go. But ye denied the Holy One, and the Juft, and defired a murderer to be granted unto you, and killed the
"Prince

SECT. XII.   *Christian Revelation.*   119

" Prince of life, whom God hath raised from the
" dead; whereof we are witnesses. And his name,
" through faith in his name, hath made this man
" strong, whom ye see and know; yea, the faith
" which is by him, hath given him this perfect
" soundness, in the presence of you all. And now,
" brethren, I wot that through ignorance ye did it,
" as did also your Rulers. Repent ye, therefore,
" and be converted, that your sins may be blotted
" out, when the times of refreshing shall come, from
" the presence of the Lord (*p*)."

This is the light wherein we must apprehend all the miraculous works of kindness that were done by the Apostles. And when we are told, that the power, whereby these works were performed, was immediately derived from God, not in the view of any man's holiness, but as God himself was pleased to dispense it; that they were all done, not upon the proper motion of the persons, to whom the power was committed, but by the express command and appointment of Heaven; and that they were to be understood, not as matter of praise to the visible Agents, (which in the particular case just now related, the *Jews* seem to have been forward to do) but only as supernatural proofs, establishing the divinity of the Gospel, which expressly condemns all affectation of vain glory; I say, when we are assured of all this, I would fain know, what have the Apostles left to themselves, upon which they can pretend to found a personal reputation? In this article, of all others, by great odds, the fairest, the most likely to raise and propagate a man's fame in the world, the Apostles honestly confessing, that they contributed nothing of their own, and that they

can

(*p*) Acts iii. 1—19.

can only be regarded as mere instruments employed to such a particular purpose; do they not thereby most effectually prevent our allowing them any share in the glory of those wonderful works they performed? And is not this a strong bar to our suspecting them of being governed, in the Ministry of the Gospel, by any passion for popular applause?

Had the Apostles been under the power of this appetite, can it enter into one's head to imagine, that they would have withstood the strongest temptations, and slighted the fairest opportunities, that could possibly offer of having their vanity gratified to the utmost? The people of *Jerusalem*, surprized at the extraordinary cure above mentioned, were in full readiness to break forth in resounding the praises of the Apostles. And would a vainglorious man have immediately checked the passion, turned the admiration of the people quite off from himself, and directed all their praising thoughts towards another object? The people of *Lystra*, no less surprized at a like miraculous cure, took the Apostles for gods assembled together, and were about to have done them religious honours: And would a vain-glorious man have, on such an occasion, had his indignation raised, and rejected as impious those flattering effects of the people's admiration? This, however, was done by the Apostles. And this cannot but lead one to conclude, that they were men absolutely free from all passion for worldly fame and glory. But their conduct will afford us some farther proofs of their innocence.

Before a man can attain to the applauses of his fellow-creatures, he must work himself into their good opinion, or gain an interest in their good liking and esteem. But how is such a purchase possible to be made, without conspiring in the views,

and

and gratifying the paſſions and appetites, that is, promoting the happineſs, real or imaginary of thoſe perſons whoſe eſteem we are courting? To take a man into our good opinion, or to regard him as an object of our inward eſteem, while we apprehend he is going croſs to our moſt valuable purſuits and intereſts, is moſt ſenſibly contradictory to the whole of our conſtitution. So that, in order to acquire popular love, neceſſary to bring about popular applauſe, of neceſſity, we muſt go along in the common meaſures, and zealouſly concur, or diſtinguiſh ourſelves, in promoting popular ſentiments and paſſions. And I would gladly know, wherein do the Apoſtles, in any degree, proſtitute themſelves to ſo inglorious an artifice? The *Jewiſh* and Heathen world, with reſpect to matters of religion, had each of them their own particular intereſts, certain principles and opinions eſtabliſhed among them, to which they were zealouſly devoted, as things ſacred and of the laſt importance. To go about, therefore, to introduce a ſet of doctrines, wholly deſtructive of all the religious ſyſtems then prevailing among mankind, muſt not this have expoſed the undertakers to the contempt and hatred of the world, to all the angry and revengeful paſſions of human nature? The religion of our anceſtors, wherein we have been educated, and which bears the ſanction of public authority, people always regard as the cauſe and intereſt of Heaven, the great means whereby our fore-fathers have been ſaved, whereby we ourſelves, and our poſterity after us, are to come to the ſame ſtate of happineſs; and ſhall a man take upon him to ſet aſide, or to overturn this eſtabliſhed religion, the foundation of all our hopes, without appearing, in our imagination, as an enemy of Heaven, a bold invader of our moſt ſacred and nighest interests, as one, who, as he would judge of things, and direct events, gives up those that went before us in our way to everlasting misery, and would reduce ourselves, and all that shall come after us, to certain endless destruction? Sure no man, in this light, can possibly recommend himself to popular liking and applause; but, as it happened in the case of the first Publishers of the Gospel, who were every-where hated, contemned, and persecuted, must necessarily incur the indignation of both Priest and people, and universally expose himself to cruelty and oppression. So that the Apostles, in their doctrines, not going along with popular sentiments, but violently opposing the superstition and idolatry, the religious principles established and professed among *Jews* and Heathens; this, by itself, without mentioning other instances that equally shew their neglect and contempt of all the arts and measures of popularity, is, I may venture to call it, a full demonstration of their innocence in this article; or that, in the discharge of their office, they were by no means seeking after popular applause. In fact, so far was the publishing of the Gospel from being the way to popular fame and glory, that the contempt and ignominy which attended the profession thereof, proved a mighty hinderance to its better success in the world (*q*). Thus we are expressly told, that some people, not enduring to be of *a sect that was every-where spoken against*, tho' they could not prevent an inward conviction of the truth of the Gospel, yet they meanly refused to profess it, and still went on in the old fashionable way, *loving the praise of men more than the praise of God* (*r*). But let us further

(*q*) John v. 44.
(*r*) Acts xxviii. 22. John xii. 42, 43.

SECT. XII. *Christian Revelation.*

further confider, how the Apoftles checked their Difciples, in foolifhly attempting to introduce popular diftinctions among their Teachers.

Vanity, indeed, is a paffion that has been always common in the world, and that never yet has failed to exert its power in the breafts of all ranks and orders of men. So ftrongly turned, and fo very forward is human nature to feek to be diftinguifhed among our fellows, that, when we have no particular accomplifhments of our own, that can raife us to a fuperior ground, where we may come to be regarded, we frequently put ourfelves under the influence of fome extraneous honourable characters, and from the relation we bear to thofe, claim a fhare in their reputation; and, in this borrowed fame, fancy ourfelves perfons of merit and diftinction. Thus, to mention only what belongs to our prefent purpofe, when public Teachers have acquired a name and become famous in the world, people value themfelves upon being their Scholars, upon following their peculiar fentiments; and apprehend that the honour of the Mafter renders the Difciples more confpicuous. So that, where the Teachers themfelves have no fuch mean ambition, as to defire to overtop one another in popular applaufe, yet the Scholars, from felf-vanity, and without all other foundation, may make the diftinction, and be mighty zealous in preferring fuch a particular perfon to a higher reputation. And when thus it happens, what more favourable opportunity can a man, covetous of fame, hope to have in his hands, whereby he may gratify his appetite for vain glory? His Difciples have their ftrongeft paffions devoted to his fervice; he needs only give way to the bent of their nature; the great power of ambition will make them active in advancing his fame above every other name

name that can pretend to rival him. Now, we are well assured, that such opportunities came in the way of the Apostles. But, so far were those Teachers of righteousness from taking advantage of any such occasion, that, when their Disciples had the folly to make distinctions among them, and would have raised the credit of one man above that of another, they do not only severely check this mischievous disposition, but industriously set themselves in such a light, wherein they must appear to us void of all personal merit, having no claim to a distinguished reputation.

In the church at *Corinth*, the humour, now so common in the world, wherein people are puffed up for one against another, was like to prevail, while one said, *I am of Paul*; and another, *I am of Apollos*; *and a third, I of Cephas*; *and a fourth, I am of Christ* (s). But this humour, probably arising from their differing about some speculations in philosophy, which the different parties, from their misapprehensions, might have the folly to imagine were favoured or condemned by this or that Apostle; I say, this factious humour, so favourable to the designs of a vain glorious man, the Apostle vehemently condemns, and represents it of so black a nature as to insinuate, that therein they had the impiety to imagine, that those persons, whom they thus distinguished, were the authors of the blessings of the Gospel, which are solely to be attributed to *Jesus Christ*. What, says the Apostle, *is Christ divided?* Or do you set up for more Saviours than one? To show the extravagancy of such an opinion, and consequently the madness of this partial distinguishing humour that implies it, he mentions himself in particular, and asks, *was Paul crucified for you?*

(s) 1 Cor. i. 12. &c.

SECT. XII. *Christian Revelation.*

you? *Or are ye baptized in the name of Paul? I thank God,* says he, *that I baptized none of you, but Crispus and Gaius, and the houshold of Stephanas;* lest any should say that I had baptized in mine own name. And as the *Corinthians* were herein highly injurious to the great *Author and finisher of our faith*; so the Apostle gives them further to understand, that by thus dividing themselves in sects, and setting up to be followers of such particular Apostles, they were acting in direct opposition to the spirit and design of the Gospel. Now, says he (*t*), *we have received, not the spirit of the world,* that delights in party and faction, *but the spirit which is of God,* that delights in concord and unity, and *by whose influences we not only know the things that are freely given to us of God,* so as to ascribe them to their only proper Author, but we live in the exercise of these amiable virtues (*u*), *love, joy, peace, long-suffering, gentleness, faith, meekness, temperance,* in short, all goodness and righteousness, and truth, which knit us together in *charity, the bond of perfectness*; and making our souls the temple of God, *we have the peace of God ruling within us, to the which also we are called in one body:* Whereas, says the Apostle to the people of *Corinth* (*x*), *there is among you,* as the fruit of your vain-glorious distinguishing humour, *envying, and strife, and divisions*; and amidst these passions *are ye not carnal?* Are ye not quite different from these *persons who by one spirit are baptized into one body whereof, Jesus Christ is the head,* and in which there can be no schism? Do ye not walk as men who are destitute of the Spirit of God? For while one sayeth, *I am of Paul*; and another, *I am of Apollos*; are ye not carnal, in a disposition of mind wherein you are

(*t*) 1 Cor. ii. 12.   (*u*) Gal. v. 22. Eph v. 9.
(*x*) 1 Cor. iii, 3, 4.

are the enemies of God; not only neglecting *to keep the unity of the spirit in the bond of peace*, but presuming to hold your redemption of another Saviour than he hath appointed, and giving way, or indulging to those contentious passions that defile the temple of God, bring along with them every evil work, to an intire forfeiture of all the blessings of the Gospel, and the suffering of that destruction which God will inflict upon those who *profane his temple* (y)? After this manner, the Apostle gives the powerfullest check possible to that spirit of vanity, that would have introduced distinctions among the Apostles, and raised one higher than another in popular applause. And to set people right in their notions about the Apostles, he lets them know, in what particular light they ought to regard their public Teachers.

It was indeed the way among Philosophers to differ from one another, and to fall into particular sects, who were always very zealous, each in preferring its own tenets, or its own system of wisdom before that of another, and in boasting of such a Philosopher as its head. But the folly of this conduct the Gospel has demonstrated, in teaching the world a divine system of truths, that expose the ignorance and folly of those wise men: *For the wisdom of this world*, says the Apostle, *is foolishness with God; and the Lord knoweth the thoughts of the wise that they are vain.* So that if any professing Christianity seem to be wise in this world, or to affect the speculations of Philosophers, and as their Disciples do, to set such a man at their head, meaning thereby to promote an opinion of their own wisdom, those persons deceive themselves, and are quite out of the way to be counted wise in the sight of

(y) 1 Cor. iii. 16, 17.

of God; *let them become fools,* as the world may call them, in renouncing the speculations and factious courses of those Philosophers and their Disciples, *that they may be wise* (z), according to the wisdom of God, in embracing the Gospel of *Christ,* that forbids all divisions, and to call any man our father or master upon earth, that commands us *to keep the unity of the Spirit in the bond of peace, and to confess only one Lord and one faith* (a). Thus the professors of Christianity must not imitate the factious humour of Philosophers and their Disciples, or look upon any man as their head or master. As for the Apostles themselves, they claim no mastership: *Who then,* say they, *is Paul, and who is Apollos, but Ministers by whom ye believed, even as the Lord gave to every man? I have planted, Apollos watered; but God gave the increase; now he that planteth, and he that watereth, are one, and every man shall receive his own reward, according to his own labour. For we are labourers together with God: Ye are God's husbandry, ye are God's building* (b). This therefore is the light, wherein we are taught to apprehend the Apostles with respect to the Christian Institution: As for the doctrines of the Gospel, and the blessings therein promised, as for the success of those doctrines in the hearts and lives of men, whereby they are led to lasting happiness; none of those things can be attributed to the Apostles; they acknowledge God for their only Author, and the glory of all must be ascribed to him alone. So that the Apostles, in the propagation of the Gospel, can only be considered as Ministers, united together in one common service, whom God employs, not for

(z) 1 Cor. iii. 18, 19, 20.   (a) Matth. xxiii. 9. 10.
Eph. iv. 3. &c.   (b) 1 Cor. iii. 5. &c.

for their own sake, but for the sake of other people, to dispense the effects of his wisdom and goodness to mankind. And, placing things in this view, they not only preclude themselves from all pretensions to merit, to superior esteem and glory; but they intimate the great folly of making distinctions among them, and how absurd it is for people to seek for credit or fame by heightening their character. Nay, they lead us to reflect, that the rest of mankind must be counted much more honourable, by far preferable to them; since its is only for their service that they are employed; only for their interest, that they are qualified, and commanded to carry on the propagation of the Gospel; and would not have been thus qualified, had not God designed thus to employ them: *We preach not,* say they, *ourselves, but Christ Jesus the Lord; and ourselves your servants for Jesus sake* (c). Must not the *Corinthians*, then, have been extremely foolish in attempting to pervert the settled order of things, while they set up the Apostles to be the heads of different parties, and the several parties were contending, each one to raise the fame of that particular Apostle for whom they had declared, thereby meanly designing to gain a name to themselves in a borrowed reputation? So worthy and honourable, so high in the love and esteem of God, are all sincere Christians, that *the world, life, and death, things present, and things to come,* all are employed by Providence in their service, as the means of their real, their eternal good and happiness: The Apostles themselves serve to no other purpose, and can be accounted of no otherwise. And, I say, does not this clearly represent the great meanness any
folld

(c) 2 Cor. iv. 5.   (d) 1 Cor. iii. 21. 22.

folly every good Christian would be guilty of, should he go about to derive his credit from the fame of his public Teacher? *Therefore*, says the Apostle (*d*), *let no man glory in men; for all things are yours; whether Paul, or Apollos, or Cephas, or the world, or life, or death, or things present, or things to come, all are yours; and ye are* Christ's, *and* Christ *is* God's. Thus it is that the Apostles do vehemently oppose themselves to that spirit of pride and vanity that prompted the *Corinthians* to make distinctions among them, and to attempt to raise one above another in popular applause. Upon the whole therefore,

Since the Apostles openly propose to the world, in the pursuit of universal goodness and righteousness, immortal honour and glory, as their great point of view:——Since upon this they expressly condemn and prohibit all passion for popular applause; shewing, at the same time, its most mischievous consequences:——Since all the doctrines they taught do strongly guard the mind against the influence of that hurtful dangerous appetite:——Since neither from the glorious truths they revealed in the Gospel, nor from the wonderful works of kindness, which, without reward, they freely did to the bodies of men, they assume any degree of praise or honour to themselves, but ascribe the glory of all to God alone, thereby honestly intending to recommend the Gospel to the acceptance of mankind as a divine institution:——Since they steadily oppose themselves to the superstition and idolatry, to all the false, absurd religious opinions that were established and professed among *Jews* and *Heathens*; whereby, as they foresaw, they came to be involved in universal contempt and hatred:——Since they are so far from using any of the mean arts or measures of popularity,

(*d*) 1 Cor. iii. 21, 22, 23.

popularity, that when some of their Disciples would have made a breach in the union of their service, and dividing them in parties, would have raised one above another; they severely check that spirit of faction and vanity, in strongly remonstrating, that therein they were highly injurious to *Jesus Christ*, to whom alone all the glory of the doctrines and blessings of the Gospel is due; and that thus acting in contradiction to the spirit and design of the Christian institution, they were cutting themselves off from all the happiness it proposes to mankind:——Since, at the same time, they depress their own character far below what people apprehended, and tell their Disciples, that while thus they set, some one Apostle, and some another, at their head, and severally professing themselves their followers, would borrow credit from their reputation, they were greatly dishonouring themselves; for that the Apostles were only their servants and ministers:——I say, since the Apostles, in all these particulars, acted a part directly cross to all the dictates of a vain glorious mind, 'tis impossible it can be suspected, that by this passion they were animated in the propagation of the Gospel. *As they were allowed of God to be put in trust with the Gospel, even so they spake, not as pleasing men but God, who searcheth the hearts. For neither at any time used they flattering words; nor of men sought they glory* (e). For all which they dare venture to appeal, not only to man, but to God himself. So that hitherto, in the judgment of every impartial man, I must presume to think, the Apostles are absolutely free from all suspicion of im-

will have the freedom of thought to allow the same weight

(e) 1 Thess. ii. 4, 5, 6.

weight to the same apology in the case of the Apostles, that they seem to allow it in justifying their own character.

It is objected to the Deists, that *" such men are afraid they shall not transmit their names to posterity with advantage, but by broaching odd and singular notions."* In answer to which, " Can they, (says Dr. Tindal) if they have any concern for reputation after death, expect fair usage then, when they are sure to be belied when alive? *For if you are not orthodox,* as an excellent Author (now deservedly in the first order of the church) says, *the most perspicuous virtue will not be believed; if you are guilty of no open vices, secret ones will be imputed to you, your inquiries will be called vain, curious, and forbidden studies; pride and ambition will be said to be the secret spring of them; a search after truth will be called novelty (f).*——How can one think any man would affect singularity in religion, when that must expose him to the hatred of the Priests, the Bigots, and the Immoral, who are ambitious of shewing their zeal to the church, the better to hide their enmity to religion. And when, by these means, one is looked on as a monster, by ninety-nine of an hundred, and others scarce dare give him any countenance; what has this unhappy man but conscience to support him (g)?" To the same purpose another Gentleman, of the same way, argues in this manner: " If any man (says he) presumes to think for himself, and, in consequence of that, departs from the sentiments of the herd of mankind among whom he lives, he is sure to draw upon himself the whole malice of the Priest, and

" of

(f) Difficulties and Discouragements, &c. p. 16, 17.
(g) An Address to the Inhabitants of London and Westminster, p. 41, 42. Vid. Christianity as old as the Creation, p. 424.)

" of all who believe in him, or who hope to make
" their fortune by pretending to believe in him, (which
" of course must be nine hundred and ninety-nine of
" a thousand) and can have no credit but what his
" virtue, in spite of his enemies, necessarily procures
" for him. Whereas, any profligate fellow is sure of
" credit, countenance, and support, in any sect or party
" whatsoever, tho' he has no other quality to re-
" commend him than the worst of all vices, a blind
" zeal to his sect or party (*h*)." Thus far the De-
ists go in their own justification. And while those *forts esprits*, those upright daring souls, that have the honesty and courage to oppose an established religion, do thus clear the sincerity of their own hearts; must they not, by the same course of reasoning, maintain the integrity of the Apostles, and pronounce them wholly free of all passion for worldly fame, to be enjoyed either before or after death? One should think that the evidence, on the side of the Apostles, is strongly fortified by the uncommon hardships, and frightful persecutions they chearfully endured, in opposing the absurd religious opinions then established in the world, or in relieving mankind from the superstition and idolatry, the bigotry which in their days every-where prevailed. Whereas; " many Free-thinkers have either
" fallen in with the reigning superstition of their
" country, or suffered it quietly to take its course,
" foreseeing how little good was to be done on so
" knavish and ignorant a creature as man, and how
" much mischief was to be expected from him (*i*)."
Wonderfully prudent! how little soever it bespeaks a free, a great and generous mind. But what can be expected from those men who tell us, " It is
" virtue

(*h*) A Discourse of Free-Thinking, p. 120. (*i*) Ibid. p. 123.

" virtue enough to endeavour to do good, on-
" ly within the bounds of doing one's self no
" harm (k)?" An unkind condemnation of *Socrates*, whom the Author had before honoured with
the character of *the divinest man that ever appeared in
the Heathen world, to whose virtue and wisdom all
ages have since done justice* (l). But passing this:

SECT. XIII.

*In publishing the Gospel to the World, the Apostles had
not the most distant Thought of thereby acquiring to
themselves worldly Power, Rule, or Dominion.*

I AM next to explain, whether the Apostles, in the prosecution of their service, were animated by a prevailing passion for worldly power, authority, or dominion. And indeed this is the passion that is most incident to great minds, and whereby fine spirits have in all ages been most apt to be strongly agitated; without regarding riches or treasures any farther, than as they are necessary to support their power and grandeur (a). And though I am not ignorant how contemptibly some people, that pretend to a more than ordinary discernment, are pleased to talk of the Apostles, as if they were only to be counted a company of poor, silly, despicable creatures; yet I will take the liberty to affirm, that the Apostles were men of the most open and generous,

---

(k) Ibid. p. 178.   (l) Ibid. p. 123.
(a) Est autem in hoc genere molestum, quod in maximis animis splendidissimisque ingeniis, plerumque existunt honoris, imperii, potentiæ, gloriæ cupiditates. Cic. de Off. lib. i. cap. 8.
In quibus autem major est animus, in iis pecuniæ cupiditas spectat ad opes, et ad gratificandi facultatem. Ibid.

rous, the greatest, and the most noble and elevated souls that ever mortals were inspired with: Nor can I think but thus much will be clearly apprehended by every man, who forms a judgment of the Apostles from their writings and course of life, and considers the character of a truly great man, as it is represented by the best Heathen Philosophers. So that I must beg leave to say, if the Apostles were incited in the service of the Gospel by any worldly motive, it does not appear, how, in a consistency with the nature of things, it could have been any other than a strong, violent passion for rule and empire. But, that the Apostles are as little liable in this, as in any other article, cannot but be obvious to every fair, impartial inquirer.

And indeed, when one reflects, that the Apostles were only a few obscure, friendless persons, neither keeping together for mutual counsel and assistance, nor setting up any one of their number to direct their acting in concert, but dispersing themselves through the world, and separating from each other to the greatest distance, in order to propagate the Gospel among all nations, having no fixed residence, but ever restlessly travelling about from place to place; it seems the wildest imagination possible, to conceive, that those men were all of them spurred on by a commanding lust of power, and had the mad ambition to conspire together in a formed design to overthrow the *Roman* empire, and all other kingdoms, and to usurp the elevation of Sovereigns, and grasp at universal dominion. The imputation is so very extravagant, and so far beyond the bounds of credibility, that, as it confutes itself, one may well think it not worth the regarding. However, as it affords an opportunity to set persons and things in a just light, I shall here go on as in the former articles,

articles, and further confider the doctrines of the Apoſtles, and their courſe of life, and from thence make it appear, that in the purſuit of their Miniſtry, they were in no degree ſtimulated by a prevailing paſſion for worldly power or dominion.

The great Author of our religion, under whoſe influence, and by whoſe authority, the Apoſtles always acted, lets us know the nature of his government, and expreſsly declares, that *his kingdom is not of this world* (*b*); that it is of no ſecular, but intirely of a ſpiritual nature. And, as the laws of this kingdom do not conſtitute any particular form of civil policy, that affects mankind in their bodies, their eſtates, or outward circumſtances; ſo its public Miniſters have no title to worldly power or dominion, and cannot, without uſurpation, pretend to rule over people in what concerns their bodies or eſtates, their natural or their civil rights or liberties. So that the kingdom of *Chriſt* having no concern but with the inward thoughts and conſciences of men, incapable of brutal force and violence, it can only be propagated and ſupported, or its Miniſters can only act, in the way of rational conviction and argument, and muſt leave all individual perſons, all the ſeveral ſtates and kingdoms of the world, to the peaceable poſſeſſion of their natural rights, their civil power and authority; being ſubject themſelves to the Civil Magiſtrate, and by their precepts and example, engaging others to obſerve a ſteady courſe of affection and loyalty.

Thus the great Founder of this ſpiritual kingdom, when upon earth, did himſelf confeſs his ſubjection, and pay tribute to the civil government, under which he then lived: He refuſed to meddle in a civil

---

(*b*) John xviii. 36.

vil difference (*c*), wherein his meddling might have been conſtructed an aſſuming or uſurping civil authority, and confirmed the *Jews* in their prejudices concerning the nature of his kingdom: And when the people, according to their miſtaken notions about the *Meſſiah*, upon a miracle wrought by our Saviour, would *have come and taken him by force to make him a King*, *he departed into a mountain himſelf alone*, and by that means prevented the deſign. (*d*): In a word, his conſtant doctrine was, to *render to* Cæſar, *the things that are Cæſar's; and to God, the things that are God's* (*e*). This was the conduct of our Saviour: And his command to thoſe particular perſons whom he was to employ in carrying on the propagation of his Goſpel, runs thus; *Ye know*, ſays our Lord, *that the Princes of the Gentiles exerciſe dominion over them, and they that are great exerciſe authority upon them: But it ſhall not be ſo among you; but whoſoever will be great among you, let him be your miniſter; and whoſoever will be chief among you, let him be your ſervant; even as the Son of man came not to be Miniſter unto, but to miniſter, and to give his life a ranſom for many* (*f*).

Now as *Jeſus Chriſt*, by his doctrine and example, declared the nature of his kingdom to be thus intirely ſpiritual, without interfering with any the ſmalleſt branch of civil juriſdiction or authority; ſo the Apoſtles do always ſteadily purſue the ſame plan. So far are they from claiming to themſelves any degree of worldly power and dominion, that they direct the allegiance of mankind to be wholly paid to their civil Governors, and command every individual to be *ſubject to principalities and powers, to obey Magiſtrates, and to be ready to every good work* (*g*).

They

(*c*) Luke xii. 14. (*d*) John vi. 15. (*e*) Matth. xxii. 21.
(*f*) Matth. xx. 25. (*g*) Tit. iii. 1.

They tell us, that government is not so much a human contrivance, as it is *an ordinance of God*, an institution which he has appointed, and which, from the circumstances wherein Providence hath placed us, he has made necessary to the peace and happiness of mankind (b). So that, by the doctrine of the Apostles, we are bound to be subject to the higher powers, not only from human compact and agreement, not only from a concern for the public peace and order of the world, or from benevolent principles that naturally prompt us to promote public happiness; but from *conscience towards God*, a regard to his sovereign authority, and as we value his protection and favour. And when the Apostles do thus enjoin obedience to our civil Governors, as an indispensable article of religion, wherein, if we fail, we become guilty of resisting the ordinance of God, and do thereby expose ourselves to his almighty displeasure; 'tis impossible they could have provided a stronger guard for the Magistrate in the possession and exercise of his civil authority; nor could they, by any other means, have more effectually engaged and secured the duty and loyalty of the subject. *Let every soul*, say the Apostles, *be subject to the higher powers. For there is no power but of God: The powers that be are ordained of God. Whosoever therefore resisteth the power, resisteth the ordinance of God; and they that resist shall receive to themselves damnation. For Rulers are not a terror to good works but to evil. Wilt thou then not be afraid of the power? Do that which is good, and thou shalt have praise of the same; for he is the Minister of God to thee for good. But if thou do that which is evil, be afraid; for he beareth not the sword in vain: For he is the Minister of God, a revenger to execute wrath upon him that doth evil.*

Vol. II.   S   *Wherefore*

(b) 1 Pet. ii. 13.

Wherefore ye must needs be subject, not only for wrath, but for conscience sake. For, for this cause pay you tribute also: For they are God's Ministers, attending continually upon this very thing. Render therefore to all their dues; tribute, to whom tribute is due; custom, to whom custom; fear, to whom fear; honour, to whom honour (*i*). This same doctrine is elsewhere thus inculcated upon us; *Submit yourselves,* says the Apostle, *to every ordinance of man, for the Lord's sake: Whether it be to King, as supreme; or unto Governors, as unto them that are sent by him for the punishment of evildoers, and for the praise of them that do well. For so is the will of God, that with well doing ye may put to silence the ignorance of foolish men* (*k*). Still reflecting, that *those who despise dominion, and speak evil of dignities, are ungodly sinners,* upon whom the judgments of Heaven shall be executed (*l*).

But not only do the Apostles, upon pain of incurring the displeasure of Almighty God, command their Disciples to be in all instances, dutiful and loyal, to pay tribute, and in every thing to answer the character of persons well affected to the civil Magistrate: But they further strictly enjoin them, in their solemn prayers and supplications to God, to intercede for all that are in authority, and to implore the blessings, the favour and protection of Heaven in their behalf. *I exhort, therefore,* says the Apostle, *that first of all, prayers, supplications, intercessions and giving of thanks, be made for all men; for Kings, and for all that are in authority: That we may lead a quiet and peaceable life in all godliness and honesty. For this is good and acceptable to God our Saviour: Who will have all men to be saved, and to come unto the knowledge of the truth* (*m*). And when one considers, with
what

(*i*) Rom. xiii. 1.—7.   (*k*) 1 Pet. ii. 13, 14, 15.
(*l*) Jude 8.   (*m*) 1 Tim. ii. 1.—4.

what uprightnefs, with what hearty fincerity, we ought, in all our prayers, to addrefs ourfelves unto God, it appears impoffible, that, in a confiftency with the difcharge of this duty, or that, without being highly impious before God, we can entertain difaffection in our hearts, or exprefs difobedience of any fort, in our lives. For it muft be owned, that to pray to God for the fafety of the civil Magiftrate, and the profperity of his government, while our difloyal thoughts or our rebellious deeds do naturally tend to the overthrow and ruin of both, is dealing doubly with our Maker, and cannot but provoke his juft indignation. This command, therefore, requiring us to pray for all that are in authority, ftrongly fecures our duty and loyalty, and affords good protection to the civil Magiftrate.

Such were the doctrines taught by the Apoftles concerning civil government, and powerfully recommended to the obfervance of mankind. How can we then conceive any the leaft fufpicion, that thefe very men who taught fuch doctrines to the world, were all the while only treacheroufly plotting together, to raife themfelves to univerfal empire and dominion, upon the ruins of the feveral ftates and kingdoms then fubfifting in the world? No imputation of this nature can be made out againft the Apoftles, without proving them, at the fame time, abandoned Atheifts, and arrant fools. Atheifts they muft have been, and impious to the higheft pitch, when they profanely meant to overturn that very power, which, in the name of God, they enjoined others always to regard and uphold as facred and religious: And muft not their folly have been egregious without example, and beyond meafure, when, from all the confiderations that heaven and earth can afford, they endeavoured, what they could, to

fortify

fortify people's minds in their loyalty to their Prince, whilst they were designing to stir them up to rebellion, and to employ their assistance in usurping his authority? But is it to be thought, that men of common sense, really engaged in such a particular plot, and endeavouring to gain a party to assist them in the execution, would, with the utmost zeal and fervency, do all in their power to inspire the minds of their followers with those principles that raise the deepest abhorrence of such a plot, and that render their opposition most certain and wholly unsurmountable? Mankind in many instances betray folly enough; but of such a degree of folly human nature is incapable. The *Roman* Pontiffs pursued another course: Having formed a design to erect a temporal universal monarchy, absolute in all things, they usurped a spiritual sovereign jurisdiction over the sentiments and actions of mankind, and thereupon claimed a power, which they frequently executed, to depose Princes, to absolve their subjects from their allegiance, to excommunicate whole nations, or lay them under an interdict, and to give away kingdoms to whom they pleased, encouraging the blinded superstitious world, to support their Bulls or Decrees, by granting them Indulgences, or publishing Crusado's. Thus likewise *Mahomet* suited his measures to the design he had formed: " His " general rule, and which he laid as a strict obli- " gation upon all his followers, was to fight for the " propagation of his religion. And there were on- " ly two conditions on which he granted peace to " any he had to do with; and these were either to " come into his religion, or submit to be tributaries " unto them (*n*)." So that the doctrines of the
Gospel

(*n*) Prideaux's Life of Mahomet, p. 91. Here is a passage of the Alcoran that declares expressly for toleration: Si Dieu l'eût
voulu,

Gospel do clearly justify the Apostles from having any design of usurping worldly power and authority. Nor is their innocence less apparent from every particular branch of their conduct.

The lust of power, like every other prevailing passion, having gained the command of the soul, will not conceal itself, nor can it keep within the bounds of justice and religion, but must produce its own genuine effects, and do all it can to make provision for its own gratification. Thus, from the conduct of the Apostles, before they fully understood the design of the Gospel, or the nature of *Christ*'s kingdom, one may easily learn, that they were animated with the prospect of coming to worldly power. They have their own ambitious aims of rising above one another in the public posts of that government, as they apprehended it: And they fail not to shew a disposition to make the world sensible of the direful effects of that passion. Their history informs us, that it was oftener than once debated among them, *Who should be the greatest* (o)? While some of them, to the great indignation of the rest, immediately petitioned *Jesus* himself, begging they might have the

---

voulu, tous les hommes qui vivent sur la terre croiroient. Serez-vous assez insensé,, vous pauvre mortel, pour contraindre, par la force, les autres hommes à croire? Non, l'ame ne croit point que par la volonté de Dieu. Alcor. ch. x. 98. So that Mahomet acted, Primierement, par la voye de la parole & de la persuasion; & ensuite à force ouverte, lorsqu'il se sentit assez appuyé. Wherein this Impostor is manifestly self-condemned. But now again; Les Mahometans ne contraignent personne pas, même leurs esclaves, à embrasser leur religion. Il y a même dans la Turquie, des villages, & des bourgs entiers, ou tous les habitans sont Chrêtiens. La seule capitale, dit-on, renferme plus de 60000 Juifs, sans compter les Chrêtiens de toutes les sectes. La Relig. des Mahomet. Tiré du Latin de M. Reland. p. 107, 233.

(o) Mark ix. 33, &c.

the promise of the most honourable places (*p*). Besides, that a certain village of the *Samaritans*, refusing to entertain our Saviour, as he was in his way to *Jerusalem*; this the Apostles counted such an instance of disaffection in those that should be under their Master's government, that their imperious spirit would have immediately commanded *fire to come down from Heaven to consume them* (*q*). And from these instances one may judge, what was likely to have been the deportment of the Apostles with respect to one another; and after what manner they would have employed that extraordinary miraculous power, with which they were endowed. No doubt, they would have acted the part of other ambitious men, fallen into intrigues and factions, endeavoured to undermine and displace one another, and exerted all their power, while they kept united together, in forcing the rest of mankind to submit to their authority. But after the crucifixion of *Jesus Christ*, when they came to a better understanding of the design of the Gospel, what is the single thought, the single action, wherein they betray a passion for worldly dominion?

Instead of the proud, the imperious thoughts of rule and empire, they express nothing but meekness and humility; they carry on their common service with great concord and unanimity; and, under the highest affronts, shew no degree of resentment, but the utmost forbearance, patience and resignation. And as there is no symptom of any passion for worldly power in the temper of the Apostles; so neither can one discern the appearance of their making any provision necessary to bring about the gratification of this appetite. One should think, that had the Apostles been engaged in any confederacy to usurp dominion over mankind, 'besides securing an infinite number

---

(*p*) Matth. xx. 20.   (*q*) Luk. ix. 54.

number of followers every where thro' the world, they muſt have found it neceſſary to have provided (for I will not mention thoſe infamous powers aſſumed by the Popes of *Rome*) a proportionable quantity of money and arms, without which, they could not but know, their deſign would prove abſolutely abortive. But as our Saviour, when alive, ſent forth his Diſciples to preach the Goſpel, and commanded them, that *they ſhould take nothing for their journey, ſave a ſtaff only; no ſcrip, no bread, no money in their purſe* (r); ſo, after his death and reſurrection, in the ſame mean and defenceleſs manner did they travel thro' the world in the diſcharge of their Miniſtry; ſhewing always an abſolute contempt of money, without which, no man can ever think of ſupporting himſelf, or his followers, in the purſuit or poſſeſſion of that power and greatneſs he intends to uſurp and maintain over others, who cannot but violently oppoſe him. So that all their arms was a ſtaff to help them by the way; and having no money of their own, they lived on the charity of other people; very frequently reduced to hunger, and cold, and nakedneſs. Such is the pomp and greatneſs they affected, and ſuch is the proviſion thoſe men made, who are ſaid to have conſpired to conquer the world. In ſhort, they make not the moſt diſtant attack upon the rights or properties of other people; but, as by their laws they ſecured every man in the quiet and full poſſeſſion of every branch of his liberty; ſo, in the whole of their practice, they keep within the bounds of theſe ſacred inſtitutions. But how could the Apoſtles, in all inſtances, have been meek and humble, patient and forgiving, univerſally temperate, juſt, and righteous, had they been go-

verned

(r) Mark vi. 8.

verned by an insatiable lust of power, which, like a common strumpet, first debauches a man's principles, and then leads him on to the perpetration of every act of impiety? A man, in the pursuit of his ambitious views, can have no regard to any thing but as it contributes towards the great end he is aiming at: So that all rights, human and divine, must be sacrificed to this one appetite; and the world cannot avoid being involved in direful oppression and misery; which, if the ambitious man does not himself perish in the attempt, will continually be breaking out, according to the opposition or success he meets withal. How contradictory is all this to the temper and conduct of the Apostles?

But, had a prevailing passion for worldly power been the motive that pushed on the Apostles to the propagation of the Gospel, must they not have found it absolutely necessary to have practised all imaginable arts of popularity? Certain it is, that they had no shadow of title, no pretensions of any sort, to set up upon, whereby people might have been induced to favour their interest, or to engage in their service. On the contrary, from their own mouths, their original and fortune were every where well known, and all the world understood, that they had no manner of claim to any the least degree of civil authority. Having therefore no support from the righteousness of their cause, they must intirely have depended on the affections of the multitude, and, for that reason, have been obliged to employ all possible methods to insinuate themselves into their favour, to prevent their revolting, when once engaged, and to keep them steady to their interest. And to compass this, must they not have had the hainous impiety to alienate men's hearts and affections from

from those civil governors, under whose authority they were living, and to pervert all their principles of common justice and honesty? And since men are seldom forward to disturb their present ease, or to expose their lives and fortunes in an attempt to change their condition, without the prospect of rendering it incomparably better; must not the Apostles have persuaded them that the advantages they might assuredly promise themselves under their government, would be infinitely greater than any they were at present possessed of? And to afford them a conviction of this, must they not, in the mean time, have entertained them with some considerable instances of their profuseness and liberality and granted them many indulgences in their prevailing humours and passions? And while they were thus carrying on their plot, what peace and quiet of mind could they possibly enjoy? Supposing them in perfect union among themselves, which rarely happens among persons of unbounded ambition, must they not have been frequently put upon racking their invention, and reduced to the utmost perplexities, how to hinder and compose differences among their followers, and prevent their proving treacherous; how to guard against their enemies penetrating into their design; and at length how to bring it into execution? It seems impossible but all these particulars must have taken place in the case of the Apostles, had they been pursuing after worldly power and dominion. But where is the single instance in their conduct, that carries the least suspicious look of their having been after any such manner involved or affected?

At an infinite distance were they from giving any countenance to any degree of disaffection and rebellion against the civil Magistrate, whose authority they enjoin us religiously to regard and to hold sacred; and for whose safety and prosperity they command us to put up our prayers to God Almighty. Nor do they buoy up the minds of their followers with any hopes of their getting above their present calamities, and of their leading them on to a golden age, wherein they should live at ease, amidst all plenty and greatness. They all along ingenuously tell the world, that as they expected for themselves no other lot upon earth, than that which had already befallen them, full of meanness, contempt, and poverty; so they could receive no man into their society, as a Disciple of *Jesus Christ*, who would not first renounce all worldly pleasures, and riches, and greatness, and solemnly profess he was well satisfied to undergo all the most dreadful miseries, even death itself, when ever he should be called to it for the sake of the Gospel, whose rewards are of another world: for that they were all of them, *through many tribulations to enter into the kingdom of heaven* (s). And if they were not at the easy charge of flattering the hopes of their followers, by shewing them some imaginary felicities at a distance; far less were they at the expence of bribing them into their interest, or securing them to their party, by any present acts of munificence. Their noble contempt of money, and all worldly treasures, as their Master had commanded them, made this popular art absolutely impracticable; without which, there is no winning the hearts of the multitude: Nay, they do not so much as grant any the least indulgence to any one of their followers, in any one single humour or appetite, that can in any measure be prejudicial to human society. For, not to speak of their severities against every open violation

of

(s) Act. iv. 22.

of the great law of universal righteousness, they will suffer no man to lead an idle life, but severely condemn those persons who do not apply themselves to some lawful and industrious business, whereby they may subsist themselves and families, and prove useful to the rest of mankind: And so zealous are they in this particular, that in the most solemn manner, they command all their other Disciples to withdraw themselves from those pretended Christians, that indulge sloth and idleness, and are busy bodies, of an inquisitive and pragmatical temper, neglecting their own proper affairs, and curiously prying into those of other people; an unhappy temper, that greatly disturbs the peace of society, by its dealing very much in censure and defamation (*t*). Such was the conduct of the Apostles. And can such a conduct give us ground to suspect, that the Apostles were designing to make a party in the world? No man that understands the humours and passions of the multitude, who in all ages have been noted for their ignorance, avarice, fickleness, ingratitude, but must own, that such measures are totally repugnant to all those arts that are necessary to gain the affections of the populace, and to secure them to one's interest. And as the Apostles are infinitely above all artifices of that nature; so they are absolutely unacquainted with those anxious perplexing passions, which continually disturb the breasts of those men that are engaged in any dark design, and who depend on the humours of a capricious multitude. As for the Apostles, they are always calm and sedate, and in one steady uniform course of action, pursue the propagation of the Gospel, with that serenity and greatness of mind, which shews them to have

such

(*t*) Eph. iv. 28. 2 Thess. iii. 6. &c. 1 Tim. v. 13. 1 Pet. iv. 15.

such things in their eye, as do not lie at the mercy of popular humours, or any turn of fortune whatsoever. From all which one should think it manifest, that the Apostles were in no degree supported by the lust of power, or by the force of any design to grasp at worldly rule and dominion, whilst they so vigorously promoted the propagation of the Gospel.

Let it only further be remarked, that as their master had it in his power, with the full consent of the people, whose notions about the *Messiah* mightily favoured an ambitious enterprise, to have made himself a King, but utterly rejected or rather greatly despised the temptation (*u*); so there is no doubt but the Apostles met with several very fair opportunities, which, to men combined together in the pursuit of power, might have appeared very flattering, and inspired them with good hopes of success. In particular, the people of *Lystra* were so much alarmed at only one miracle done by the Apostle *Paul*, in healing a man that had been cripple from his mother's womb, that they verily believed *the gods had come down among them in the likeness of men*. And of this, it would seem, they were so very confident, that judging *Barnabas* to be *Jupiter*, and *Paul Mercurius*, because he was the chief speaker; *the priest of Jupiter brought oxen and garlands to the gates of the city, and would have done sacrifice with the people*. And is it to be thought, that men insatiably ambitious, grasping at worldly power and dominion, and carrying on a plot to that very purpose, would have failed to improve so favourable a conjuncture? What safety to their persons, what submission to their commands, what success might they not have expected in any attempt the most dangerous, while their followers were persuaded, that they

---

(*u*) 2 Joh. vi. 14, 15.

they had the gods themselves visibly at their head? One cannot imagine, that men, absolutely devoted to the lust of empire, would totally have neglected this opportunity, or have been so far from making use of it to serve the end they were intending, as to do their utmost to suppress such notions among the people, to convince them of their being highly absurd and impious, assuring them that those, whom they took for gods, were but *men of like passions with themselves*: One cannot imagine, that by the strongest arguments, with great vehemence, they would have gone about to persuade them, to embrace those principles, which for the future should determine them to worship the one only living and true God, to be in all instances charitable and just to one another, and particularly to be dutiful and loyal to their present civil governors. Such measures, quite contradictory to all past experience, would only serve to defeat their ambition, and to render their attempt to usurp worldly power extremely ridiculous. And yet this was the conduct of the Apostles; for no sooner did they hear what the Priest with the people were about to do, but, with the utmost concern and indignation, *they rent their cloaths, and ran in among them, crying out and saying, Sirs, why do ye these things! We also are men of like passions with you, and preach unto you, that ye should turn from these vanities unto the living God, who made heaven, and earth, and the sea, and all things that are therein.——And with these sayings scarce restrained they the people that they had not done sacrifice unto them* (x). A clear demonstration, so far as I am able to judge of human nature, that the Apostles were under the commanding influence of no worldly ambitious passion, as the great spring that

---

(x) Act. xiv. 8. &c.

that set them a-going, that supported them in the propagation of the Gospel. To conclude,

"In reflecting upon the whole, it appears, that the kingdom which the Apostles gave out they were commanded, by the authority of Heaven, to erect and establish among mankind, was purely of a spiritual nature, relating wholly to the minds and consciences of men; and to be supported and propagated only by the considerations of another world, the rewards and punishments of a future state:——— That they powerfully recommended affection and loyalty towards civil Governors, and bound the subject to obedience, particularly from conscience towards God, a regard to his sovereign authority, which cannot be contemned without infinite hazard: ———That in pursuing such measures, while they only meant to usurp worldly power, they must have deliberately renounced the favour of God, armed their disciples to defeat their design, and rendered their own ruin certain and unavoidable:———That under the highest indignities, the most provoking affronts and injuries, they expressed nothing but meekness and humility, patience and forgiveness, and were utterly void of all pride and resentment, of every symptom of an aspiring imperious spirit:——— That they made no provision, that could help forward the designs of an ambitious mind; but, in all instances, showed a noble contempt of money, without which no attempt for empire can prove successful:———That they employed no popular arts to gain followers, or to secure people to their interest; but pursued measures, that must have alienated the heart of every worldly man from their enterprise; and proposed encouragements that could take with none, but such as were dead to this world, and lived in the hopes of a glorious immortality:———That they were

were altogether free of all those torturing thoughts, that ever afflict the minds of men engaged in a dangerous conspiracy; and carried on the propagation of the Gospel, with that resolute compoſure and ſedateneſs of ſoul, that ſhows them infinitely above all worldly regards:——That in thoſe inſtances wherein they might find people diſpoſed to ſupport them in the purſuit of any ſuch deſign, they checked the temper, and deſpiſed the opportunity: I ſay, all theſe particulars appear manifeſt in the character of the Apoſtles; and as every one of them ſeems to be a clear proof, ſo, taken all together, they muſt make up a full demonſtration, that in the propagation of the Goſpel, the Apoſtles were no Impoſtors, or that they were concerned in no plot; under the pretence of that Miniſtry, to attain to worldly rule and empire. They did every thing neceſſary to fruſtrate ſuch a deſign, and no one thing did they do calculated to promote it. Had their ſucceſſors, down to our times, every where inherited the ſame temper, and kept themſelves at as great a diſtance from every branch of civil authority, one is tempted to think, that the truth of the Chriſtian inſtitution had not at this day been ſo much contraverted. It ſeems too true, that the power of Clergymen, whoſe proper buſineſs ought to confine them to preach faith and repentance, from the conſiderations of another world, has always proved fatal to religion: It fills their heads with foreign concernments, it nouriſhes in their hearts the baſe paſſions of human nature, and has dreadful effects upon the world, in all the cruelties of dire perſecution. May God maintain the ſword always in the hands of the civil Magiſtrate and ever preſerve his church from the uſe of ſo deſtructive an inſtrument. Happy our days, wherein no man can complain of oppreſſion of conſcience, wherein the ſacred liberties of mankind ſuffer no force or invaſion.

SECT.

SECT. XIV.

The Conclusion, from what has hitherto been explained, viz. The Apostles having been animated, in the Prosecution of their Enterprise, by no worldly Motive of any sort, they were certainly no Impostors.

THUS far have I endeavoured to explain, that the doctrines taught by the Apostles, are, in the whole of their contexture, in their general precepts, infinitely above, and directly opposite to all purposes whatsoever that can be thought base or criminal; and in their particular prohibitions, do expressly condemn every particular passion, to which a man can be thought capable of indulging, to the disturbance, the hurt or prejudice of the world about him: ——That as the conduct and situation of the Apostles was such, that had they conspired together in any carnal secular design, it was impossible for them to avoid being detected and ruined; so the constant zeal they employed in recommending their doctrines, by the most powerful arguments, to the belief and practice of their followers, served directly to arm those very persons against them, from whom alone they could hope to be supported: ——That in their deportment and conduct of life, they express nothing but an exact rectitude of manners, universal righteousness, steadily pursuing a course of actions, in all instances, answerable to their doctrines, and visibly tending to the glory of God and the good of mankind:—That this their virtue and integrity they still maintained without the least blemish, or giving the smallest ground of suspicion, (but every thing to the contrary), even amidst those opportunities and temptations, that can be thought

fairest

fairest and strongest, or most favourable to the designs of a worldly minded man: I say, from such considerations, I have endeavoured to make it appear, that the Apostles, in the propagation of the Gospel, had no regard to the riches, or pleasures, or honours of this world, that they were animated with no worldly design whatsoever; and consequently, that they were no Impostors, while they assured the world, that in the course of their Ministry, designed to reform the world, and to promote universal righteousness and goodness, *they were only pressing forward towards that joy that was set before them*, their great recompence of reward, a blessed life, and immortality. Nor is it possible that a charge of imposture can be laid against them, without supposing them void of all sense of this or another world, void of humanity, and void of common understanding.

Openly to profess, that in every article of their Ministry they are determined by the authority of God, and from the considerations of another world: And under this profession, to be deliberately carrying on a plot in defiance to what they expressly declare to be the will of God, and against all the hopes they pretend to have of future happiness, can belong to no persons, but to such as are obstinate, confirmed Atheists.——Indeed, to suffer one's self, and to encourage others to suffer in the cause of virtue and religion, is noble and generous, and most worthy of all the sentiments of human nature; but to involve the world in sufferings, or to expose mankind to be every where massacred and butchered, as by the objection the Apostles must have done, for the sake of some base infamous project, is cruel and barbarous, and totally void of humanity.——And what degree of common understanding can one ascribe to the Apostles,

postles, when all the measures they pursued are absolutely unfit, notoriously repugnant to the worldly end they are supposed to have intended? So that, I say, had the Apostles been Impostors, or had they been put upon propagating the Gospel from any worldly design, they must, at the same time, have been a set of silly, barbarous Atheists: A character of the Apostles that can enter into the suspicion of no man, who has any the least acquaintance with their history.

SECT. XV.

The Apostles were guilty of no Fraud or Imposture in the Matter of the Resurrection of Jesus, *as alledged by Mr.* Woolston.

THE considerations hitherto advanced, one would think, are fully sufficient to clear the Apostles of the charge of imposture, or to satisfy every impartial man, that the great power or motive that supported these first Publishers of the Gospel in the discharge of their Ministry, had nothing in it of this world. But, though it must be confessed, that the Apostles were under no sort of influence in the universe, that could induce them to deceive mankind in any one article whatsoever; yet our Infidels are pleased to accuse them of a particular instance of fraud, which, as it directly strikes at the foundation of the Christian institution, I cannot but here examine, before I conclude this part of our argument.

And we are told, *The Apostles were guilty of a villainous theft, in stealing away the dead body of* Jesus, *upon which they pretended,* whilst in their consciences they knew it was quite otherwise, *that he was risen from*

from the dead, and therein have impofed a moft monftrous cheat upon the world. This is the heavy charge. But how contradictory it is to all the known certain principles whereby one can judge of perfons and things, to alledge, that the Apoftles were Impoftors in any one article, efpecially in that of the refurrection of *Jefus*, without the truth of which, the credit of the Gofpel falls immediately to the ground, is apparent from what I have hitherto largely explained. Nor, in truth, is it an eafy matter to conceive, as this charge againft the Apoftles would have us, how men, with all their fenfes about them, could deliberately, and with great obftinacy, renounce every prefent and future enjoyment, and that upon no motive in the univerfe, but purely to live in mifery, to expire in torments, and to go into another world, there likewife to be miferable to eternity! Till human nature comes to fet up mere pain as the great object of its warmeft purfuits, fuch an event lies far beyond the bounds of poffibility. But we fhall proceed to examine the force of thofe particular reafons, upon which our Infidels take upon them to affure us, that the Apoftles ftole away the body of *Jefus*, and thereupon grafted the bare-faced, infamous cheat of his refurrection. And,

Firft of all, they inform us, " That 'tis hard and " even impoffible to imagine, that God would vouch- " fafe the favour of a miraculous refurrection to one " who, for his crimes, defervedly fuffered and un- " derwent death (*a*)." But was it a crime to relieve the world from Heathen Idolatry, and *Jewifh* fuperftition? Or, was it a crime to introduce among mankind the knowledge of the true God, and of a future ftate of rewards and punifhments; and to teach them a fyftem of morals, the pureft and

beft

(*a*) Woolft. 6th Difcourfe, p. 6.

best the nature of things can afford, and of infinite consequence to the human species? If these are crimes, *Jesus* was most certainly guilty;——of what other, I am not able to comprehend. I confess, that, in order to engage the world to submit to his institution, he wrought miracles, in healing diseases, and raising the dead, works of the same beneficent nature with his doctrines; he foretold his own resurrection, and upon this event staked his character, and put the whole credit of his Ministry: And in all this, wherein was *Jesus* criminal? Why, the Deists tell us, that those miracles of *Jesus* were all fraud and deceit, had nothing real, and therein he grossly *abused the credulity of the people*. A most hainous crime! I readily grant. But by what authority do our Infidels contradict the universal voice of all history, that ascribes real truth to the works of *Jesus?* Must stubborn facts, clearly supported by the most unquestionable evidence, lose all existence, or be reduced to mere delusion by the mighty breath of bold arbitrary assertions to the contrary? When the Deists shall have disproved the testimony of Heathen and *Jewish* Writers, concerning the reality of the miracles of *Jesus*, then may they have leave to call them delusions.

In the mean while, I would gladly know, is this the reasoning that becomes a Freethinker; " *Je-*
" *sus Christ* foretold, that he would rise again from
" the dead; but on this very account, his pre-
" suming to take upon him the fulfilling of such an
" event, he must be held a wicked deceiver, hate-
" ful to God. And therefore, nothing can be more cer-
" tain, than that his prediction never took effect, it
" being impossible to imagine that God would vouch-
" safe a miraculous resurrection to so great a criminal?"
A criminal! merely because he foretold his resurrection!

rection! and before we knew whether the event will juftify the prediction! Whoever, like Mr. *Woolfton*, is capable of putting upon the world fuch an argument, or of thereby forming his own judgment of perfons and things, does not feem to be overftocked with modefty, or to want an appetite fitted to relifh any abfurdity.

In a word, from all the lights we can have, and every poffible way of judging, the whole life of *Jefus* is fo intirely irreproachable, that to charge him with crimes, one muft be guilty of a moft notorious contradiction to the obvious naked truth of things. Nay, the accufation feems quite inconfiftent with Mr. *Woolfton*'s open profeffion, wherein he affures us, that *if Chriftians, in procefs of time, had not fophifticated the primitive religion of* Jefus,——*the world might have enjoyed great happinefs under* Jefus's *religion, even that happinefs——of the ftate of nature, religion and liberty*, for the recovery of which Mr. *Woolfton* has had the greatnefs of mind to labour fo inceffantly (*b*). Thus, I fay, had the primitive religion of *Jefus* ftill fubfifted, (fo compleatly, by his own confeffion, was the work done to his hand) Mr. *Woolfton* would have been faved the trouble and hazard of repairing the religious interefts, the moral happinefs of mankind. Whatever therefore may be objected to his Difciples of after ages, it muft be allowed, that as to *Jefus* himfelf, his moral character was intire, and rendered it in noways unworthy of God to be concerned in his refurrection. But,

In the *next* place, it is alledged, " That the chief " Priefts and Pharifees having fealed the ftone at " the mouth of the fepulchre; by this fealing we " are to underftand nothing lefs than a covenant
" entered

(*b*) Woolfton, ibid. p. 37.

" entered into between the chief Priests and the
" Apostles, by which *Jesus's* veracity, power and
" *Messiahship* was to be tried. It is true, we read
" not of the Apostles giving their consent to the
" covenant, yet it was reasonably presumed, and
" could not have been refused, if asked, and as for
" the condition of the sealed covenant, it was this;
" If *Jesus* arose from the dead in the presence of
" the chief Priests, upon their opening the seals of
" the sepulchre, at the time appointed, then was
" he to be called the *Messiah*: But, if he continued
" in a corrupt and putrified state of mortality, then
" was he to be granted to be an Impostor. Very
" wisely and rightly agreed! [Say the Deists.]
" And if the Apostles had stood to this covenant,
" Christianity had been nipt in its bud, and sup-
" pressed in its birth. But they had other views,
" and another game to play at all adventures. The
" body was to be removed, and a resurrection pre-
" tended. Nor did the Apostles neglect to use
" means to accomplish their design; at last an op-
" portunity they got for that purpose. The watch
" that was set to guard the sepulchre having drunk
" so largely that night, either by the contrivance
" of the Apostles themselves, or upon the bounty
" of some other people, that they were quite in-
" toxicated, *fell fast asleep*: Upon which the Dis-
" ciples being aware of the lucky opportunity, car-
" ried the body of *Jesus* off safely, and executed
" that fraud, which has been the delusion of na-
" tions and ages since (*c*)." Thus far the accusation goes, and the sealing of the sepulchre seems
to be the grand topic from whence they pretend to demonstrate the villany of the Apostles,
and that the resurrection of *Jesus* is a mere imposture.

(*c*) Id. ibid. p. 15, 20, 21.

fture. But, before I come particularly to confider this mighty argument, I would beg to be informed,

Upon what evidence do the Deifts pretend to know, that *Jefus* was crucified, and lay dee'd in his grave at the time of the *Jewifh* Paffover——That the chief Priefts fealed the ftone of the fepulchre ——and from *Pilate* the *Roman* governor obtained a watch of foldiers to guard it? The Apoftles have indeed recorded fuch events in their hiftory of the tranfactions of thofe times: And is it upon the truth of this hiftory, that the Deifts believe the truth of thefe matters of fact? Why then do they difbelieve other facts, that are as pointedly attefted by the fame witneffes? Is there good reafon to fufpect the Apoftles when they report, that for fear of the heavenly Meffenger who rolled back the ftone from the door of the fepulchre, *the keepers did fhake and become as dead men*; and that *early in the morning fome of the watch came into the city, and fhewed unto the chief Priefts all the things that were done*; I fay, is there good reafon to fufpect the veracity of the Apoftles in thofe articles; but no reafon to call their teftimony in queftion, when they tell us, that the chief Priefts fealed the ftone, and placed a guard upon the fepulchre? It is true, thefe precautions taken by the chief Priefts, though they could not poffibly prevent, yet they do not infer the refurrection of *Jefus*; whereas the account we have concerning the behaviour of the watch, would lead one to that conclufion. But muft nothing have credit that makes for the refurrection, and every thing that would make againft it be admitted?——In examining into the truth of a main fact, attended with fo many collateral facts or circumftances, all attefted by the fame authority, whereby the main fact is
fupported;

supported; is it fair, has it any shew of honesty, to garble, if I may speak so, those collateral facts, and to forge others, so as to lead one to apprehend that the main fact in question is a downright forgery? Thus,

The great event about whose truth we would be satisfied, is the resurrection of *Jesus Christ*. Now, along with this main fact, we have so many collateral facts whereby its credibility may be judged, such as the sealing the stone of the sepulchre, and setting a watch; the trembling of the keepers, and their becoming as dead men, upon some astonishing incidents at the time of the resurrection; the coming of some of the watch into the city, and informing the chief Priests about what had happened; the calling of a council by the chief Priests, and their giving large money to the soldiers, bribing them to say, *his Disciples came by night, and stole him away while we sleep:* These, I say, are so many collateral facts; and what evidence we have for any of them, the very same we have for each and all of them. What then is the law of reason, or where is the rule of honesty, that can intitle a man to assure the world, " The sepulchre indeed was sealed
" and guarded, as *Matthew* reports: But he lyes
" when he tells us, that the *chief Priests bribed* the
" soldiers to say, *his Disciples came by night, and*
" *stole him away:* For this report of the soldiers
" which the Historian would here make to be the
" effect of a bribe, and therefore a mere falsehood,
" is the real account of things as they actually happened; since the whole truth of the matter, is
" plainly this; either by the contrivance of the A-
" postles themselves, or by some other means, (one
" cannot positively determine, how) the soldiers
" that night being quite intoxicated with excess of
" drink,

Sect. XV.   Christian Revelation.

"drink, and in a deed-sleep, the Apostles took the opportunity, and having stole away the body of *Jesus*, pretended a resurrection." I say, what is the rule of reason or honesty, upon which a man gives credit to *Matthew* in some articles; but offers him the lye in others? Can our Infidels justify a man's differing so widely from this Historian, by the testimony of any other Historians of better authority, or by an interfering and clashing of facts told by the Apostles themselves; or from any blemish in their moral character? I am afraid, that to alledge that the Apostles contrived to have the guards intoxicated; that they gained their design; and by this means throwing the watch into a deep sleep, that, in the mean while, they carried off the body of *Jesus* safely, must be held the forging of facts at pleasure, not only without, but contrary to the faith of history. Such management must totally overthrow all history whatsoever; and while a man pretends to make use of it, render it absolutely useless: Nor can those who follow this course ever prevent their being suspected of being wholly in the power of mere passion and prejudice. And how very partial our modern Deists are in representing the character of the Apostles, there is abundant proof from their opinion concerning the soldiers that guarded the sepulchre.

    "Your Evangelists (say they) would hint, that
"the chief Priests gave money to the soldiers to
"say, they were asleep, when the Disciples stole
"the body of *Jesus* away, as if they were bribed
"to a false testimony; but there neither was nor
"could be any such thing. If there had been a
"real resurrection to their astonishment and amaze-
"ment, as it is represented in your Gospels, *no
"money could so soon have corrupted them to a false,*

Vol. II.   X   "*witness,*

"*witness*, being under such fears of God and of
"*Jesus* (d)." Thus those drunken unconscionable
soldiers must not be held capable of telling a
lye, tho' under the temptation of a large bribe, for
fear of that God whom they knew nothing of, and
of *Jesus*, whose real character they were totally
ignorant of: And yet the Apostles, amidst the
most solemn appeals to the true God, and the most
awful representations of an approaching judgment,
a future state of rewards and punishments, *when all
lyars shall be damned eternally*, were not only capable,
but they were actually guilty of a deliberate horrid
lye, and for which, by their own doctrine, they must
suffer torment for ever hereafter! If this be a freedom of thought in judging of persons and characters,
upon which a man has reason to value himself, I
appeal to the whole world. For my part, as I pretend to know nothing about antient facts but from
the history of former ages, so I as little know what
other way I can arrive to the certain knowledge of
the truth of those facts, but by carefully considering the nature and circumstances of the facts themselves, and the character and principles of the persons concerned in them. 'Tis after this manner that
I now come impartially to inquire into the truth of
those particular facts that relate to the resurrection
of *Jesus*, and concerning which the best authentic
records we have are those of the Gospel, as they
come from those persons who are said to have been
eye-witnesses.

In the *first* place, 'Tis agreed that *the sepulchre
was sealed and guarded:* But then our Infidels alledge, that this *sealing* must signify, "There was
" a covenant betwixt the chief Priests on one side,
" and the Apostles on the other, wherein both parties

(d) Woolst. ubi supra, p. 21.

" ties mutually agreed, That the seal should not be
" broken up, but in the presence of all concerned:
" That if, upon the opening of the sepulchre, the
" body of *Jesus* should be found still dead, he
" should be held an Impostor; but, if alive and
" risen, he should be esteemed the *Messiah*. From
" whence it follows, that the Apostles were an-
" swerable for the intireness of the seals; and that
" *Jesus*, should he return to life again, must not
" presume to stir out of the sepulchre, till the chief
" Priests should be present to take off the seals, and
" to open the door for him." This is our modern
account of things, which is reckoned new and ingenious, and upon which the Author values himself
extravagantly. But alas! in this covenant their is
nothing real to be seen but a man's wit straining
itself to amuse people with an imaginary conceit,
and to render them mistrustful of the resurrection.
Not to mention other reflections that might be
made on it, I shall only observe, that, from the
truth of things, as recorded in the History, 'tis absurd to imagine, either that the chief Priests made,
or meant to make such a covenant with the A-
postles, or that the Apostles could or would agree
to it.

On the whole face of the History, it is apparent,
that, upon the crucifixion of their Master, the A-
postles gave up all for lost, and had the comfort of
no hopes of any sort. So that the controversy a-
bout the *Messiahship* of *Jesus* being intirely at an
end, and the Apostles no longer pretending to maintain his credit in that character, which they certainly thought he had now forfeited; what need of
a covenant to settle the matter, as if the question
were still intire, and both parties were yet insisting
on their different claims? Had such a covenant been
proposed

proposed to the Apostles, they would have esteemed it a cruel insult over their miseries; or had they judged the chief Priests sincere and in earnest, no doubt, had the sting of their disappointments suffered them, they would have laughed at the proposal, frankly owning they gave up the point, and their cause was ruined beyond remedy. But,

Supposing the Apostles to have been in hopes of the resurrection of *Jesus*, (which, in real fact, was the thing in the world farthest from their thought) how could they possibly become bound, as this covenant would have them, that *the seals should be preserved whole and intire*, and that *Jesus*, arise when he would, should not stir out of the sepulchre, till the chief Priests and all concerned should be present to witness it? I hope it is not pretended, that the Apostles, by the exertion of their own power, were to restore *Jesus* to life again. Indeed, had this been the case, they might have made such a covenant, and brought themselves under such engagements. But their Master had told them *he had a power to lay down his life, and a power to take it again* (e). And can it be thought, that the Apostles would take upon them to enter into any articles about the precise particular circumstances of the exertion of a power that was none of their's, that was absolutely at the disposal of another, and in relation to which they had no commission to treat with any man living? As the agreeing to such a covenant would have been extremely ridiculous on the part of the Apostles; so the proposal of it would have been equally absurd and extravagant on the part of the chief Priests and Rulers. To alledge, therefore, that the Apostles, upon any such covenant, (or upon any other consideration whatsoever, unless a man can

(e) John x. 18.

can be bound to impossibilities) were answerable for the seals on the mouth of the sepulchre, and that those seals having been broken, they must be held guilty of a most villanous theft in the matter of the resurrrection.; is giving judgment, not only without all foundation or just reasoning, but in open defiance to the truth of things. What then shall we think of this pretty conceit of a covenant, whose infringement is counted no less than a demonstrative argument of a manifest and bare-faced cheat in *Jesus*'s resurrection? Those are but empty airs of triumph which the Deists give themselves, when they vauntingly tell us, that " the fracture of the seals " (which the Apostles were no more obliged to pre- " serve whole, than Mr. *Woolston* was) against the " law of security, against the laws of honour and " honesty, is such a manifest and indisputable mark " and indication of fraud committed by the Apo- " stles, as is not to be equalled in all, or any of " the Impostors, that ever were attempted to be put " upon the world *f*)."

That they might satisfy themselves, or the rest of the world, as to the truth or imposture of *Jesus*'s character, upon his rising or not rising from the dead; had the chief Priests and Pharisees designed to transact any thing about the hour of the day, and the witnesses to be present, when the resurrection should happen, if it was to happen; *Jesus Christ* himself was certainly the only person in whose power it was to receive and agree to articles. And I much wonder that our Infidels, since they had the whole at their own invention, did not make the chief Priests to stipulate with *Jesus* himself, who, before his death, in publicly declaring *he was to rise again the third day*, had encouraged them to propose further articles,

---

(*f*) Woolst. ub. supr. p. 15, 17.

cles, or whatever particular circumstances they should judge necessary to afford them satisfaction, as to the certainty of that event, whereby the whole was to be decided. This, in my apprehension, would have represented those sage Gentlemen, the chief Priests and Pharisees, acting much more within the bounds of common sense; than the setting them forth as covenanting with the Apostles, who had no degree of power in the matter, or at whose disposal; not to speak of their not expecting it, there was not one single circumstance of the resurrection. But to tell the world, that the chief Priests were in covenant with a man, about the circumstances of his rising from the dead, whom they were crucifying as an infamous malefactor, might have been counted a little too gross and contradictory. And indeed the greatest credulity could not possibly believe the truth of such a covenant, unless at the same time we are told, it was in the way of barbarous insult, of cruel mockery and ridicule: As something very like it seems to have happened, when *the chief Priests mocking him with the Scribes and Elders said, he saved others, himself he cannot save: If he be the King of Israel, let him now come down from the cross, and we will believe him* (g). When therefore it is said, that " the chief Priests intending to be present on the " day appointed, at the opening of the sepulchre, " they did not doubt, what no body could questi- " on, but *Jesus*, in accommodation to the sealing of " the stone, would wait their coming, and arise to " life, if he could, in their sight (h)?" I hope the Deists do not hereby mean to fasten likewise upon *Jesus* a breach of covenant. The chief Priests disdained the thought of transacting any such thing with *Jesus* when alive——His Disciples after his death,

---

(g) Matth. xxvii. 41, 42. (h) Woolst. p. 12.

death, had no shadow of power to stipulate for it in his name——Had not *Jesus* then, independently of the chief Priests, of all their seals and guards, the absolute disposal of his own body! And was he not, reasonably speaking, and as it becomes a Freethinker, at full liberty to return to life, if he could, at that hour of the third day, and in those circumstances which he should judge the least ostentatious, the most commodious, and the safest?

The Deists, however, may still insist, that granting it was in *Jesus*'s power to arise to life when he would, or that there was no restraint from any express agreement that could hinder him; yet for the satisfaction of the chief Priests, &c. he ought to have waited their coming, and to have arisen in their sight, when they should have opened the sepulchre. But as this will come to be considered in a following article, I shall only here again remark, that, at any rate, this conceit of a covenant, upon which the Deists boastingly lay the stress of a demonstrative argument for a villanous cheat in the matter of the resurrection, is a silly, rediculous imagination, without any thing real to support it: Such, I say, is the pride of Mr. *Woolston*'s demonstration. But,

In the *next* place, The Deists assure the world, " that the guard having that night drunk to excess, " they were fast asleep on the morning when the " resurrection is said to have happened——That ei- " ther the Apostles themselves, or some of the *Jews* " who were then keeping the Passover, had by " their bounty ministred to this excess of the sol- " diers."——*But which way soever this drunken sleepy fit of the watch came to pass, certain it is,* say they, *the Apostles took the advantage, and stole away the body of Jesus.* Now, these are matters of fact,

for

for which the history itself affords us no degree of evidence, but every thing making to the contrary. And do the Infidels of our day, set up to inform the world of what was passing at *Jerusalem* more than 1700 years ago, in contradiction to the pointed reports of an Historian, who was upon the spot when the things are said to have happened, and upon whose sole authority the Deists themselves do depend for the truth of many articles? As such bold arbitrary assertions do plainly tend to make the resurrection of *Jesus* to pass for an imposture, so one is tempted to suspect, that they were only forged for that purpose, and have no other foundation but the mere passion and prejudice of our modern Infidels. Ay, but, say those Gentlemen, " It is not
" at all improbable, that so few soldiers should be so
" fast asleep at that time of night, or so early in the
" morning when the clandestine work was done;
" especially after keeping such a gaudy day as was
" the feast of the Passover, which, like the festi-
" vals of other nations, was celebrated with excess.
" Foot soldiers then, you may be sure, upon the
" bounty of one or other, did no more want, than
" they would scruple to take their fill, which,
" like an opiate, lock'd up their senses for that
" night, when the Disciples, being aware of the
" lucky opportunity, carried the body of *Jesus*
" off safely (*i*)." Thus the bare general circumstance of its being the feast of the Passover, wherein the Heathen soldiers were noways concerned, without any thing else, must of itself conclude the certain existence of particular facts, *viz.* the *guards being drunk*, and *fast asleep*; upon which must be built the credit of another fact, namely the *stealing away the body of Jesus*, which at once overthrows the

(*i*) Woolst. p. 20.

the belief of ages, the whole of the Christian institution. What a mighty stress is this very circumstance, the gaudiness of a day, which no *Roman* soldier had any thing to do with, able to bear? If our Freethinkers can rest their faith on such sort of evidence, I cannot but think, they are the last men in the world, who should have the front to accuse Christians of credulity. But since those Gentlemen are pleased to pay so great a regard to mere arbitrary conjecture, grounded on a general circumstance, which, without other proof, can, with no equitable judge, affect any man in particular; I would fain presume to hope, if they are not the blind Zealots they would have the rest of the world to be, they will allow their due weight to some high probabilities, arising from human nature, and particular known circumstances, that seem to lead one to apprehend, "The truth of the fact rather "stands on the other side of the question." Thus,

Had it been one of the Heathen gods whose feast was then celebrated, there might be some shew of reason to suspect, that Heathen soldiers would join in the gaudiness of the day, and share in that riot, which possibly might have ended in locking up their senses. But as it was a festival of the *Jews*, and in honour of the true God, whose serve the *Romans* despised and rejected, the *Roman* soldiers at the sepulchre were under no motive, they had no temptation to indulge any particular chearfulness. Accordingly the Deists do by no means pretend, that this excess of the guards was at their own charges; but it happened, as they alledge, either by the bounty of the Apostles themselves, or of some other *Jews*. As for the Apostles, how little liable they are to suspicion in this article, I shall shew afterwards. And as for any of the other *Jews*, is it not somewhat extravagant to imagine, that whilst, within the walls of the city, among their friends and neighbours, they were joyfully celebrating the feast of the passover, in honour of the true God, they would leave their chearful company, walk out of the city, and go to some distance, either to make merry with Heathen soldiers, with whom their religion forbad them to eat, or to give them money that they might be chearful on account of that solemnity, which would have been profaned by their presence?——I say, does it not seem somewhat extravagant to imagine, that any of the *Jews* would have acted this part towards Heathens, especially those Heathens under whose yoke the *Jewish* nation was then groaning? Since therefore, the Deists are far from pretending, that the soldiers got themselves drunk at their own charge, and there is good reason to believe, they had no temptation to excess from the bounty of the *Jews*, it is certainly highly probable they were sober and awake in the morning, when it is said the resurrection happened. Again,

Were the soldiers ignorant of the duty of guards, and what military discipline would inflict on them, should they drink themselves drunk, and fall asleep, when they ought to be sober and watching (*k*)? I confess, there are instances of guards that have exposed their lives in thus neglecting their duty. But as the contrary instances are infinitely more numerous, the probability, as every reasonable man will judge, lies greatly on our sides and comes very much to be heightened, not only from the situation of the guards

---

(*k*) Ὅτι τε γὰρ νόμοι παρ᾽ αὐτοῖς ὁ λειποταξίε μόνον ἀλλα ᾗ ῥᾳςώνης ὀλίγης θανατικοὶ. Joseph. de bell Jud. l. 3. cap. 5. § 7. vid. Polyb. hist. l. 6. cap. 34, 35.

guards in a lonely place, at a diftance from the temptation of what one would call gin-fhops and alehoufes; but in a particular manner, from the hiftory of their behaviour, wherein there is not the leaft hint that can make us fufpect them of the want of faithfulnefs to their truft; and is it not an event fomewhat wonderful, that not one of the guards was awake, but every foul of them faft afleep, the commanding Officer as well as the private centinel! In fhort,

The Chief Priefts witneffed the crucifixion; they, no doubt, were fure to fee *Jefus* fully dead; and feeming to fufpect, there might be a defign of fraud, they took the precaution of placing a guard upon the fepulchre. And after all this, had they no farther thought about the matter? Or, did it never more enter into their heads, what might be a-doing at the fepulchre? From their eagernefs in the profecution; from their apprehending, even after the death of *Jefus*, that their affairs were not altogether fafe; and from their being fenfible, that the ftealing away the dead body would occafion among the people a latter delufion, as they underftood it, much worfe than the former they had been under, while *Jefus* was alive; one may eafily conceive, that the Chief Priefts had not yet loft all thought, and quite abandoned the care of the fepulchre. Curiofity itfelf, much more an anxiety of mind, feveral violent paffions that had not yet had time to abate, and apprehenfions of great danger, far from being wholly over, that ftill threatened their moft valuable interefts, would certainly prompt them to look after the guards, and to have a watchful eye upon their behaviour. And if there was but a chance, from its being the feaft of the paffover, that the foldiers at the fepulchre, fhould venture their necks in the neglect of their duty, get themfelves drunk, and fall faft afleep; had not the

the chief Priests and Rulers so much sagacity and good sense as to forsee it? And if they foresaw it, would they not have taken effectual measures to prevent it! The Deists would have us believe, that in the guards drinking themselves drunk at the sepulchre, there was a great deal more than chance: In their apprehension, the certainty of this event, arising from its being the time of the passover, was so infallible, that it is now counted a clear demonstration of villany in the Apostles, in carrying off the body of *Jesus*. But if there was so probable, or rather, so very necessary a connection betwixt that festival of the *Jews* and the intoxication of Heathen soldiers, what was to hinder it from having been then observed, as well as it is now at so great a distance of time? Or, did the chief Priests connive at it, and suffer the fraud to go on and be executed? It is hard, that the chief Priests should be fools, and the Apostles villains, and our Infidels the only wise and honest men!

Thus the bare general circumstance of its being the feast of the passover, as it would infer the guards were drunk and fast asleep, is greatly overbalanced, and amounts to nothing, by the weight of the particular known circumstances of all parties concerned, that afford us the highest probabilities that the guards were cool and sober, and in the watchful discharge of their duty. And when these many strong probabilities are clearly justified by every article of the history itself, to which the arbitrary conjecture from the bare general circumstance is wholly repugnant, one would think, we have as great certainty, that the watch were awake, at the time when the resurrection of *Jesus* is said to have happened, as we can have for any matter of fact

whereof

whereof our knowledge depends on testimony, and is not the immediate perception of our senses.

But if it must be so, that the guards were then drunk, and fast asleep; and the Deists are far from pretending, that this fit of excess was occasioned by the soldiers clubbing their own money; may not one beg to be informed, who were the persons who brought about their being thus intoxicated? The history itself is indeed absolutely silent as to this article: And since our Freethinkers had it therefore intirely of their own framing, one may count it a shame for them, that by their avowed uncertainty on this head, they should have betrayed the cause they have undertaken. Why, they tell us, they cannot be positive whether it was the Apostles themselves, or some other of the *Jews*, whose bounty was the occasion of this excess; but which way soever it came to pass, they are well persuaded, the guards were asleep. In the mean while, till they shall have settled this point, and made it evident, that the Apostles were the very persons who found the means to drink the watch into a base and dangerous neglect of their duty, what title have they directly to charge the Apostles with the horrid crime of stealing away the body of *Jesus*? For ought they know, this drinking-bout of the soldiers, was the effect of the bounty of other *Jews*, in no confederacy, but in downright enmity with the Apostles. And does it follow from hence, that the Apostles took the advantage and stole away the body of *Jesus*? Indeed, if once you prove they certainly had a design of this nature, the matter, I confess, will look very suspicious: But our Freethinkers, I hope, will never esteem it fare dealing, or a method of arguing suited to their character, first to suppose a design of fraud, and from this supposition, immediately

ly to conclude the fraud was executed: or, without any degree of proof, boldly to assert the fraud was executed, and from thence to conclude the design was certainly formed. And yet after what other method, than this of going round in a circle, proving an arbitrary assertion from a groundless supposition, and again the groundless supposition, from the arbitrary assertion; I say, after what other method of proof our Infidels can make out a theft in the business of the resurrection of *Jesus*, I am not able to comprehend. It is true, in either case they seem to alledge, that the testimony of the sleeping soldiers must be held valid and good. But if it was by the bounty of other *Jews*, and not by means of the Apostles, that the guards were drunk into a dead sleep, would it not be ridiculous in this case to depend on the testimony of those persons, whose senses were intirely locked up, who heard and saw nothing, while the matter of fact in question is said to have been a-doing? But where is the absurdity, say the the Deists, " to suppose that the Disciples themselves might contrive the intoxication of the guards(*l*)." In this case indeed I should be satisfied, that the testimony of the soldiers, notwithstanding their being asleep, was true: But my conviction would arise, not at all from the testimony of the sleeping watch, but from the evidence I had, that the Apostles themselves contrived and effected the intoxication of the guards; which every reasonable man will allow, could have been done on no other but the wicked design of stealing the body of *Jesus* away. After all, it appears to me quite contradictory, wholly absurd to imagine, that any man, or number of men, in the circumstances of the Apostles, and endowed with human understanding, would make an attack of any sort, upon the
guards

(*l*) Woolst. p. 19.

guards, in order to steal away the body. For, as some years ago I observed, in the Preface to the other part of this Discourse, when published by itself,

What is the temptation that could have determined the Apostles to disturb the dead body, and carry it away? We are indeed told plainly, that thereby they intended to impose upon the world, and to make it pass that *Jesus* was risen. But what is the purpose they meant to serve by this sham-resurrection? Whilst *Jesus* was alive, they confidently expected, that he, in his own person, at the head of his Disciples, would subdue their enemies before them, and, as their glorious Deliverer, raise the power and greatness of their nation, upon the ruins of all other states and kingdoms. This, and particularly this, did the Apostles hope for and expect from their *Messiah*; nor had they the least thought that this could be accomplished without his being present in person among them, and openly appearing in the world as their great Leader and Commander. How could it then enter into the heads of men, of such hopes and sentiments, to steal away the body of *Jesus*? What is it they were to make of the carcass? They wanted a living worldly Deliverer, and could perform or attempt nothing without him. After what manner, therefore, could it serve their purpose to move the lifeless body out of the sepulchre, on the third day after it was crucified, and to lay it somewhere else for worms to devour it? To say, he was risen, without their being able to show and follow him, was, in their sense of things, arrant folly; as it could be of no sort of consequence to their views and interests. No, they all considered him as a person in whom they had been grievously disappointed, and having no hopes of his ever returning to life again,
gave

gave-up his body to corruption. Nor is it possible, that men of their prepossessions could have conceived any other notions concerning him. Indeed, if the Apostles had had the hopes of restoring life to the dead body, and of raising up their *Messiah*, that he might lead them on to victory and triumph, they would, it is likely, have inclined, if possible, to steal away the body, in order to perform the wonderful operation. But, to imagine that so ridiculous a conceit ever entered into the thoughts of the Apostles, is highly absurd and inconsistent; and I am apt to think the Deists would find no great account in it, should they have the folly to make the extravagant supposition.

Thus, I cannot but think, there is good reason to rest confident, it was impossible for the Apostles to conceive one single thought about stealing away the body of *Jesus*; and consequently it was impossible for them to go about to bribe or intoxicate the guards for that purpose. And since an impossibility, arising from human nature, either to bribe or to drink the guards into a neglect of their duty, is, so far as it concerns the event, fully equivalent to its being impossible to evade the guards (upon which the Deists have agreed to confess, *then there was a real resurrection* (m). I would fain flatter myself, they will now be reconciled, at least, to a little more moderation, and no longer indulge a licentiousness of thought, and an extravagance of language, in condemning the resurrection of *Jesus* as the " most notorious and monstrous imposture that
" ever was put upon mankind!" But our Freethinkers further insist, That,

" Had *Jesus* really arose from the dead, he would
" certainly have appeared to the chief Priests, to
" *Pilate*,

(m) Woolst. p. 19.

"*Pilate*; and to others his crucifiers and insultors. Nor can it be questioned (say they) but that, in reason, for the conviction and conversion of unbelievers, he ought to have done so. In their apprehension therefore, *Jesus*'s non-appearance to the chief Priests is a confirmation, that he did not arise from the dead, but that his body was stolen away." Here I must observe, it is confessed by the Apostles themselves, that Jesus *did not shew himself to all the people, but unto witnesses chosen before of God*, particular persons whom Providence had placed about *Jesus*, and who, by their having lived long with him in great friendship and intimacy, could not be imposed on in the business of a resurrection, and ought therefore to be counted, as they certainly are in the judgment of every considerate man, the most proper and the surest evidence. Meanwhile, as it was easy to foresee, that this circumstance, *Jesus*'s not appearing publicly, would come to be abused by the enemies of the Gospel; so, the recording it notwithstanding, seems to be a plain proof of the honesty of the Apostles, and that they were sensible, they had no need of any of those arts and disguises, that are always necessary in the case of an imposture. And indeed, had the history of the Gospel been the mere contrivance and forgery of the Apostles, I doubt not but their speculations would have led them to apprehend, as *Celsus* does, Mr. *Woolston*, and other Infidels, that the better to procure credit to their story, it was necessary to introduce *Jesus* appearing to his crucifiers and insultors, and upbraiding them with their infidelity and ill-treatment of him: For, judging by human passions, this, we are sure, had the case been ours, we would have done, and thereby have had the pleasure of insulting in our turn. But, passing this

As to the objection itself; having already settled the matter of fact, and made it clearly evident, that the Apostles cannot possibly be suspected of stealing away the body of *Jesus*; his non-appearance to the chief Priests, &c. can be counted of no force or consequence. In itself it is a mere, arbitrary, extraneous circumstance, wholly depending on the good pleasure of the Agent, that has no connection with his action, and in whose absence there is nothing to hinder his deed or action from having a true and real existence. Nor is it possible to imagine, how the non-appearance of *Jesus* to his murtherers, can satisfy any man that he never did appear to his Apostles; as if it were not strangely ridiculous to pretend, that a matter of fact, attested by eye-witnesses of good credit, must be held a forgery, because other people had not the same means of knowing it. They alledge, indeed, that *Jesus* ought, in reason, to have done so and so. And thus we are brought to debate a metaphysical question about the fitness or reasonableness of some foreign circumstances, in order to ascertain a matter of fact, that has no dependence on speculation, and which of itself can very well subsist without the help of such circumstances. I confess, *Jesus*'s not appearing alive to the chief Priests might greatly shake the credit of his resurrection, would Infidels be so good as once to favour us with a demonstration, that *Jesus*, should he arise, was indispensibly obliged thus to shew himself. But after what manner such a demonstration can proceed, I am not sagacious enough to discern. So far as I am able to understand, the great and only argument whereby one can pretend to demonstrate, there was such an obligation upon *Jesus*, must be taken from the particular end or purpose, which his public appearance was necessary to serve.

serve. So that, if the necessity of the end be absolute and indispensible, it must be granted, that the necessity of the means, without which the end cannot be attained, is of the same absolute and indispensible nature. Now the Deists tell us of two purposes which this public appearance was to serve:

First, " *Jesus* ought, and had he really arose from
" the dead, would have personally appeared to the
" chief Priests, to *Pilate*, and to others his cruci-
" fiers and insultors, to upbraid him with their in-
" fidelity and ill-treatment of him." But where was the necessity of his appearing for this purpose? True it is, that *Jesus*, during the whole course of his Ministry, and especially at his death, was oppressed with the highest insults and injuries: And, placing ourselves in his circumstances, had it been in our power to arise from the dead, no doubt, in our apprehension, as I have just now observed, the passions of resentment would have made it necessary for us to appear to our murderers, that we might insult over them, and upbraid them with the baseness and cruelties of their indignities. But let us reflect a little——Supposing we should lay aside all resentment, and had no angry passions to gratify, what is the particular obligation we have violated? There is thus far no reason for our appearing personally: And surely our murderers will not complain of our having done them an injustice, in saving them the confusion they must be in, upon their seeing us returned to life again, or in our not making up to them in order to requite them as they have deserved. Had the Deists, therefore, the wisdom not to fasten upon *Jesus* the silly passions of our character, or had they the patience to consider not only that *Jesus* left the world, *praying to his Father to forgive his enemies*, in a temper of mind that gives us no ground

to

to expect, he would return again with anger and resentment; but that he had it wholly in his own power, so far to forgive his murderers, as not to upbraid them with any of the crimes they had committed against him; I say, had the Deists the freedom of thought to attend to these things, they would never have the folly to alledge, that *Jesus* ought to have personally appeared to his crucifiers, to upbraid them with their infidelity and ill-treatment of him; and that he would certainly have done so, had he really come back to life again. As there was no sort of tie, far less an absolute, indissible obligation upon *Jesus*, to have acted this part; so the contrary opinion, maintained by our Freethinkers, must arise from a shameful ignorance of the nature of things, particularly of the character of the meek, the merciful and compassionate *Jesus*, and from too great an indulgence to the revengeful passions of human nature. But,

The other end or purpose to be served by *Jesus*'s appearing publicly, " is the conviction and " conversion of unbelievers." And, I confess, this argument is a great deal more plausible. No doubt, before a man can be indispensibly bound to admit the resurrection of *Jesus*, he must be convinced, (without which there can be no rational conversion) or he must have the means indispensibly necessary to convince him of the reality of this event. So that if the Deists will demonstrate, that *Jesus*'s personal appearance to the chief Priests (which never happened) was indispensibly necessary to assure them of the truth of his resurrection, or that there was no other means, in their own nature sufficient, to afford them a rational conviction of this matter of fact, I will then allow, that the chief Priests, *&c.* were under no obligation to believe it, and, what is more,

more, that *Jesus* did not arise from the dead. The question therefore comes of course to this, Whether, independently from the personal appearance of *Jesus*, the chief Priests, &c. had sufficient evidence, upon which any man, by the law of reason, as it requires in all such cases, is bound to confess the truth of the resurrection? And if such evidence there was, which the chief Priests had access to, the consequence was unavoidable; by no means was *Jesus* under any sort of tie, far less an indispensible obligation, personally to appear to his crucifiers and insultors: Upon which again it will necessarily follow, that the rejecting of the resurrection of *Jesus* as an imposture, merely upon the account of its wanting such a circumstance, which *Jesus* was not bound to regard, is acting without reason, and in a most absurd and arbitrary manner. I say, therefore, before the Deists can have reason to justify their laying the whole stress of the argument, concerning the resurrection of *Jesus*, upon the single circumstance of his personally appearing to the chief Priests, it is incumbent on them to demonstrate, that all the other evidence we have, is insufficient to satisfy a reasonable man, as to the certainty of that event. And, when they shall have done this, they will have gained their cause. But, till then, their insisting on this personal appearance of *Jesus* as indispensibly necessary, and without which the whole must be a cheat, will be counted by every sober, free thinking man, altogether shameless.

But, let us see what sort of evidence was sufficient to satisfy the chief Priests, that the resurrection of *Jesus* never happened: From whence one may learn, whether the want of evidence on the other side made them take up with that opinion. It is agreed, that those sage Gentlemen having no more witnessed the supposed theft at the sepulchre, or seen the dead body

body afterwards, than they witnessed the resurrection, or saw the living body at any other time, they could, in neither case, plead the information of their own senses, but were left to depend on the testimony of other people. Accordingly, they prefer the testimony of the soldiers before that of the Apostles. And, as they report the story themselves, if we add what is now alledged, to render it more feasible, we are told, that " the guards set to watch " the sepulchre, having drunk to excess that night, " they were all fast asleep in the morning when the " resurrection is said to have happened." Now, these very guards, without the least insinuation, that the Apostles had treacherously brought about their being thus intoxicated, take upon them, as it is pretended, to testify to the chief Priests, what they neither saw themselves, nor could hear of from other people; they testify, that *while they slept*, while their senses were all locked up, and could discern nothing, *his Disciples came by night, and stole him away!* This is the testimony, on which the chief Priests confidently rely; and with this testimony so well are they satisfied, that Mr. *Woolston* doubts not, but " they might reward the soldiers for speaking the " truth, and exhort them to persist in it, with a pro- " mise to secure them against the anger of *Pilate*, " for their sleeping and neglect of their duty (*n*)." Thus we see the whole evidence upon which the chief Priests proceed, in giving their verdict against the resurrection of *Jesus*. Should the Deists meet with such proof in favour of Christianity, one may easily conceive what reception they would give it. But the bare repetition of such an argument is all the confutation necessary. And what can be trusted

(*n*) Woolst. p. 21.

ed to the decision of those men, who are capable of grounding their judgment on such evidence? Or, what is the disposition of our modern Freethinkers, who are capable of thinking, that such a judgment is just and equitable?

As for the evidence on the other side of the question, which the chief Priests are pleased to reject: Those learned *Rabbis* were extremely sensible, that the body of *Jesus* was gone out of the sepulchre: That it was not in their power to shew the body; or to inform the world whither it was carried; or to prove that the Apostles stole it away, but by witnesses, whose situation exposes their testimony to the contempt of mankind. They might have known, that the Disciples of *Jesus* did not expect his resurrection; but that, after his death, they looked upon their cause as desperate and lost; that upon the rumour of *Jesus*'s having risen from the dead, they gave no credit to each other's relations; but continued obstinate in disbelieving it, till they saw him with their eyes, handled him with their hands; till they conversed with him personally; till they ate and drank with him; and had all the evidence that their waking senses could afford them: That in testifying the truth of this matter of fact, the Apostles had no visible interest to serve; but in being conscious it was a fiction, (as they must have been, had they stole the body away) did, without any compensation in the universe, deliberately forego the favour of God and man, willingly forfeit all the comforts of this life, all the happiness of an after-state, and, with all their senses about them, expose themselves to present pains and cruelties at the hands of man, and to future eternal miseries from the righteous judgment of God: This, I say, among other numberless circumstances, is the evidence on the

other

other side: This is the evidence which the chief Priests have rejected, and to which they can oppose nothing but the testimony of men without the use of their senses. I appeal therefore to all mankind, Whether the chief Priests had reason, or any shadow of reason, to prefer the testimony of drunken, sleeping soldiers, before that of the sober, waking Apostles: Whether those persons, who are capable of relying on such evidence against the resurrection, can decently reject the truth of that event, as not sufficiently attested: And whether, to such people, *Jesus Christ* ought in reason personally to have appeared? By the violence of passion, the chief Priests had hurried on the crucifixion of *Jesus*; wherein, one should think, they justly forfeited all title to any extraordinary favour: By the violence of the same passions, they took up with a senseless, stupid report (supposing there was in it no forgery) in contradiction to pointed and clear evidence in favour of the resurrection. And as this cannot but be counted an incontestible proof, that the chief Priests were carried away by strong prejudice, and absolutely determined, at all adventures, to deny the truth of the resurrection; so, to what purpose can any one imagine, ought *Jesus* to have appeared to those persons, who were despising sufficient valid evidence, in preferring a testimony of no imaginable value, and whose hearts were pre-occupied, hardened against the power of rational conviction? To talk, that in such circumstances, *Jesus* ought, in reason, to have shewn himself personally, is making reason dictate the most needless thing in nature, the greatest extravagance. How much soever it may blacken their memory, there appears to me a great deal more of sense and consistency in the conduct of the chief Priests, when, as the history represents them, we
consider

consider those resolute Politicians, as conscious there was no theft in the matter, and therefore bribing the soldiers to publish a ridiculous falshood, the only way they had left, whereby to disappoint the belief of *Jesus's* resurrection; which, if possible to effect, they were obstinately determined should never gain credit in the world.

After all, it may be thought, " That had *Jesus* " waited in the grave the coming of the sealers of " the stone, and their regular opening of the sepul- " chre, or had he afterwards appeared to the chief " Priests; either of these, (as our Freethinkers al- " ledge) would have been effectual to the convicti- " on and conversion of all who might be present; " and therefore of full satisfaction to the whole na- " tion of the *Jews* then, and tended to the confir- " mation of the faith of all ages and nations since " (*o*)." Here, again, our Infidels seem to shew their partiality in thinking favourably of every man, except *Jesus* and his Apostles. They apprehend, that had *Jesus* personally appeared to the chief Priests, then those Rulers would have had reason to believe and confess the truth of the resurrection: And, having reason, they cannot but think, they would have yielded to it. But why so partial in judging of characters, where the nature of the things, as little as the history itself, affords us no ground to make such distinctions? If it be thought, that the chief Priests would have yielded to reason in such a case, why must we think the Apostles are acting against reason, or that they are speaking a downright falshood, when they tell us, the case happened to them; *they saw* Jesus, and therefore believed the truth of his resurrection; as the Deists imagine, the chief Priests

Vol. II. A a would

(*o*) Woolst. p. 25.

would have done in the like circumstances? Let our Freethinkers, without the help of mere supposition, distinctly inform us, what there is in the several characters, that assures us of the integrity of the chief Priests, and demonstrates the villainy of the Apostles. In the common opinion of mankind, civil Governors and Politicians are not always held so strictly honest, or so religiously devoted to truth itself, but they will take the freedom to represent things, as they may best suit their political interests. But to come directly to the objection:

What reason have our Infidels to be so positive, that the personal appearance of *Jesus* would have convinced the chief Priests, and brought them to confess the truth of the resurrection? One cannot but incline to think quite otherwise, when one considers what sort of regard the chief Priests had to the truth of things, in forming their sentiments about *Jesus* when alive. Thus, though the life of *Jesus*, his whole conduct was, in all instances, absolutely irreproachable; though the doctrines he taught were all worthy of God, and of infinite benefit to mankind; though, in his wonderful works, he gave manifest proofs of his incontestible power over all the several parts of this lower world; over the winds and seas, which he calmed and made still; over earth and water, which he disposed, and made fit to cure a man of his blindness; over plants and vegetables, in causing a fig-tree to wither away; over the animal world, in suffering a herd of swine to be hurried away and drowned in the sea; over the necessaries of life, in multiplying food for many thousands; over the bodies of men, in healing all manner of diseases; over their souls, in raising their thoughts and turning them to proclaim his character, as he rode amidst the acclamations of the people

SECT. XV. *Christian Revelation.*

to *Jerusalem*; over their dead bodies and their departed souls, in bringing both back to this mortal life again; and though (all his other numberless works being wholly beneficent) he only, in one single instance of each kind, *viz.* in the case of the herd of swine, and of the barren fig-tree, gave mankind to understand, that the power he had over the animal and vegetable world, was no fatal thing, a blind impulse necessarily determined such a particular way, but a natural faculty intirely at his own disposal, and which he might have employed in bringing judgment and ruin on his enemies: I say, though the whole life of *Jesus*, all his doctrines, and all his miracles, clearly expressed a spotless purity, a divine wisdom and goodness, and a sovereign power over all the several parts of the creation, extending so far as to raise the dead to life again; yet the chief Priests obstinately despised all this, and were so far from being thereby induced to think, in any sort, favourably of *Jesus*, that, on the contrary, they conceived the most malicious and revengeful passions against him, and could not rest satisfied till they had brought about his being crucified as a malefactor, a notorious Impostor, who dared to pretend to the character of their *Messiah*, whilst he meant to overturn their national constitution, and, at the same time, leave them enslaved and oppressed under the *Roman* government.

Thus it was, that the chief Priests were affected towards *Jesus* in his life-time: And that their prejudices still subsisted after his death, one has abundant proof from their forging (as the history informs us) or their believing a senseless report, which a sober man would be ashamed in the least to regard; which, nevertheless, they imposed upon the world, and thereby only expressed how forward
they

they were to discredit or suppress every thing that might justify the character of *Jesus*. And are these the men whom we must apprehend disposed and ready to follow impartial reason, in what relates to the resurrection of *Jesus*? Before such men can be thought capable of confessing the truth of the resurrection, they must overcome, not only all those strong prejudices, but the violent aversion they will surely have at acknowledging their gross mistake, as to *Jesus*'s real character, the baseness and injustice of those cruelties they used against him, and the hainous guilt they had contracted, in shedding his innocent blood. And has any man reason to be positive, that the personal appearance of *Jesus* would have given them such conquest over themselves?

Indeed, had the chief Priests been Freethinkers, men void of prejudice, quite free from bigotry and superstition, had they acted a cool, a fair and equitable part towards *Jesus* while alive, and kept themselves always open to conviction, or in a disposition of mind, honestly to settle their belief as the truth of things, the event of his rising from the dead, the concluding proof of his character, upon which the whole depended, might come out to direct them; one may reasonably admit, that upon seeing *Jesus* alive in the sepulchre, they might have confessed the truth of his resurrection, and that he was no Impostor. But when one reflects, that the exertion of so much goodness, wisdom, and power, as are apparent in the life, the doctrines, and miracles of *Jesus*, was not able to satisfy them, that the Author of those doctrines and miracles, must be some very extraordinary person; or to prevail on them to judge it reasonable, at least, to wait the final decision of his character, by that particular event, upon which he himself had put it; what else can one apprehend,

but

but that those men had withdrawn their minds from the influence of reason, and delivered themselves over to the arbitrary commands of mere passion and prejudice? And to such men, what signifies the clearest evidence, even ocular demonstration? Reason is a principle to be dealt with, and whereby one may be led to a certain conclusion: But passion cannot be laid hold on, it slights every thing, even the strongest addresses that suit not with its views; it is subject to no control, and sways the mind by its arbitrary over-powering influence. So that in despising such a certain degree of evidence, which impartial reason calls one to listen to, a man puts himself out of the reach of all conviction: And hence the observation is extremely just, *If we hear not* Moses *and the Prophets*, if we hearken not to reason, or refuse to submit to sufficient evidence, there being no bounds to contain us, *neither will we be persuaded though one rose from the dead* (*p*). In such a case the mind may be alarmed, but never will be convinced: For the sudden fright over, the stubborn passion prevails.

When, therefore, the chief Priests, instead of yielding to the strong evidences of wisdom, goodness, and power, shining forth in the doctrines and miracles of the holy *Jesus*, sufficient to raise in their minds a favourable opinion concerning this extraordinary person, at least to persuade them to suspend their judgment as to his real character; till they should see what became of his resurrection, to which, in his own justification, he had made his last appeal, and which they had good reason to apprehend, he was capable of effecting; I say, when instead of this, the chief Priests give way to the most furious passions,

(*p*) Luk. xvi. 31.

passions, that violently prompt them to persecute *Jesus* to death, as a gross deceiver, and malefactor; what can one imagine would have been the conduct of those men, had they happened to see *Jesus* alive in the sepulchre?

Attended with great crowds of people, they come to the sepulchre, they open the seals, which they found intire, and entering the tomb, they see *Jesus* alive: Upon this sight, will the whole power of their prejudices immediately vanish, and all their resolute designs to secure their constitution and government, against the dangers that threatened them from a belief of his rising from the dead, that moment forsaking them, will they forthwith confess a miraculous resurrection, take upon them the shame and guilt of crucifying their *Messiah*, and yielding themselves to his authority, heartily conspire in his measures, to abolish their national religion and constitution, all their public posts and preferments, and now aim at nothing but the overthrow of every thing, which, to that instant, they tenaciously held most sacred and valuable? I say, would the personal appearance of *Jesus* have brought about such a revolution in the passions and sentiments of the chief Priests and Pharisees? I violently suspect, that their revengeful passions still subsisting without abatement, would still have represented *Jesus* in the same odious light, wherein they had all along beheld him. And in this light, would not the same passions, now more enraged because of their disappointment, have powerfully stimulated them to seize him again, or immediately to cut him off a second time; judging that by collusion, or stratagem, or by some accident or other, he had not been quite dead in the crucifying? For my part, I am not able to conceive that men, in the power of those passions, to which the chief Priests were enslaved, could have acted otherwise. From hence therefore one may judge, whether the personal appearance of *Jesus* to the chief Priests would have been of satisfaction to the chief Priests themselves, to the whole nation of the *Jews* then, and to the confirmation of the faith of all ages and nations since? But,

Let it be granted, that upon seeing *Jesus* alive in the sepulchre, the chief Priests would have confessed a miraculous resurrection, and acknowledged him for their *Messiah*. In this case one must consider under what particular notions or ideas *Jesus Christ* would appear to them, while they apprehended him in this character. As every body knows the notion about the *Messiah* that universally prevailed among the *Jews*, and to which they were obstinately devoted, was that of a secular Prince, who by the success of his victorious arms, should deliver their nation from all oppression, and raise and establish them in a sovereign dominion over all other states and kingdoms. It was the contradiction which the mean appearance, the low circumstances of *Jesus*, bore to this pompous touring notion, that determined the chief Priests to reject him in his lifetime: It was this notion that made the people (when from a miracle that *Jesus* did, they came to be persuaded, that this is of a truth that Prophet that should come into the world) enter into a design, to take him by force and to make a king (r): And with this notion were the Apostles strongly possessed till after the day of *Pentecost*. So that the whole nation of the *Jews*, without exception, being thus carried away by the flattering notion of exchanging their slavery under the dominion of the *Romans*, for universal empire under the reign of their *Messiah*; and the

(r) Joh. vi. 15.

the chief Priests being particularly animated with such high expectations, what else could they do, under the commanding influence of those ambitious views, but in a triumphant manner carry off their *Messiah* at their head, and immediately enter into a resolute design to shake off the *Roman* yoke, to recover the freedom and glory of their nation, and to extend their dominion all over the earth? And in this prospect of things, a spirit of insurrection overspreading the whole nation, their preparations for war would, undoubtedly, have brought upon their heads the destructive vengeance of the *Roman* arms. This, I say, beyond all peradventure, would have been the case, had the chief Priests, upon *Jesus's* shewing himself alive in the sepulchre, come to be thoroughly persuaded, he was in very deed their *Messiah*.

Altho' therefore it may be thought, that the personal appearance of *Jesus* would have satisfied the chief Priests as to the truth of his general character; yet, to prevent the nation from being involved in blood, he must either not appear, or, if he does, he must immediately find means by a miracle to get out of their hands. Nor could his acting this last part have saved the nation from the destruction of war, unless we suppose, what most probably would have happened, that the sudden disappearance of *Jesus* would have effectually revived the old prejudices; too deep and strong to be in a moment wholly eradicated, wherein the chief Priests had but the other day crucified him as a malefactor. Upon which it is apparent, that the personal appearance of *Jesus*, to the chief Priests in the sepulchre; or any where else, supposing they had thereby been convinced of the truth of the resurrection, was infinitely far from being a proper means to afford satisfaction

faction to the whole nation of the *Jews* then, or to confirm the faith of all ages and nations since. Such satisfaction and confirmation, capable of being provided for, as they really are, by means much fitter and far more reasonable, would have been purchased at too high a price, when they would have cost the blood of the whole *Jewish* nation, or reduced that people to utter ruin without their reaping any benefit from it, either here or hereafter: For what advantage in another world could have accrued to the *Jews* from their having here acknowledged *Jesus* as a secular Prince?

But what do people mean when they tell us, that, had the Chief Priests been favoured with the personal appearance of *Jesus*, their confessing the truth of the resurrection would have been satisfactory to the rest of the world, or have induced those of that, and of every future age, who could not be eye-witnesses, to rest assured of the certainty of that extraordinary event? I am apt to think, that notwithstanding the most open confession we can suppose to have been made by the chief Priests; yet the whole matter, as to the conviction of other people, who had not their means of knowledge, must have rested, as it still does, on human testimony, or moral evidence. No body, sure, can imagine, that the faith of mankind was blindly to have been given to the bare assertions of the chief Priests, without examining into their character, whether they were men worthy to be trusted, and upon what particular grounds they came themselves to be persuaded. And since even the most ample attestation of the chief Priests, concerning the truth of the resurrection, could have made no alteration in our way of judging, or of our settling our belief about the certainty of that event; but

we must still have had recourse to the principles of moral evidence; what matters it who were the witnesses, provided they were men of sense and discretion? Or, of what greater importance would have been the testimony of the chief Priests, than that which we now have of the Apostles? I know not but one may suspect, that our Deists, for all their telling us, it would have been satisfactory to them, would have made a shift to assure the world, that the evidence of the chief Priests, had they given it in favour of the resurrection, was not a little exceptionable. They were men at the head of the government, and no doubt were subject to all those passions that for the most part prevail in publick characters: And might not the story of the resurrection, in the mouths of those intriguing politicians, have been only an engine of state, a mere political contrivance, or a national plot, whereby they designed to accomplish some worldly purposes? Might it not have been said, that those Rulers, having the power in their hands, prevented all inquiry, and checked every examiner who might have detected the forgery: Nay, had the chief Priests taken the truth of this article into their protection, it is to be feared, they would have promoted its belief by persecution, the means they employed to suppress it; which, I confess, would have been a considerable argument against the Christian institution. In short, it appears to me, that the testimony of the Apostles is every way unexceptionable; and I cannot but think, that to every sober considerate man, it affords the highest satisfaction that can arise from moral evidence; upon which the truth of the resurrection must necessarily rest. And let me here, in a few words, take notice of some of
those

SECT. XV. *Christian Revelation.* 195

those reasons that might have hindered *Jesus* from personally appearing to the chief Priests in the sepulchre.

Our Saviour having openly foretold his resurrection, he assures his Disciples, that *they should see him again* (*s*); but he no where intimates that he was to appear to the chief Priests, or to the body of the people; on the contrary, he seems expressly to tell them, that after his death *they were not again to see him* (*t*). And indeed, when one recollects the character of *Jesus*, and what was his conduct in the world, there is no reason to expect his making any public appearance. During the whole course of his Ministry, he never affected any degree of ostentation, but was always guided by the dictates of meekness and humility. The wonderful works he performed were capable of being set off with great pomp and solemnity, but the meek and holy *Jesus* neglected all those circumstances, that serve to alarm the passions of mankind; he chose to do his works, only in a manner that would affect the judgment of sober thinking persons; and in several instances rather studied concealment; nay, he set some cases in such a light, as would lessen the greatness of the miracle (*u*). I confess, *Jesus* once rode to *Jerusalem* amidst the acclamations of the people. But as this is the single instance, wherein *Jesus* was pleased to raise himself in the applauses and admiration of mankind; so the power he therein exerted over the affections of human hearts, only gives us to understand, that had he been only aiming at worldly grandeur and authority, he was able to have gained abundance of followers: As the power he put forth upon the swine and the fig-tree, upon those who came to apprehend

(*s*) Joh. xvi. 16, &c. (*t*) Matth. xxiii 39. Joh. vii. 33. 34. xiv. 19. (*u*) Vid. Mark. i. 40. &c. v. 35. &c. vii. 32. &c. Joh. ix. 1. &c.

hend him (*x*), and by means of his Apoftles, upon *Ananias,* and *Sapphira,* is abundant proof how capable he was to diftrefs his enemies, and totally to overthrow them ; certain, therefore, it is, that, during his life, *Jefus* never affected any degree of parade and vain-glory: And fince all his works were done with meeknefs and humility, what elfe can be looked for in his rifing again from the dead? To fet forth his refurrection with glare and fhow, or to appear among wondering crouds, does not feem to fuit his character, or to afford that fort of evidence, upon which, he feems all along to have defigned, the faith of mankind fhould be founded. And having had no defign, for afcertaining the truth of his pretenfions, to engage the common paffions of men, that always rife high upon every thing glaring and oftentatious, as it would have happened, had he perfonally appeared to the chief Priefts and to the infinite numbers of people that would have been attending them; but only meaning to fecure the rational conviction of mankind, arifing from moral evidence; he judged it fufficient, for that purpofe, as it certainly is, to fhew himfelf to credible witneffes, and in thofe circumftances wherein cool reafon might be fully fatisfied as to the reality of his refurrection, or that the appearance was no impofition on the fenfes; and in order to difcover the real truth of the fact, one fhould think, that the appearing after fuch a manner, is infinitely preferable to the moft open and public appearance that could be made before the greateft crouds. I fhall therefore obferve,

In the next place, that *Jefus*'s perfonally appearing to the chief Priefts could ferve to little good purpofe, and would have been extremely incommodious, and attended with bad confequences. For

(*x*) Joh. xviii. 6.

For let us imagine that about the sepulchre, as it could not but have happened, there are gathered together infinite numbers of people to witness a most extraordinary event, *the resurrection of a man from the dead*. Now, the chief Priests open the seals; they enter into the sepulchre; and finding *Jesus* alive, they are satisfied themselves; and they lead him forth, in order to afford the like satisfaction to the multitudes. But as yet *Jesus* standing on even ground, how many, do we think, will have it in their power to be satisfied? A few about him may indeed have access to examine the truth of the fact thoroughly: But as to the infinite numbers of people that are present, and who ought likewise to be satisfied, the situation of *Jesus* renders it impossible for them to have any degree of evidence from their senses. Let us then suppose, that to remedy this, the chief Priests set *Jesus* upon an eminence, from whence he is exposed to the view of the whole multitude. But should *Jesus* have submitted to so pompous an appearance, and so much pageantry, what sort of satisfaction could those infinite numbers have received from seeing a man at a distance? The Apostles, tho' for several years intimately acquainted with *Jesus*, would not believe the truth of his resurrection, without far stronger evidence, without not only seeing him, but handling him, and perceiving the wounds he had got when he was crucified. And how in reason could those multitudes depend on a distant view, without being able to examine into particulars? For any satisfaction they had received from their senses, to which the appeal was made, it might be all delusion and imposture: And indeed, one cannot but rest confident, that after such an appearance of *Jesus*, the number of those, who, as to any rational conviction from their senses,

must

must be held to doubt, or to deny the truth of the resurrection, would have infinitely exceeded those few, who thought they had reason, from the testimony of their senses, to believe it. To what little purpose, therefore, such an appearance would have served, every man must be sensible.

Nor is it less evident, that it could not but have proved extremely incommodious and mischievous. The whole city of *Jerusalem*, some hundred thousands of people being brought together, what could the consequence be but noise and uproar, tumult and confusion? In such a prodigious confluence of people, many, no doubt, would have been squeezed to death, many would have been trod under foot, and all the other mischiefs must have happened, that constantly attend vast crouds of people pressing upon one another, and struggling every one to get a fairer view. And in such circumstances, can any man judge it was fitting or proper for *Jesus* to have appeared? To this let me only add, that,

The personal appearance of *Jesus* to the chief Priests at the sepulchre, would have been very dangerous, either to *Jesus* himself, or to the whole nation of the *Jews*. As I have before observed, it is more than probable, that the chief Priests would by no means have been satisfied from the personal appearance of *Jesus*, as to the truth of his character: So that the finding *Jesus* alive in the sepulchre, would only have put it in their power, to attempt the again imbruing their hands in his innocent blood. But supposing that this appearance would have afforded full satisfaction to the chief Priests: As I have likewise formerly observed, the notions they entertained concerning their *Messiah* would have determined them *to take him by force and to make him a King*, which would have provoked the *Roman* arms, and brought on the ruin of the nation;

at

at no rate, therefore, was it safe for *Jesus* personally to appear to the chief Priests. Now,

From these several particulars laid together, it seems clearly manifest, that, according to the law of reason, *Jesus* ought not to have appeared to the chief Priests: Upon which the Deists have been so good as to promise to turn Christian; and to grant, that in their attempt to prove a plain fraud in the resurrection, there's no force nor truth (*y*). And indeed *Jesus's putting out all those who laughed him to scorn*, for saying that *Jairus's daughter was not dead but asleep*, or his refusing to suffer these persons to witness the miracle he was about to perform, is as strong an argument against the truth of his restoring that damsel to life, in the presence of her father and mother, and of his Apostles, *Peter, James, and John*, as his non-appearance to the chief Priests can be thought against his resurrection. But the former was wise and prudent, and shews an aversion to all ostentation, while the fact itself had enow of witnesses to attest it: And, in the latter, the same qualities are most conspicuous.

Thus having shown, there is no force or reason in those objections which our Infidels make against the truth of the resurrection of *Jesus*; it now comes to be remarked, that how much soever our Freethinkers may insist on the necessity of *Jesus's* personally appearing to the chief Priests, and pretend, that, for want of this evidence, the resurrection must be counted a cheat; yet the chief Priests themselves do not seem to have wanted any such evidence, in order to convince them, there was no imposture in the case, or that the resurrection really happened.

For three hundred years after the first promulgation of the Gospel, it was not then, as the Deists complain

(*y*) Woolst. p. 25.

complain it is now. During that long space of time, the Christian religion had no shadow of secular power to support it; on the contrary, the civil Magistrate, and the established Priesthood, every where set themselves zealously against it, and jointly exerted all their authority to prevent its propagation, cruelly punishing those resolute Freethinkers, who durst be bold to oppose themselves to the public religions then subsisting. In those days, therefore, when the means of information were most favourable, every man was at full liberty, there was nothing to hinder him from searching out the truth of the matter, he was under no restraint either as to argument or passion, but had all possible encouragement to expose Christianity after what manner his heart should incline him; and the more effectually any one exposed it, the higher he thereby raised his own reputation, and the greater service he was then held to do, as well to the interest of the state, as to that of religion. Now, this liberty, or rather encouragement, to ruin the credit of the Gospel, having been preserved for so long a time, can it be thought, that its enemies, either through ignorance were not able, or through indifferency carelessly neglected, to make a thorough inquiry? Every body knows, that those first ages, wherein the Gospel appeared, were learned and knowing; so that an imposture could have had no advantage, from the darkness and ignorance of the times: And the violent opposition that was every where made to the progress of Christianity, is abundant proof, that men's hearts were in those days far from being in a state of indifferency. What then is the reason, why the Deists now complain, they are under restraint, and have not leave to speak out their sentiments?

ments? At this time of day, have they found out any thing that can blacken the credit of the Gospel, which the penetration and zeal of the first ages was not able to discover, or durst not publish to the world? If they have, I wish, with all my heart, they would make it public. Only, from the liberties they have taken of late years, one is tempted to think, they are guilty of no concealments. To save, however, a man's decency in still adhering to a baffled cause, it seems prudent, always to pretend the strongest argument is still in reserve, so strong that the opposite party now in power, would crush a man in pieces for urging it. But be that as it will:

I hope the chief Priests were under no such apprehensions: They surely had no restraint laid upon them by any authority whatsoever: They imprisoned, they scourged, they threatened the Apostles, they stoned *Stephen* to death, *James the brother of John was killed with the sword*. And having all power in their own hands, and being possessed of every passion that could prompt them to detect the fraud; why did they not search it out, and expose it to the indignation of all mankind? How the guards at the sepulchre came so soon to be rouzed out of their dead sleep, I know not. It could not be the noise of the Apostles in stealing away the dead body, otherwise the theft would have been prevented: Perhaps it was the earthquake, and the rolling away the stone when the Angels descended. But leaving this difficulty to be explained by our Freethinkers; the history tells us, that *early in the morning, the soldiers came to the city, and informed the chief Priests of what had passed.*

Upon this indeed a council is held immediately. But in this council, had they had so much as a suspicion,

spicion, not to talk of their being certainly perfuaded, that the body of *Jesus* was stole away, in order to impose upon the world a sham-resurrection, the belief of which, they were sensible, would endanger their whole national constitution; why did they not express their resentment against the guards, and make some strong propositions to have them punished; which the great confusion and danger all their affairs, notwithstanding their precautions, were now brought into, could not, in the nature of things, but provoke them passionately to pursue; which might have assured the world, that the watch (in their opinion at least) had been really guilty of an infamous neglect of duty, and would have answered their purpose a great deal better, than the stupid testimony of sleeping soldiers? Why did they not, in so dangerous a juncture, immediately resolve upon the most obvious and necessary measures, the dispatching away their officers to raise town and country to go in search of the dead body, which, in so short a space of time, could not have been carried far off, and which, in so general a search, wherein every honest man would have gladly lent his assistance, could not possibly miss of being discovered? Why did they not immediately give orders to apprehend the Apostles, the main actors and every one whom they had reason to suspect as their accomplices? And had the general search disppointed them, why did they attempt to bring none of the Apostles themselves, none of their associates to a confession, either by bribes, or by torture, having found the success of the former upon *Judas*, and knowing, as one may reckon, that the fear of something like the latter, had formerly tempted *Peter* to deny his Master? And, in the interim, why did they not issue out a proclamation, setting forth the

hainous

hainous nature of the impofture, exhorting all, as they regarded God, their religion, their country, to contribute their endeavours to detect the fraud; and promifing a large reward to any man who fhould find out the body, or difcover the place where it was depofited? They were at the trouble and charge of difpatching meffengers to all nations, every where through the world, with letters to their country men, in order to prepoffefs them againft *Chrift* and his Gofpel, and to prevent their giving countenance to that novel impious herefy; alledging againft its broachers, moft difhonourably to themfelves, that very fenfelefs ftory, which they had publifhed at *Jerufalem* (z). But why all this buftle and expence about foreign difpatches, when proper meafures at home would at once have crufhed the defign, and prevented its being heard of without the walls of the city? I fay, under the perfuafion of a villanous theft, with refpect to the body of *Jefus*, and fenfible of the great mifchiefs it would certainly bring, as they thought upon the whole nation; why did the chief Priefts, in order to bring about a difcovery, and thereby fave themfelves and the nation from the impending ruin, ufe none of thofe plain obvious means which common fenfe dictates, and are univerfally employed on the like occafions? It cannot but be thought furprifing, that inftead of purfuing thofe meafures, wherein they could not have failed of detecting the whole villany, and of bringing immediate ruin upon the whole project;

They not only protect the guards in that provoking treachery they were guilty of, which had brought upon them the very dangers they dreaded, and which they fet them to prevent; but they give
them

(z) Vid. Juft. Mart. dialog. 2. cum Tryph. p. 335. Eufeb. in Ifai. xviii. 1. 2.

them money, as if their unfaithfulness to their trust had done them good service. So far were they from searching after the dead body, or seizing upon the contrivers and actors of the theft, that from the time the resurrection began first to be spoken of, for the space of fifty days, they suffered the Apostles and other Disciples to live peaceably at *Jerusalem*, tho' all that while they were confident in reporting to all about them, that at such particular times and places, they had seen and conversed with *Jesus* alive from the dead, and that at length they saw him ascend into heaven. Nay, tho' the circumstances that attended the beginning of the Ministry of the Apostles, occasioned a great noise all over the city, and their converting at that time to the Christian faith, several thousands of people, was not a little threatening; yet the chief Priests permitted the Apostles to go on, they made no attempt to confine them, in order to expose the fraud they alledged against them, or to punish them for so monstrous a piece of wickedness.

Indeed, when they found that the Apostles had the boldness to come to the very temple and work their miracles, this so much alarmed them, that *they laid hands on Peter and John and put them in prison*; wherein, I confess, they began to act in their own defence. And may not one now expect, to find the charge pointedly laid, and clearly made out against the Apostles? But so it happened, that after a night's confinement, those two Apostles being brought before the Council, and boldly asserting, in face of their Judges, that *that Jesus whom they crucified was risen from the dead, and had empowered them to work such miracles*; the chief Priests, after a solemn consultation, come only to this resolution, *straitly to threaten the Apostles that they speak henceforth*

forth to no man, nor teach in the name of Jesus (a). A strange judgment this! in the case of so impious a fraud as was said to have been committed. But the Apostles openly profess their resolution not to obey, and appealing to the chief Priests themselves, *whether it be right in the sight of God to hearken unto them, more than unto God,* they dare be bold to tell them, that *they cannot but speak the things which they have seen and heard.* Nor does this resolute answer any farther provoke the chief Priests, than to renew their threatening to the Apostles, and to let them go; *finding nothing,* as the history informs us, *how they might punish them, because of the people.* But in the name of wonder! had they not the stealing away of the body of *Jesus* to lay to their charge and make out against them? Durst they not, for the people, so much as mention the villanous theft that had been committed? Or, would the people have opposed them in carrying on the accusation, and bringing the imposture to light? Every honest man, all the people, had they but suspected the smallest fraud in the case, would, no doubt, have gladly assisted in detecting it, and have had great pleasure in seeing the Authors of it condignly punished. And is it not surprising, that, in all their accusations, at no time do the chief Priests ever once mention against the Apostles or any of the Disciples, their carrying off the body of *Jesus*, and imposing upon the world a most wicked imposture, in pretending a resurrection? So far are they from going on such a supposition, that in all their resolutions they clearly proceed upon quite other apprehensions of the matter.

Thus,

(a) Acts iii. 4.

Thus, having seized the Apostles a second time, and brought them before the Council. the chief Priests only accuse them of having violated the strict orders they had formerly laid upon them; *did not we*, say they, *straitly command you, that you should not teach in this name? And behold, you have filled Jerusalem with your doctrine, and intend to bring this man's blood upon us.* To which the Apostles returning their former answer, that *they ought to obey God rather than men*; and still charging them with the murder of *Jesus*, whom they still boldly professed, *God had raised up from the dead, and that the holy Ghost as well as they were his witnesses of these things*; this at length so exasperated the chief Priests, that the proposition was made to slay the Apostles. Upon which *Gamaliel*, one of the Council, and a Doctor of law, gave his opinion thus: *Take heed* (says he) *to yourselves what ye intend to do as touching these men.——Refrain from them, and let them alone; for if this counsel or this work be of men, it will come to nought; but if it be of God, ye cannot overthrow it; lest happily ye be found even to fight against God* (b). But, in his right senses, can any man ever in the least come to suspect, that that counsel, or that work may be of God, may have his countenance and protection, which one is persuaded takes its rise from a villanous forgery; and that the cutting off the contrivers of so monstrous a cheat, may be found a fighting against God? The Rulers of the *Jews* forming their resolutions upon such an argument, gave no credit to their own story, but despised the testimony of the sleeping soldiers, and must have been conscious of a notorious lye, when they assured the world, that *his Disciples came by night and stole him away.*

And

(b) Acts v. 17. &c.

And that this was their guilty case, one cannot but the more be satisfied, when one further considers, that tho' the *Jews* could not but know, that their Heathen judges never cared to meddle in questions purely relating to their Law, yet, as we learn from their eager prosecution against *Paul*, they insist on nothing else in their accusations, and wholly neglect that article of fraud with respect to the body of *Jesus*, which comes under the cognizance of the common justice of all nations, and which, sufficiently made out, would have exposed to the severest punishment, not only the immediate actors in the theft, but all who should obstinately unite with them, as *Paul* had done, to carry on the design they had grounded upon it. Here is the account of *Paul*'s case, which *Festus* gives to King *Agrippa* : *You see this man,* says Festus, *about whom all the multitude of the Jews have dealt with me, both at Jerusalem, and also here, crying that he ought not to live any longer. But when his accusers (Ananias the high Priest with the Elders, and Tertullus an Orator) stood up against him, they brought none accusation of such things as I supposed: But had certain questions against him of their own superstition, and of one Jesus, which was dead, whom Paul affirmed to be alive* (c).

Thus, I must beg leave to think, whoever attends to the principles of human nature, and considers the conduct of the chief Priests and Rulers of the *Jews*, cannot fail to be satisfied, that in their consciences the chief Priests did not believe, the Apostles were guilty of stealing the body of *Jesus* away. And as the chief Priests, thro' the whole of their management, give us all ground to rest confident, that they did not themselves believe there was any fraud committed in the matter of the resurrection ;

(c) Acts xxv.

surrection; so the conduct of the Apostles clearly demonstrates, how much they are above all suspicion of imposture with respect to that grand article of Christianity. For let us reflect,

Had any plot been contrived to steal away the body of *Jesus,* and to put upon the world a sham-resurrection, can it enter into one's head to imagine, that the plotters themselves, instead of carefully concealing what they intended, would have alarmed all mankind, and awakened them to take measures that would effectually prevent the execution? Now, we know that *Jesus*'s design of rising from the dead was kept no secret, nor yet the day when it was to happen neglected to be published: So that the world had fair warning given them, all concerned were called to be upon their guard; and so well were the chief Priests apprised of the design, that they took all possible precautions to prevent a cheat in the matter. Thus far, I am certain, there is a strong appearance of honesty, and the presumption is irresistible, that no sort of fraud is intended.

After this public warning to the chief Priests, and to all the enemies of *Jesus,* the crucifixion comes on; *Jesus* dies, and guards are placed on his sepulchre; whilst all his Disciples had forsaken him and fled, without expecting to see him any more. But the third day approaches, and on that day the body is a-missing; the guards could not keep it; the chief Priests cannot show it; and the Disciples do not believe it is raised from the dead. Amidst this perplexity, *Jesus* appears to some of his Disciples; their eyes and other senses convince them he is risen; they report the fact to the rest; but the rest will give no credit to their testimony:——In a word, they refuse to trust one another; and all of them

them continue obstinate unbelievers, till every man's own senses makes it impossible for him, not to confess the truth of the resurrection. And as the Apostles were the chosen, the particular witnesses pitched upon, who should publish this fact to all nations, and who, in attesting it, were to undergo great sufferings; that their conviction of its certainty might be strong and lasting, having deep root in their minds, *Jesus* was pleased, during the space of forty days, frequently to appear to them, familiarly to eat and converse with them, and, as he was wont to do before his death, to work miracles in their presence.

Nor did the Apostles delay the publication of this event, till they were at a distance from the place and time of its happening; but upon the spot, where the things were transacted, and where every man had all opportunities of inquiring, and of examining into the bottom of the matter; they began, as soon as they were convinced themselves, confidently to report it to all about them: Nay, so open were they and honest, that they put it in the power of numbers of other people, to satisfy themselves from the testimony of their own senses, by letting them know, that on such a day, and at such a place, they might see *Jesus* himself, and witness his ascending into heaven. And so it happened, that a great many were present at this extraordinary event.

So that *Jesus* having left this lower world, and gone to his father; his Apostles, a few days after his ascension, being *endowed with power from on high*, entered upon their public Ministry, and beginning at *Jerusalem* itself, they every where openly and avowedly proclaim the resurrection of Jesus, and even in the face of his murderers, boldly maintain the

the truth of that event. Nor did they confine people to their testimony alone, but they tell the world, if they want further evidence, they may have access to the attestation of several hundreds of other eye-witnesses.

And, that no man might be negligent in examining into the truth of the fact, or satisfy himself with slight evidence, they do not fail to make mankind aware of what consequence it is; of such consequence, that if *Christ* be not risen, *then*, say they, *our preaching is vain, and your faith also is vain,* your believing in *Jesus* is to no purpose, and you gain nothing by exposing yourselves to any hazards for the sake of the Gospel. *Yea, and we are found false witnesses of God, because we have testified of God, that he raised up Christ, whom he raised not up.* Nay, so secure are they against all imputation of fraud, that they awaken people's passions, while engaged in the heat of controversy, for the most part then very keen, so keen that they frequently hurry a man to deny first principles; I say, in these circumstances, the Apostles provoke human passions to inquire into the truth of a matter of fact, and to bring forth what they know about it; whilst they appeal to the resurrection of *Jesus*, as an infallible proof of a general resurrection from the dead, which in their day was by some people openly denied.

In short, in attestation of the certainty of this fact, of no moment as to any worldly purpose, the Apostles willingly lay down their lives, and expiring in torments persist in declaring what their eyes had seen, and their hands had handled, what all their senses forced them to confess; while they might have escaped by barely promising to fall in with the public religion for the future, or, which is less, to talk no more of the matter. And let me now ask;

Can

SECT. XV. *Christian Revelation.*

Can those people be counted cheats and Impostors, who, witness a matter of fact, which the world, being forwarned was to happen, took the most effectual measures to prevent being falsified? Who, as to their own particulars, were the farthest in the world from expecting it was to have happened; who did not believe it had happened, till they were assured of its reality, not from the testimony of others, which they rejected, but every man from the testimony of his own senses; who, upon the spot, and at the time when it happened, openly proclaimed it to the whole world; who, for the truth of it, appealed to a great many others, who, they said, were eye-witnesses, as well as themselves; who, in the strongest manner, invited and provoked other people carefully to inquire into its certainty; who, without variation, in the face of dangers, in the presence of death itself, still persisted in their evidence, and left the world, with their last breath proclaiming to all, " The matter of fact " is certain ;" having it, at the same time, in their power to secure their peace, and to save their lives only by complying with the religious opinions then prevailing, and in which they had been educated; or barely by being silent as to what related to *Jesus Christ?* I say, can such people be counted Impostors (*d*)? If they must——moral evidence is at an end, and no man can rely on human testimony. Besides,

In those days, nothing was more notorious, than that, to undertake the profession of Christianity, was
infinitely

(*d*) That the Apostles were no Impostors, but that they were under the most penetrating conviction of the certainty of the resurrection of Jesus, Chrysostom, in his Reflections upon 1 Cor. i. 25, 31. (p. 264, 265, 270, 271, 272. Oper. tom. 3) clearly demonstrates, from their undertaking and pursuing the propagation of the Gospel.

infinitely hazardous: And yet, at that very time, even in *Jerusalem*, the place where all was transacted, the number of Disciples came soon to be very great; nay, even then and there it was, that a great company of Priests themselves, with their eyes open upon the sad sufferings, that would follow their conversion, renounced their national principles, and *become obedient to the faith* (*e*). But, those people, well knowing the whole weight of the Christian profession, then so extremely dangerous, rested on the truth of the resurrection of *Jesus*; can any man seriously think, that, upon the spot, where they had it in their power to inquire and to know the whole truth of the matter, they would examine nothing; but, at the hazard of their lives, blindly take up with a religion utterly repugnant to all their former sentiments, or run headlong into an imposture, that would ruin them here, and damn them hereafter? If people in those days were capable of acting such a part, they must have been creatures not of our make (*f*).

Upon the whole, I would now fain flatter myself, that every man who thinks freely, will find himself at full liberty openly to profess, the Apostles did not deceive the world about them; they were

no

(*e*) Acts vi. 7.

(*f*) An numquid dicemus istius temporis homines usque adeo fuisse vanos, mendaces, stolidos, brutos, ut quæ nunquam viderant, vidisse se fingerent? et quæ facta omnino non erant, falsis proderent testimoniis, aut puerili assertione firmarent? cumque possent vobiscum & unanimiter vivere, & inoffensas ducere conjunctiones, gratuita susciperent odia, & execrabili haberentur in nomine?——Imo quia hæc omnia & ab ipso cernebant geri, & ab ejus præconibus, qui per orbem totum missi beneficia patris & munerandis animis hominibusque portabant, veritatis ipsius vi victi, et dederunt se Deo, nec in magnis posuere dispendiis membra vobis projicere, et viscera sua lanianda præbere. Arnob. lib. I. p. 19.

no Impostors in the business of the resurrection. And indeed, as the Apostles have reported them, such are the circumstances of this event, that the truth of the fact requires their existence; or, the resurrection really happening, it must have been attended with such circumstances. And as supposing the fact true, such circumstances must have existed; so those people who oppose the truth of the resurrection, being forced to forge or suppose other circumstances, do therein seem to be determined, at any rate, to deny the certainty of this event: First laying it down with themselves, as an undoubted maxim, that the resurrection is a mere falshood; and then framing the circumstances, as in the case of a fraud, one may imagine they must have happened: Which is a freedom of thought not so well adapted to the discovery of truth.

But, before I conclude this article of imposture, I shall presume to lead the Reader to consider, that, by the same arguments, whereby the Deists go about to justify themselves, and whereby one may justify *Socrates*, it must be confessed, the Apostles are clearly vindicated.

SECT. XVI.

The Apostles are vindicated from the Imputation of Imposture, by the same Arguments whereby the Deists go about to clear themselves and to justify the Character of Socrates.

THE Author of a Discourse of Freethinking, giving out the great characteristic of a Freethinker, to be upon one's having thought freely, " the op-
" posing one's self to the established opinions, to popu-
" lar superstition and bigotry," he favours us with

a roll of persons, whom he reckons of this character; and among them we find Heathens, *Jews*, Christians, Atheists, Theists, men of the most contradictory principles, mixed together. The Apostles indeed have not the honour of a place in this catalogue; but if opposition to established opinions, from a generous freedom of thought, be the chief criterion of a Freethinker, one should think, that never were there men in the world who have a better title to this character. But that which I bere design, is to leave it to the world to judge, whether what the Deists alledge, in vindication of their own virtue and honesty, does not equally serve to clear the reputation of the Apostles? It is objected to the Deists, as we learn from the same Auhor,

" That Freethinkers themselves, are the most in-
" famous, wicked, and senseless of all mankind (g)."
And to clear them from this charge, he forms this apology:

" This objection, says he, of wickedness and ig-
" norance is made by all sects one against another,
" and serves to keep the several herds and folds of
" men united together, and against one another:
" And tho' in reality men of all sects are much a-
" like as to sense, where literature equally pre-
" vails, and every where the same as to their lives
" and conversations, (as is obvious to any indiffer-
" ent person) yet through such spectacles do men
" see the defects of others, so partial are they to
" themselves, so ready to believe ill reports of those
" with whom they have any difference in opinion
" and to believe good of those with whom
" they agree in opinion; so apt to put an ill
" construction on any actions of the former,
" and a good one on any actions of the latter;
" that nothing but the most familiar intercourse
" imaginable

(g) A Discourse of Freethinking. p. 118.

" imaginable can make men, who are governed by
" one fort of Priests, think they are like those in
" understanding and morals who are governed by
" another sort. But this objection, as it is urged
" against Freethinkers, is still with more difficulty
" to be removed by them; because they who have
" leisure, application, ability, and courage to
" think freely, are so few in number in respect of
" any other sect, that they must be less able, by
" conversation in the world, to answer an objecti-
" on against themselves, so early planted in men's
" minds, and so carefully cultivated. However, I
" think it may be much easier answered upon pa-
" per, and may be shown to be more unjustly ur-
" ged against Freethinkers, than against any other
" sort of men whatsoever. In answer to it there-
" fore, I observe,

" I. That men who use their understandings must
" have more sense than they who use them not; and
" this I take to be self-evident. And as to the o-
" ther part of the objection, I assert, that Free-
" thinkers must, as such, be the most virtuous
" persons every where.

" 1. Because, if any man presumes to think for
" himself, and in consequence of that departs from
" the herd of mankind among whom he lives, he
" is sure to draw upon himself the whole malice
" of the Priest, and of all who believe in him,
" (which must of course be nine hundred and nine-
" ty nine of a thousand) and can have no credit, but
" what his virtue, in spite of his enemies, necessari-
" ly procures for him. Whereas any profligate
" fellow is sure of credit, countenance, and support,
" in any sect or party whatsoever, tho' he has no
" other quality to recommend him than the worst
" of all vices, a blind zeal to his sect or party.
                                             " The

"The Freethinker therefore is, for his own fake, in this world, obliged to be virtuous and honest; but the Bigot is under no such obligation; and besides, has the temptation to become a knave, because so many weak people of all parties are ready to put their confidence in him purely for his bigotry.

"2. Because whoever applies himself to any action, much more to freethinking (which requires great diligence and application of mind) must by that habit expel all those vicious habits and passions, by which every man out of action is tossed and governed.

"3. Besides, by much thinking only, are men able to comprehend in their minds the whole compass of human life, and thereby to demonstrate to themselves, that misery and unhappiness attend the practice of vice, and pleasure and happiness the practice of virtue, in this life: And that to live pleasantly, they must live virtuously. *For who*, says Cicero (*b*), *lives pleasantly, except him who delights in his duty, and has well considered and settled his manner of life; and who obeys the laws not out of fear, but observes and regards them, because he judges it the best thing he can do?* Wherein we see by experience, that most men, for want of considering the whole compass of human life, mistake their own happiness, and think it wholly consists in gratifying their present passions and inclinations: And accordingly are very little moved even by their belief of future happiness and misery, to become virtuous, while they are under such a mistake. And thus, of
"course,

(*b*) Quis igitur vivit ut vult, nisi qui gaudet officio? Cui vivendi via considerata atque provisa est, qui legibus non propter metum paret, sed eas sequitur atque colit, quia id maxime salutare esse judicat? Cic. oper. Gron. p. 417c.

"course, all unthinking people are vitious, unless
"they are prevented by some natural defect or im-
"pediment, or are moral by the goodness of
"their natural temper. *Cicero* admirably describes
"the bad effects of this wrong judgment about
"the rule of morality. Says he (1), *Whoever*
"*places happiness in any thing besides virtue, and jud-*
"*ges of happiness by his* present *interest and advantage,*
"*and not by the rules of honesty,* or what is good upon
"the whole; *if he be consistent with himself, and is*
"*not carried away by his own good natural disposition,*
"*can neither be friendly, nor equitable, nor generous.*
"*No man can be courageous, who takes pain to be*
"*the greatest evil; nor be moderate in the enjoyment of*
"*pleasure, who takes that to be the greatest good.*

"II. I answer, that tho' there has hardly been
"a country, where the Priests have been so few in
"number, or have had so little credit, or where
"superstition has been at so low an ebb, as not to
"draw some inconveniencies on men for thinking
"freely; and by consequence, many Freethinkers
"have either fallen in with the reigning superstition
"of their country, or suffered it quietly to take
"its course, foreseeing what little good was to be
"done on so knavish and ignorant a creature as
"man, and how much mischief was to be expected
"from him: Yet they who have been most distin-
"guished in all ages for their understanding and
"virtue have been Freethinkers.

"*Socrates*, the divinest man that ever appeared in
"the Heathen world, and to whose virtue and
"wisdom

(1) Qui summum bonum instituit ut nihil habeat cum virtute conjunctum, idque suis commodis non henestate metitur; hic si sibi ipsi consentat, et non interdum bonitate naturæ vincatur, neque amicitiam colere possit nec justitiam, nec liberalitatem; fortis vero dolorem summum malum judicans aut temperans voluptatem summum bonum statuens esse certe nullo modo potest. De Offic. lib. 1. cap. 2.

"wisdom all ages since have done justice, was a ve-
"ry great Freethinker. He not only disbelieved
"the gods of his country, and the common creeds
"about them;——but obtained a just notion of
"the nature and attributes of God———As a fur-
"ther evidence of his freethinking, *Socrates* had
"the common fate of Freethinkers, to be calumni-
"ated in his life-time for an Atheist; (tho' the God
"*Apollo* by his oracle declared him the wisest man
"upon earth) and at length suffered that punish-
"ment for freethinking, which knavery and folly,
"whenever they are arrived to a due pitch, and
"are well confederated together, are ever ready
"to inflict on all those who have the honesty and
"courage to endeavour to imitate him." Upon
which, by the way, one cannot but observe, that as
our present Freethinkers have little ground upon
which to claim an interest in *Socrates*, who believed
revelation and confessed its necessity, against both
which they are pleased to declare; so if the number of Deists be in proportion to the instances of
honesty and courage in imitating *Socrates*, one may
venture to say, there are at this day few or none
of that character.

After this manner, the Deists defend their virtue
and innocence. And if such speculations are judged
sufficient to vindicate their conduct, or to shew, that
in their opposition to established opinions, they
hearken only to the dictates of honesty, and are governed by no worldly consideration; since the Apostles, as I have hinted, were the most open and determined Freethinkers that ever lived; must not
the same speculations equally justify their conduct,
and satisfy the world, that in the opposition they
made to the established opinions of their day, both
among *Jews* and Heathens, they were sincere and
honest,

honeſt, and felt nothing from the power of any worldly motive whatſoever?' So that while the Deiſts, upon ſuch topics, would induce the world to confeſs, they are themſelves fair, honeſt men; it is to be feared, that their attacking the character of the Apoſtles, clearly ſupported by the ſame topics, may chance, with ſome people, to ruin all the force of this ſpeculative argument in their own favour, and ſtill to keep their honeſty in queſtion. But it is not ſpeculation only upon which we can ſettle the character of the Apoſtles; there are numberleſs *phænomena*, plain matters of fact, in their courſe of life, from whence we can aſſuredly know, what were the particular, inward ſprings, whereby they were moved and directed in the proſecution of their Miniſtry. Of thoſe matters of fact I have mentioned ſo many in the preceeding *Sections*, and upon thoſe I appeal to the conſciouſneſs of every man, Deiſt or Chriſtian, who conſiders human nature, or who attends to the operations of his own mind; whether a ſet of Impoſtors, having their views fixed on a determinate end of a ſecular nature, would have acted the part the Apoſtles did in the propagation of the Goſpel? In my apprehenſion, the principles of human nature, as they would infallibly operate in ſuch particular circumſtances, do loudly proclaim quite the contrary. Groundleſs, therefore, and unnatural is the ſuſpicion of thoſe who are called ſceptical, " That the holy Records themſelves are no other " than the pure invention, or artificial compile‑ " ment of an intereſted party, in behalf of the " richeſt corporation, and moſt profitable monopo‑ " ly which could be erected in the world (*k*)." A moſt violent contradiction to the whole tenor of
the

(*k*) Characteriſt. vol. iii p. 118.

the Apostles conduct, who strictly command their successors in office, to entertain the same sentiments, and to act upon the same principles, wherein they had gone before them. Let those unhappy men, who prostitute the sacred office, and basely pervert it to a gainful trade, answer for their conduct, condemned by the Apostles, and by all good men (*l*).

I shall

(*l*) To enter into holy orders, or to assume the character of a Minister of the Gospel, only with a view to grasp at the revenues of the church, and upon those to live in the gratification of worldly appetites, without any regard to the laws and interest of the Gospel, is most certainly, beyond expression, wicked and infamous. Among other melancholy consequences, it gives a handle to some inconsiderate people, who set up for Philosophers, to deny the truth and usefulness of the Christian Revelation. But, as Philosophers do not seem, in their profession, to act a more honourable part, will any man say, that, from their vitious lives, one may reasonably conclude the falshood and uselesness of philosophy? Let us hear Cicero upon the subject:

Quotusquisque, says he, Philosophorum invenitur, qui sit ita moratus, ita animo ac vita constitutus, ut ratio postulat? Qui disciplinam suam, non ostentationem scientiæ, sed legem vitæ putet? Qui obtemperet ipse sibi et decretis suis pareat? Videre licet alios tanta levitate et jactatione, iis ut fuerit non didicisse melius: alios pecuniæ cupidos, gloriæ nonnullos, mulios libidinum servos: ut cum eorum vita mirabiliter pugnet oratio Quod quidem mihi videtur esse turpissimum.— Philosophus in ratione vitæ peccans, hoc turpior est, quod in officio, cujus magister esse vult, labitur, artemque vitæ professus, delinquit in vita. Upon which it is objected: Nonne verendum igitur, si est ita, ut dicis, ne philosophiam falsa gloria exornes? Quod est enim majus argumentum, nihil eam prodesse, quam quosdam perfectos Philosophos turpiter vivere? To this Cicero answers: Nullum vero id quidem argumentum est. Nam ut agri non omnes frugiferi sunt, qui coluntur;—sic animi non omnes culti fructum ferunt. Atque, ut in eodem simili verser, ut ager, quamvis fertilis, sine cultura fructuosus esse non potest; sic sine doctrina animus. Ita est utraque res sine altera debilis. Cultura autem animi philosophia est: hæc extrahit vitia radicitus, et præparat animos ad satus accipiendos, eaque mandat his, et, ut ita dicam, serit, quæ adulta fructus uberrimos ferant. 2 Tuscul. cap. 4. 5. All this is finely illustrated, Matth. xiii.

I shall only say, whatever ground there may be now, from the mean conduct of some of the Clergy, for this imputation, every impartial man will allow, there was not the shadow of one in the days of the Apostles (*m*); who, for themselves, as to this life, had no prospect, and met with nothing but misery. And can it be imagined, that with great chearfulness, they designedly bore all the hardships of this world, that their successors might securely riot in all its profuseness and luxuries.

Thus, having vindicated the character of the Apostles, by the same reasoning whereby the Deists go about to clear themselves; let me next propose to the consideration of every thinking Deist, whether the character of the Apostles has not still as good a title to their favourable opinion, as that of *Socrates* can have, in whose commendation they are so loud and frequent?

This wonderful man, who deserved a better fate, falling a sacrifice to the infidelity of his ignorant and malicious countrymen, proceeds in his defence, before his Judges, after this manner: " Now (says
" he) that I am a person of whom it may be pre-
" sumed, I am sent to you of God, you may learn
" from hence: It looks not like any thing human,
" that, neglecting all my own private concern-
" ments, and persisting in this neglect for so many
" years, I should be continually attending your in-
" terests, and addressing every man singly, like a
" father or an elder brother, recommend to people
" to be mindful of virtue. If thereby indeed I pro-
" moted

(*m*) Νῦν μὲν ὖν τάχα τολμήσει τις λέγειν διὰ τὸ δοξάριον προΐςασθαι, τινας τῆς κατὰ Χριςιανὲς διδασκαλίας. ὰ μὲν κατὰ τὴν ἀρχὴν, ὅτε πολὺς ὁ κίνδυνος μάλιςα τοῖς διδάσκυσιν ἦν οἷόν τε τὸ τοιῦτον εὐλόγως ὑπονοεῖν. —Orig. contra Celf. b. iii. p. 117.

" moted any particular end of my own, and made
" gain of my inſtructions, there might be some
" reaſon to ſuſpect me. But you yourſelves ſee,
" that my accuſers, who have ſhamefully accuſed
" me of every thing elſe, have not had the face to
" charge me with any thing of that nature, alled-
" ging, that I ever, at any time, either received or
" demanded a reward. And, as a full proof, in
" my apprehenſion, of my innocence, I propoſe to
" you my poverty (*n*). For the ſake of the ſer-
" vice of God (ſays he) I chuſe to live in extreme
" poverty." Now, if this vindication be of any force, as I think it is, in the caſe of *Socrates*, I leave it to the Deiſts to inform the world, why the like vindication, ſupported by much ſtronger circum-ſtances, muſt not be confeſſed of equal force in clear-ing the Apoſtles? Again,

As I have before obſerved, upon the ſingle in-ſtance of *Socrates*'s ſhewing himſelf in the theatre, while the Poet was expoſing him to public ridicule, Lord *Shafteſbury* concludes, " There could be in
" the

(*n*) Ὅτι δ' ἐγὼ τυγχάνω ὢν τοιοῦτος οἷος ὑπὸ τοῦ θεοῦ τῇ πόλει δεδόσθαι, ἐνθένδε ἂν κατανοήσαιτε. οὐ γὰρ ἀνθρωπίνῳ ἔοικε τὸ ἐμὲ τῶν μὲν ἐμαυτοῦ ἁπάντων ἠμεληκέναι, καὶ ἀνέχεσθαι τῶν οἰκείων ἀμελουμένων τοσαῦτα ἤδη ἔτη, τὸ δὲ ὑμέτερον πράτ]ειν ἀεὶ, ἰδίᾳ ἑκάςῳ προσίοντα, ὥσπερ πατέρα ἢ ἀδελφὸν πρεσβύτερον, πείθοντα ἐπιμελεῖσθαι ἀρετῆς. καὶ εἰ μέν τοι τὶ ἀπὸ τούτων ἀπέλαυον, καὶ μισθὸν λαμβάνων ταῦτα παρεκελευό-μην, εἶχεν ἄν τινα λόγον· νῦν δὲ ὁρᾶτε δὴ καὶ αὐτοὶ ὅτι οἱ κα-τήγοροι τἄλλα πάντα οὕτως ἀναισχύντως κατηγοροῦντες, τοῦτο γε οὐχ οἷοί τε ἐγένοντο ἀπαναισχυντῆσαι, παραχόμενοι μάρτυρα, ὡς ἐγώ ποτε τινὰ ἢ ἐπραξάμην μισθὸν ἢ ἤτησα. ἱκανὸν γὰρ, οἶμαι, ἐγὼ παρέχομαι τὸν μάρτυρα, ὡς ἀληθῆ λέγω, τὴν πε-νίαν. Plat. Apolog. Socrat. p. 31. A. vol. i. Ἐν πενίᾳ μυρίᾳ εἰμὶ, διὰ τὴν τοῦ θεοῦ λατρείαν. Ibid. p. 23. B.

SECT. XVI. *Christian Revelation.* 223

" the world no greater testimony of the invincible
" goodness of the man, nor a greater demonstra-
" tion, that there was no imposture either in his
" character or opinions." What shall we then say
of the Apostles, who present their Master on the
theatre of the world, dressed up in all the ridicule
of mock-majesty, *having on him a scarlet robe, with
a crown of thorns upon his head, and a reed in his right
hand,* while *a band of soldiers bowed the knee before
him, and mocked him,* saying, *Hail King of the* Jews
(o)? What shall we say of their representing him
amidst his enemies, standing *blind-folded,* and *those
about him striking him on the face, and asking him,* saying, *prophesy who is it that smote thee* (p)? If it was
good humour in *Socrates,* and an unanswerable vindication of his character and opinions, to shew his
real figure in the theatre, that it might be compared
with a man in a basket hanging in the air; is it
not as good humour in the Apostles, and as thorough a vindication of their character and opinions,
when, in the case of their Master, with whom they
must share every thing, they set his true and his
false by one another, or leave it to the world to
compare his real figure with that which his witty
enemies had brought as his representative on the
stage? But not only do the Apostles represent their
Master with all the ridicule about him, in which
his enemies exposed him, and which must rebound
upon themselves, but they further confess, that they
themselves, in particular, were every where made the
objects of raillery and derision. Upon their very
first appearance in the service of the Gospel, they
tell us they were openly ridiculed, as men full of
new wine (q); and that ever after they continued

to

(o) Matth. xxvii. 28, 29.   (p) Luke xxii. 64.
(q) Acts ii. 13.

to be made *a gazing-stock by reproaches, a spectacle unto the world, and to Angels, and to men* (r).

The noble Author just now mentioned, is persuaded, that had the truth of the Gospel been any way surmountable, the Heathen would have bid much fairer for silencing it, if they had chosen to bring our primitive Founders upon the stage in a pleasanter way than that of bear-skins and pitch-barrels (s). But in the then state of things, what occasion was there for the assistance of comedy in order to expose the Apostles? Could the stage have represented any thing more ridiculous, than the Apostles, in themselves, to the view of mankind did really seem to be? A dozen of poor, mean, illiterate creatures, in the condition of vagabonds, owning the authority of a dead man, crucified at *Jerusalem*, who, in his life-time, was loaded with mockery and reproaches, dispersing themselves through the world, and wandering about, sometimes singly, and sometimes by pairs, in hunger, and thirst, and cold, and nakedness; and yet boldly setting up to confound the wisdom of Philosophers, to overthrow the religion of nations, and upon the ruins of every other institution, against all the powers on earth, to establish their own principles; at the same time confident of success, and that, in spite of hell itself, their doctrines should prevail, not only in their day, but after their death, to the end of the world! This, one should think, was comedy enough, and being openly acted upon the stage of the world, must have exposed the Apostles to much more ridicule, than any representation, within the walls of

---

(r) 1 Cor. iv. 9. Hebr. x. 33. The word θεατριζόμενοι, here used, properly signifies their having been exposed upon the stage.

(s) Characterist. vol. i. p. 29.

SECT. XVI.   *Christian Revelation.*   225

of a house, could have done. I say, could the stage have set the Apostles, and their enterprise, in any light more ridiculous, than that whereby they actually appeared? To the Heathen world *the Gospel was mere foolishness* (*t*). And we may believe that those Epicurean and Stoic philosophers, who encountered *Paul* at *Athens*, were not sparing of their raillery in ridiculing that babler, as they called him (*u*). But so far was the ridicule every where thrown upon the Apostles, from putting a damp upon their spirits, that they went resolutely on in the prosecution of their Ministry; and so far was it from sinking their reputation, or suppressing their philosophy, the doctrines of the Gospel, that they each increased the more for it; and they apparently grew to be more the envy of other teachers. They were not only contented to be ridiculed, but they bore it with good humour, nay, they gloried in their reproaches, the railleries they endured. Concerning St. *Paul*, in particular, this is the noble Author's opinion; " I do not, says he, find that he declines the way " of wit or good humour; but, without suspicion " of his cause, is willing generously to commit it " to this proof, and try it against the sharpness of " any ridicule which might be offered (*x*)." So that if ridicule, as some people think, be the great test of opinions and characters, the Apostles having stood it in all its different attacks, they were men of real truth and honesty, incapable of having any sort of imposture fastened upon them. In short, they were men of great minds, superior to the calamities of life, they looked ridicule and calumny in

Vol. II.   F f   the

(*t*) 1 Cor. i. 23.   (*u*) Acts xvii. 18.   (*x*) Characterist. vol. 1. p. 30.

the face, and went on undisturbed in the discharge of their duty (*y*).

Thus Lord *Shaftsbury's* vindication of *Socrates*, seems to be of equal force to justify the Apostles. But as I have before hinted, a small degree of attention will satisfy us, that the character of the Apostles is infinitely superior to whatever the world can ascribe to that great and good man. And without stating the comparison, in other instances;

By how much the distinct genuine knowledge of the true God, and the certainty of a future state of rewards and punishments, clearly taught and explained by the Apostles, are of consequence to mankind, above a confused knowledge of God, including false deities as the objects of worship, and some uncertain conjectures about an after life, given out by *Socrates*; by so much is the character of the Apostles preferable to that of the divinest man that ever appeared in the Heathen world: And as it is infinitely more noble and generous, to attempt the reformation and happiness of all nations, which was the great design of the Apostles, than to attempt only the reformation and well-being of one single city, which was the case of *Socrates*; so the character of the Apostles is infinitely more illustrious than that of *Socrates* (*z*). Indeed, to refuse money, freely

---

(*y*) Τὰ σκώμματα κ̣ αἱ λοιδορίαι ὐδέν μοι δοκεῖ δύνασθαι. ἐὰν γὰρ ϛερεᾶς γνώμης λάβωνται, κατα λέλυνται· ἐὰν δὲ ἀγεννῦς κ̣ ταπεινῆς, ἴσχυσε, κ̣ ὐ μόνον ἐλύπησε πολλάκις, ἀλλὰ κ̣ ἀπέκτεινε. Τύτων ἀπόδειξις ἐκεῖνα ἔϛω. Σωκράτης μὲν ὂν κωμωδύμενος ἐγέλα: Πολίαγρος δὲ ἀπήγξατο. Ælian. var. hist. lib. 5. cap. 8. vid. lib. 2. cap. 13.

(*z*) Τίς ἂν ὁ σοφώτερος; ὁ πολλὺς πείθων, ἢ ὁ ὀλίγυς, μᾶλλον δὲ ὐδένα; ὁ περὶ πεγίϛων πείθων, ἢ ὁ περὶ τῶν μὴ δεόντων;

SECT. XVI. *Christian Revelation.* 227

freely to employ all one's time and labour, to bear poverty, and to submit to reproaches, and to death itself, in the service of reforming the world, and promoting the happiness of our fellow creatures; are glorious instances of a most magnanimous love towards mankind, and are to be found both in the Apostles and *Socrates*. But to forsake one's house and goods, to leave one's relations, and friends, and good acquaintances, and one's native country, and to travel abroad through the wide world, every where oppressed with want, with reproach and ridicule, with misery of all sorts, and worn out with dangers and hardships, to die the most cruel deaths, in recommending religion and virtue, and propagating the happiness of mankind, which was the case of the Apostles; as this is a situation of life very different from one's living in peace, tho' poorly, at home with one's family, while one has all freedom to go abroad to enjoy the company of one's friends; but, among some people, for the sake of one's instructions, comes to be involved in calumny and reproach, and at length happens to be condemned to a gentle death (*a*), wherein one has the comfort of being

δεόντων; πόσα ἔκαμε Πλάτων ᾗ οἱ κατ' αὐτὸν περὶ γραμμῆς, ᾗ γωνίας;—— πόσα ἔκαμε διῖξας ἐπιχειρῶν ὡς ἀθάνατος ἡ ψυχή, ᾗ ὐδὲν σαφὲς εἰπών, ὐδὲ πείσας τινὰ τῶν ἀκυόντων ὕτως ἀπῆλθεν; ὁ δὲ ςαυρὸς διὰ ἰδιωτῶν ἔπεισε, ᾗ τὴν οἰκυμένην ἅπασαν ἔπεισε, ᾗ ὐχ ὑπὲρ τῶν τυχόν των πραγμάτων, ἀλλὰ περὶ Θεῦ διαλεχθεὶς ᾗ τῆς κατὰ ἀλήθειαν εὐσεβείας, ᾗ τῆς εὐαγγελικῆς πολιτείας, ᾗ τῆς τῶν μελλόντων κρίσεως. ᾗ πάντας ἐποίησε φιλοσόφυς, τὺς ἀγροίκυς, τὺς ἰδιώτας. Chrysost. in 1 Cor. i. 25.

(*a*) Ἐμοὶ μὲν ὖν δοκεῖ θεοφιλῦς μοίρας τετυχηκέναι. τῦ μὲν γὰρ βίυ τὸ χαλεπώτατον ἀπέλιπε, τῶν δὲ θανάτων τῦ ῥᾷςο ἔτυχεν. Xenoph. Apol. Socrat. p. 707. C.

being attended by one's friends, which was the case of *Socrates*; I say, as these two situations of life are very different; so, if we measure the value, the generous strength of one's love towards mankind, from the compass wherein one exerts it, and the hardships one chearfully undergoes in serving the interests of one's fellows; the love of mankind must appear with an incomparably greater lustre in the character of the Apostles, than in that of *Socrates* (*b*).

I

(*b*) It should seem that Socrates might have saved his life, by submitting to a voluntary banishment. But, to leave a vagabond, and to be persecuted from town to town for the sake of his doctrines, this he could not endure the thoughts of. And therefore death before banishment is his choice; how useless soever and necessary he apprehended his instructions were to mankind. (Ἀλλὰ δὴ φυγῆς τιμήσομαι; ἴσως γὰρ ἄν μοι τύτυ τιμήσαιτε. πολλὴ μὲν τ᾿ ἄν με φιλοψυχία ἔχοι, ὦ ἄνδρες Ἀθηναῖοι, εἰ ὕτως ἀλόγιστός εἰμι, ὥςε μὴ δύνασθαι λογίζεσθαι ὅτι ὑμεῖς μὲν ὄντες πολῖται μυ, ἐχ ὅιοί τε ἐγένεσθαι ἐνεγκεῖν τὰς ἐμὰς διατριβὰς ᾗ τὺς λόγυς, ἀλλ᾿ ὑμῖν βαρύτεραι γεγόκασι ᾗ ἐπιφθονώτεραι, ὥςε ζητεῖτε αὐτῶν νυνὶ ἀπαλλαγῆναι. ἄλλοι δὲ ἄρα αὐτὰς οἴσυσι ῥᾳδίως. πολλῦ γε δεῖ, ὦ ἄνδρες Ἀθηναῖοι. καλὸς ὖν ἄν μοι ὁ βίος ἔιη, ἐξελθόντι τηλικῷδε ἀνθρώπῳ ἄλλην ἐξ ἄλλης πόλεως ἀμειβομένῳ ᾗ ἐξελαυνομένῳ ζῆν. εὖ γὰρ οἶδ᾿ ὅτι, ὅπη ἂν ἔλθω, λέγοντος ἐμῦ ἀκροάσονται οἱ νέοι, ὥσπερ ἐνθάδε. κἂν μὲν τύτυς ἀπελαύνω, ὗτοί με αὐτοὶ ἐξελῶσι, πείθοντες τὺς πρεσβυτέρυς· ἐὰν δὲ μὴ ἀπελαύνω, οἱ τύτων πατέρες τε ᾗ οἰκεῖοι, δι᾿ αὐτὺς τύτυς. Ἴσως ὖν ἄν τις εἴποι, σιγῶν τε ᾗ ἡσυχίαν ἄγωι, ὦ Σώκρατες, ἐχ οἷος τ᾿ ἔσῃ ἡμῖν ἐξελθὼν ζῆν; τυτὶ δή ἐςι πάντων χαλεπώτατον πεῖσαί τινας ὑμῶν, ἐάν τε γὰρ λέγω ὅτι τῷ θεῷ ἀπειθεῖν τῦτ᾿ ἐςι, ᾗ διὰ τῦτ᾿ ἀδύνατον ἡσυχίαν ἄγειν, ὖ πείσεσθέ μοι ὡς εἰρωνευομένῳ. ἐάν τ᾿ αὖθις λέγω ὅτι ᾗ τυγχάνει μέγιςον ἀγαθὸν ἀνθρώπῳ τῦτο, ἑκάςης ἡμέρας περὶ ἀρετῆς τὺς λόγυς ποιεῖσθαι, ᾗ τῶν ἄλλων περὶ ὧν ὑμεῖς ἐμῦ ἀκύετε διαλεγομένυ, ᾗ ἐμαυτὸν, ᾗ ἄλλυς ἐξετάζοντος, ὁ δὲ ἀνεξέταςος βίος ὖ βιωτὸς ἀνθρώπῳ,

ταῦτα

SECT. XVII.   *Chriſtian Revelation.*   229

I would therefore ſtill hope, if the Deiſts regard *Socrates* as a character extremely valuable, and at an infinite diſtance from all impoſture of any ſort, they will think freely and without prejudice, and entertain the ſame favourable ſentiments concerning the Apoſtles.

SECT. XVII.

It being apparent that the Apoſtles were no Impoſtors; if they were not really animated from Heaven, nothing remains, but that they muſt have been Enthuſiaſts.

BUT, however abſolutely free from all intrigue and impoſture the Apoſtles might in reaſon be held,

ταῦτα δ᾽ ἔτι ἧττον πείσεσθέ μοι λέγοντι. τὰ δὲ ἔχει μὲν ὕτως ὡς ἐγώ φημι, ὦ ἄνδρες, πείθειν δὲ ὐ ῥᾴδια. Plat. Apol. Socrat. p. 3. 7. C.) So that however Socrates, as the Apoſtles did, made it his firſt concern to promote the happineſs of his own countrymen or citizens: (Ταῦτα ἢ νεωτέρῳ ἢ πρεσβυτέρῳ, ὅτῳ ἂν ἐντυγχάνω, ποιήσω, ἢ ξένῳ ἢ ἀςῷ. μᾶλλον δὲ τοῖς ἀςοῖς, ὅσῳ μοι ἐγγυτέρῳ ἐςὲ γένει. ταῦτα γὰρ κελεύει ὁ Θεὸς, ἐυ ἴςε. ἢ ἐγὼ οἶμαι ὐδέν πω ἡμῖν μεῖζον ἀγαθὸν γενέσθαι ἐν τῇ πόλει ἢ τὴν ἐμὴν τῷ Θεῷ ὑπηρεσίαν. Id. ibid. p. 30. A.) Yet, upon their condemning his inſtructions, he was far from acting the generous part the Apoſtles did, who, being rejected by their countrymen the Jews, had the noble reſolution to turn to the Gentiles; and were not frightened from doing good to mankind of all nations, by the hardſhips and miſeries of a life of vagrancy and perſecution. Their brave magnanimous conduct is thus reported: " And the " next Sabbath-day came almoſt the whole city of Antioch toge-" ther to hear the word of God. But when the Jews ſaw the " multitudes, they were filled with envy, and ſpake againſt thoſe " things which were ſpoken by Paul, contradicting and blaſpheming.

held, yet from hence one cannot immediately conclude, that the inftitution of religion they eftablifhed in the world, is of divine original. It is poffible for men to be fincere and honeft, or to have no defign to impofe upon other people, and yet thofe very men may impofe upon themfelves, they may apprehend they have a commiffion from Heaven to inftruct mankind in fuch particular doctrines, and that a crown of glory is waiting them in another world as the reward of their miniftry; while in truth, there is nothing in all this but pure fancy and delufion: So that we muft next inquire, whether the Apoftles were not thus, mere unfortunate Enthufiafts. And indeed, I am apt to think, that whatever be the original caufe of people's infidelity, whether a proud felf-fufficiency, or a paffion for fingularity, or an averfion to the Clergy, or a ftrong prejudice againft the doctrines of the Gofpel;

One of the chief reafons whereby they would juftify their difbelief and contempt of the Chriftian inftitution, as an idle fancy they have taken up concerning the Apoftles, as if they were only a company of poor deluded creatures, going about the world under the power of enthufiafm, and indifcreetly expofing themfelves to all forts of miferies, without any commiffion from Heaven, to propagate the Gofpel, which was the only thing that involved them

---

" pheming. Then Paul and Barnabas waxed bold, and faid;
" It was neceffary that the word of God fhould firft have been
" fpoken to you: But feeing ye put it from you, and judge your-
" felves unworthy of everlafting life, Lo, we turn to the Gentiles.
" For fo hath the Lord commanded us, faying, I have fet
" thee to be a light of the Gentiles, that thou fhouldeft be for
" falvation unto the ends of the earth. And when the Gentiles
" heard this, they were glad, and glorified the word of the
" Lord." Acts xiii. 44.——48.

them in all their sufferings. This, I say, I vehemently suspect is the case of our unbelievers. And therefore, to remove all such groundless prejudices, and to open people's minds to the just character of the Apostles; that so the doctrines which they taught the world may be received according to their true importance and certainty, I shall, in the following Sections, directly inquire into the nature of enthusiasm, and endeavour to make it manifest, that the Apostles were in no sort governed by such a wild extravagant principle. And as the doing justice to this argument may oblige me to set the spirit of enthusiasm in a strong light; so I hope no sober man will take offence at what I may happen to say; or imagine I have encroached upon the regard that is due to serious godliness and religion. I can safely say, from my conscience, there is nothing farther from my thoughts and intention; and I should count myself deserving the highest censure, if I acted a part that brings along with it so much prejudice to the real interests of mankind, and which is so inconsistent with the Gospel of our blessed Saviour, which I here professedly undertake to defend.

In the mean time, since I have unanswerably cleared the Apostles from the charge of imposture, not only by the same arguments whereby our Deists go about to justify themselves, but by other arguments that appear to me incomparably stronger; and as upon this it follows of course, that the only way left whereby one can attempt to discredit the testimony of the Apostles, is to prove them mere Enthusiasts (which may seem to be the most probable imputation) I would presume to beg of our Gentlemen Freethinkers, that in the following branch of our argument, they would condescend to

go

go along with me, with that freedom of thought, wherein the mind, void of all biafs, clearly perceives the truth, and, be the confequences what they will, chearfully embraces it, as its greateft good, its beft and moft valuable enjoyment. And as I thus invite thofe Gentlemen to favour me with their unbiaffed attention; fo I promife them, they fhall find me *in meckne/s inftructing thofe that oppofe themfelves; if God peradventure will give them repentance to the acknowledging of the truth.* At any rate, I am in hopes I fhall put them to filence, or make them fenfible they have it not in their power to fhow the weaknefs or fallacy of my argument in vindication of the Apoftles, or to object any thing to the prejudice of their character. This indeed bears the face of a challange: I confefs it is. And as mankind are greatly delighted with the hiftory of the rife and advancement, the declenfion and fall, the revolutions of ftates and kingdoms, and all fuch events as affect public bodies and communities of men, I am confident, it would be highly gratifying to the world, if our Deifts would, after the fame manner, give us an impartial diftinct account of the rife, the progrefs, and the prevalency of the Chriftian inftitution over the religions of the *Roman* empire. The conduct, and the fuccefs of the Apoftles, a few obfcure illiterate men, their boldly attacking, and, in the event, their actually overthrowing all the religious inftitutions then prevailing in the known world; and, in place thereof, their eftablifhing a new fet of principles and doctrines, are *phænomena* in the moral world, the moft extraordinary that ever happened among mankind. A curious inquifitive mind would like to fee the fprings and caufes of fuch ftrange uncommon events, of fuch a wonderful revolution, clearly laid open

and

and explained. Hitherto our Deists have done nothing of this nature. They tell us in general, the Apostles were either knaves or visionaries. But what instruction or satisfaction can this afford to a thinking considerate mind? Neither the Impostor nor the enthusiasm of the Apostles are so very obvious, as not to need a particular explication. If therefore our Infidels will condescend to think, that the world about them have a title to be treated as reasonable beings, they must not dogmatise, they must reason, and by a fair rational deduction make us sensible, that the conduct and success of the Apostles, in relation to the Gospel of our Lord, are *phænomena*, very extraordinary events, that owe their existence, either to knavery or enthusiasm. For my part, having fully explained the particular grounds upon which I rest my confidence, and upon which I would persuade gainsayers, that the Apostles were no Impostors; I shall now proceed to the other branch of our argument, and in like manner explain the particular reasons, upon which I am well assured, and upon which, if I convert not Infidels, I am in hopes I I shall fully justify Christians in their belief, that the Apostles were no Enthusiasts. And if the Deists shall find that my arguments do not here conclude in a fair vindication of the Apostles, let them show their regard for truth, and their charity to mankind, in publishing to the world wherein I have failed in my reasoning. But this they must be left to do when they shall judge it convenient. I go on in the task I have undertaken: And in order to discharge it in the best manner I am able, in the manner that may prove most satisfying to the Reader, I shall begin with an impartial explanation of the nature and influence of enthusiasm.

SECT. XVIII.

Wherein the Nature and Influence of religious Enthusiasm are impartially explained.

ENTHUSIASM, in the proper meaning of the word, signifies *divine inspiration*. And of this there are two sorts: One common and ordinary, consisting in those influences from Heaven, that are necessary to form a really good man: And the other, uncommon, of an extraordinary and miraculous nature, importing those illuminations and impulses, which, upon some signal occasions, are imparted by the Divinity to those persons whom he is pleased to employ in the execution of some particular design.

As to the *first*, people in all ages have confessed the truth of it: The Heathen, in many instances, seem to acknowledge it: And every man who understands the Gospel, must certainly know, that it is an undoubted article of the Christian faith. Nor in some cases have mankind been backward in admitting the latter: 'Tis particularly after this manner that Christians contend, the Gospel was at first revealed and propagated in the world.

I willingly confess, that people's pretensions to supernatural illuminations and impulses, have not always been well founded. Not to speak of designed trick and imposture, from which I have justified the Apostles; a man, merely by the strength of pure fancy and imagination, may come to conceit himself thus wonderfully animated: Which, with us, in common language, is called *enthusiasm*. And indeed, in some circumstances, a religious contemplative mind seems to be in great hazard

hazard of deviating into such flattering deceitful apprehensions. Thus, if we consider the natural influence of things over intelligent minds,

So immensely glorious is the nature and perfections of God, that a mind engaged in the devout contemplation of those sublime objects, cannot miss being sensible of the warmest and most ravishing emotions. These indeed are powerful encouragements to indulge ourselves in those exalted meditations, which, rightly managed, would raise an ambition, that would effectually employ us in forming ourselves, as we are capable, upon those divine excellencies that are the objects of our love and admiration. But a human soul, when under any sort of devout raptures, being very apt to be exceedingly elated, and from its inward extasies of joy, to draw conclusions very much to its own advantange, wherein it conceits itself high seated in the peculiar favour and esteem of God; one cannot but apprehend, that in such circumstances, either a luxuriant and wanton fancy, or a gloomy and melancholy imagination, may come to expose a man to very extravagant or very dangerous mistakes. For the mind, in its devout raptures, receiving the flattery of the proud or sullen fancy, as if it were now a mighty favourite of Heaven; and not being duly balanced by a just understanding of the nature of things, is thereby deluded into a vain opinion, that these manifestations it thinks it has of the nature and excellencies of God, are supernaturally communicated to its thoughts; and those inward ravishments it feels upon such pretended revelations, are divine joys poured in upon it by the immediate hand of God himself. And certain it is, when people suffer themselves, in the fervours of their devotion, to be carried away by the extravagant conceits

ceits of an over-heated imagination, greatly supported by the mechanism of the body; there is nothing in the world which they may not work themselves to believe is supernaturally revealed and impressed upon them by the divine Spirit. Nay, such people, amidst their extraordinary emotions, having their thoughts, as they imagine, full of God; and in the mighty warmth and elevation of their spirits, fancying themselves admitted to an immediate intercourse with the Divinity; whatever may then chance suddenly to strike their imagination, provided it suits their humour, and goes along with the commanding bias of their mind, the flattering thought will prevail, it is darted in upon them immediately from Heaven.

With great care, therefore, ought the religious contemplative person to keep a strict watch over all the emotions of his soul, lest, in the heat of his devotion, he should be transported beyond the bounds of reason and religion, and fall under the delusive suggestions, or the wild ravings, of a proud, sullen, irregular fancy, whereby people are in great danger of becoming visionary to the utmost degree of extravagance, in all things whatsoever, whether they concern present opinion and practice, or future events.

I am far from denying but that God may, and has manifested himself to some people in a miraculous and extraordinary manner, that has affected them with very warm and sensible emotions. But, I must beg leave to say, where there is one that has enjoyed this uncommon privilege in reality, there are thousands who have had it only in mere pretence, conceit and delusion. And this pretending, or extravagant conceit of being peculiarly blessed with such supernatural communications from Heaven,

Heaven, makes up the very life and foul of enthusiasm. So that

An Enthusiast is one, who, in the course of his devotion, keeps not within the compass of reason and religion, but having given up himself to the power and influence of an over-heated fancy, is mechanically wrought up into such extraordinary heats and fervours, that he verily believes he is immediately under the benign emanations of Heaven, and has divine revelations made to him; whilst there is nothing really in his case, but pure mechanism and strong imagination.

Upon which I shall observe, there are two things that are essential to this character, and in which the enthusiasm particularly consists:

First, The imagination being greatly chafed and heated, and therefore raising in the machine an high tide of animal spirits; there are thence some inward emotions or fervours of soul, which feeling very warm and extraordinary, (while the mind under an apprehension of the divine presence, in which it conceives itself immediately placed, is agreeably filled with a kind of solemn gloomy awe and reverence,) are passionately regarded as divine joys and endearing emanations flowing down directly from God himself.

Secondly, The mind, in so melting a frame, as it is now under, being very soft and tender, and the things themselves that are the subject-matter of its devotion, and for which it hopes God will declare himself, being such as fall in with its prevailing temper, or some or other of its favourite notions, the impressions it receives with respect to those things, must necessarily prove deep and strong; and these strong impressions being at the same time accompanied with what is fondly thought to be su-

pernatural

pernatural joys and raptures, the extravagant conceit prevails; that those very things, which amidst such heavenly raptures, are thus warmly impressed, have certainly the immediate approbation and countenance of God. For,

'Tis to be remarked, that those inward heats and fervours, which are sensibly felt by devout melancholy minds, the common temper of Enthusiasts, are always imagined to be the great seals of Heaven put upon those notions, whether of a speculative, or practical, or prophetic nature, that have come to settle strongly on their fancies, whereby it is expressly declared, they are of divine original, and are justified and supported by the authority of God. And thus it happens, that as those heats and fervours do not always rise to the same height, or continue of an equal force or degree, but ebb and flow according to the various turns of a man's constitution and temper, or his outward circumstances in the world; so it is in proportion to their influence, and the strength of the impressions of those things about which his devotion happens to be employed, that an Enthusiast fancies himself more or less countenanced and inspired from above.

Now, in those two particulars, we have, in my apprehension, a just enough view of the nature of enthusiasm. And let it be observed, that a man may be thus visionary, not only in those things which in themselves are absurd and wicked, but in such likewise as in their own nature are indifferent, and even in the most undoubted truths of religion. This indeed must always happen, just according to the turns of a man's irregular imagination, which may sometimes chance to fix on proper or lawful objects, and at other times prove out of measure extravagant. And whatever be the object, true or false,

false, good or bad, which an Enthusiast may take into his devout contemplations, or upon which he may address himself to the throne of grace, the warm way in which he performs his spiritual exercises, will soon heat the imagination, and raise in the mind those fervours which such people never fail to regard as divine heavenly influences. And this, I say, is reckoned to put a stamp of divinity upon whatever the mind is devoutly fixed on.

But what I would lead the reader particularly to consider, is, that as enthusiasm can have no bounds set to it, and its only measure is the extravagance of fancy; so people, in the power of this melancholly distemper, may come to imagine they are illuminated from Heaven, when they figure to themselves the wildest and most extravagant absurdities, which, the more absurd and extravagant they are, may, in their conceit, have the better title to divinity, or immediate revelation: And by what is counted a divine impulse, or a call from God, may zealously destroy all the peace and order of the world, and commit the greatest outrages and barbarities; not only in defence of their own wild imaginations, but in pursuing those things which they want to have established, and which, in their own nature, may be good or indifferent. And all this seems really unavoidable in the case of those persons, in whom an enthusiastic spirit happens to prevail. For

Such high pretenders having given up themselves to their own fancy and imagination, without any fixed principles that can bound them; and being accustomed to feel some very warm emotions in their minds, which are always apprehended to come immediately from Heaven, and which they always regard as symbols of the divine presence, endearing tokens of his peculiar love and favour towards them;
they

they cannot but entertain an extravagant conceit of their own worth and excellency, as if they were the beloved, the peculiar people of God, to whom he hath revealed himself in so extraordinary a manner. And thus viewing themselves in high favour with the Deity, from which, they believe, the rest of mankind are excluded; it being very natural for the mind of man to be ever fond of those things that flatter his sullen pride and vanity, especially in such instances, as raise him above the common rank of mortals; hence those visionaries have their minds always turned, in their gloomy manner, to contemplate God and heavenly things, and particularly the high station, to which, they vainly think, they are exalted in the divine grace and favour. And with this sullen frame of devotion, which is continually hanging about them, do they spiritualize and sanctify all things whatsoever, even the greatest absurdities and the blackest villanies, according as they happen to suit their particular temper and circumstances.

For those conceited people being so far from submitting themselves to the government of reason, that they look upon this *dim light*, as they are pleased to call it, and all its fixed principles, and every stated rule whatsoever, especially such as are of human authority, to be fit only for common servile souls, and much below the notice of those who have immediate access to the fountain of all light, and who distinctly perceive all the measures of their behaviour in supernatural revelations; whenever any growing imagination or passion is like to settle upon their minds, which they have a strong inclination to indulge and pursue, they do not consult and hearken to the dictates of reason, but they take a more easy and compendious, and as they judge,

a

a more honourable method; abusing the language of men truly godly, and profaning the highest privilege mortals can enjoy, and without which mankind would be miserable; they go to God with it, and lay the matter before the Lord, as they are used to speak, and in their familiar and devout manner, implore his light and direction, and loudly call for an answer. Now, in their opinion, a favourable answer of prayer (and they will have no other concerning those things they are fond of) consists in divine joys and raptures that seize upon the soul, and make it sensible of the immediate presence and countenance of God. So that till they find something of this nature springing up within them, and warming and agitating their breasts, they have received no return from Heaven; and therefore do they still insist, and, with great importunity, labour hard, till they wrestle themselves into those mechanical heats and emotions which they take for a gracious return to their fervent supplications, and as a full approbation from God, in reference to those things about which they were consulting the throne of grace: Whereupon their minds are at ease, and they make no doubt but they have the authority of Heaven to indulge their absurd imaginations, or to pursue and gratify their villanous passions. And what is able to check them in the course of their enthusiastic madness?

Such fanciful people being preferred, as they imagine, to such close communion, and near intimacy with God, that they verily believe (not from a participation of the divine nature, but from strong conceit and delusion) they are his darling sons or daughters; one can apprehend nothing sufficient to restrain them from maintaining or pursuing any notion or action, how wild or wicked soever, to which they may have conceived a strong inclination. For God, certainly, in their apprehension, will not condemn any sort of grateful enjoyments, which his *dear children*, to whom he is always indulging such heavenly communications, have a hearty and passionate liking for, and without which they could not live any way comfortably. No:——This would make them look but very little in the esteem and favour of Heaven, and represent God without that tender love and concern for them, which, in their own most undoubted experience, they are well assured he indulgently bears them. And for their part, they are very conscious to themselves, that nothing is able to abate, far less extinguish their holy zeal, their melting affections towards God: For whatever way they are employed, they are still in a religious mood, in a devout and spiritual frame, and are always full of heavenly contemplations. So that, I say, the mutual love and friendship which those people have the impious presumption to think, is established between God and them, still going on, without any interruption, and probably increasing to higher degrees of fervour and intimacy, whilst they are gratfying their worldly passions and carnal appetites; what is it that can withold them from giving a loose to their wild notions, to all their most vitious and mischievous lusts and inclinations? Nothing, sure, can extinguish that light, or overbear that impulse which they firmly believe to be communicated to their minds immediately from Heaven. And how amazingly head-strong and vigorous must a man necessarily prove, when his favourite opinions and commanding passions, are all strongly supported by a supernatural light, and a divine impulse! It is impossible but he must exert himself with the most furious zeal imaginable, when all his powers

are

are awakened, and put upon the stretch, by a lively sense, that therein he is fortified and directed by the immediate hand of God himself.

And does not the character, which the sullen pride of those gloomy visionaries chuse to bestow on the rest of mankind, give us to understand, with what peace and quiet of conscience they will invade and usurp upon the just rights and liberties of other people, and reduce the sober part of their species to ruin and misery! On the crazy imagination of men of their distemper, we are all painted as miscreants, infidels, reprobates, and I know not what,——*as dogs that devour the children's bread.* And having it in their power, will they fail to acquire the merit of doing justice upon the enemies God, of asserting the liberties of his people and children, and of recovering those rights which they have from their heavenly Father, by casting out the wicked of the world, (all the human race except themselves) from those comfortable possessions which belong to their betters? Most certainly, when people fall into the merciful hands of Enthusiasts, if they escape being cruelly butchered, they shall have oppression and slavery for their portion. Nor must we neglect to mention one principle in particular, that seems to prevail among those poor deluded creatures, whereby the whole of reason and religion is intirely overthrown, I mean this most impious opinion, namely, *the goodness of the end* (which in their case, without doubt, is never but simply and purely the glory of God) *sanctifies all the means,* be they what they will, *that lead to it.* Nay, as I have before hinted, by the fervency of their prayers, they are capable of putting a stamp of divinity on end and means, on every thing.

I

I confess, however, every Enthusiast is not quite so abandoned as to be capable of committing any piece of villany whatever. This happens according to the particular constitutions and tempers of such people; whereof some, for instance, may be naturally fierce and barbarous, and others humane and merciful; some lascivious and sensual, and others chaste and temperate; some ambitious and covetous, and others not obnoxious to these worldly passions. So that very possibly there may be persons of this character, who so far retain such just notions of the Deity, and of the authority of his laws, as rather to hate and detest every gross enormity. But as I have above explained the natural tendency of enthusiasm; so what I have observed proves but too true in experience: And when it happens otherwise, it is their natural tempers, or their outward worldly circumstances, and not their principles, which restrain them.

Nevetheless, I think, I may venture to say, without breach of charity, there are not many of them who scruple to allow themselves, in their own little tricks and knaveries, that are all swallowed up in the depths of their devotion, or that, like the spots of the sun, are not discernible to their own eyes, for the brightness that surrounds them. And one thing is certain, they are all, without exception, so excessively puffed up and self-conceited, that they set an inestimable value on themselves, and entertain a mean contemptible opinion of all other mortals: By which means, their minds are so miserably contracted, that they are notorious offenders against the divine law of universal love and charity; and are so far from allowing to other people, the free use and government of their own sense and reason, that they would have the whole world to be
under

under their discipline, to submit to their dictates, and to copy after them in all points whatsoever: And this they will always attempt, as the strength of their enthusiasm may happen to prompt them, or as they may chance to be encouraged from the circumstances of the world about them. In their general character, they put me much in mind of these lines of the Poet,

Asperitas agrestis, et inconcinna, gravisque,
Quæ se commendat tonsa cute, dentibus atris;
Dum vult libertas mera dici, veraque virtus.
——————— scilicet ut non
Sit mihi prima fides, et vere quod placet, ut non
Acriter elatrem, prætium ætas altera sordet (c).

Upon the whole, let the reader reflect, whether he can judge it possible for Enthusiasts, in framing their own lives, to pursue, in all instances, a manly regular course of social behaviour; and, for the conduct of other people, to propose to the world, in every article, a just rational scheme of religion and virtue.

SECT. XIX.

Explaining some Particulars, on which the Truth and Force of the Argument seem to depend.

IN the preceeding Section I have endeavoured to lay open the true nature and real tendency of enthusiasm, without setting it in a false light, for the sake of my present argument. And, from what I have said, because they will be of use to us in the course of our reasoning, I shall make these three observations; and as to the justness of them, I desire
the

(c) Hor. Epist. 18. ver. 6. 16. lib. 1.

the Reader may be pleafed to fatisfy himfelf, before he enters upon the following Sections:

I. As I here only fpeak of religious Enthufiafts, it may be obferved: In whatever a man happens to be vifionary, that certainly muft have been the fubject-matter of his devotion: wherein having overftrained his paffions, and inflamed them into mechanical heats and fervours; thefe fervours feeling very warm and extraordinary, he verily believes they are fupernatural.

II. It is impoffible that a man, with refpect to thofe things againft which he is is violently prepoffeffed, can become an Enthufiaft all of the fudden. For,

As enthufiafm muft always terminate or be converfant in thofe matters, to which people ftand well difpofed, or toward which they have an inward biafs and propenfion, and even fuch things muft have been for fome time entertained with good liking and approbation; fo it is only after they have conceived a ftrong propenfion towards them, that their devotion, in fuch inftances, begins to be warm and elevated, fo as to fcrew them up to thofe mechanical fervours, that are accounted fupernatural communications. Indeed, when a man's fancy is very much heated, fome fudden things may ftart in upon him, and ftrike him very furprizingly as unexpected revelations: But as this manifeftly implies, that his enthufiafm did not begin upon thofe objects, (for it is amidft his enthufiaftic fervours he receives them) fo, unlefs they correfpond with his prevailing opinions and paffions, certain it is, he never will entertain them as divine truths or impreffions. Hitherto, with a fettled indignation, he has been accuftomed to reject them as quite contradictory to his eftablifh-ed notions of things, and wholly deftructive of all thofe principles, of the certainty whereof he has
been,

been, after a very fenfible manner, fupernaturally convinced and illuminated.: How then is it poffible that fuch objects can appear to him in any other light, than in that wherein heretofore he never but beheld them? And regarding them in that light, muft not the fixed and unalterable averfion he bears to them, and the heavenly fervours he is now under, when fuch fudden fuggeftions, fo repugnant to all his inward feelings and fentiments, are darted in upon him, ferve as a demonftration, that God immediately from heaven exprefsly commands him to abhor and reject them, as the fuggeftions or temptations of *Satan.*

And fince a man, already an Enthufiaft, can never, in thofe particulars againft which he is violently prepoffeffed, become on a fudden purely vifionary, it may well be judged altogether impoffible for a man to begin his enthufiafm all of a fudden, in apprehending thofe things as undoubtedly true and highly eligible, declared to be fo, and as fuch impreffed upon him by the Divinity himfelf; which very things, to that moment, in his cool and fober thoughts, he had all along condemned as mere falfhood, and againft which he had all along entertained the ftrongeft and moft inveterate prejudices. Such a fudden turn, all at once, to enthufiafm of any degree, not to fpeak of what is furious and violent, plainly implies a total fudden change of a man's fixed fentiments, and an utter fudden extirpation of all his ftubborn prejudices; events abfolutely repugnant to the nature of things.

III. Every Enthufiaft being, more or lefs, under the influence of mere fancy or a diftempered brain, muft, of courfe, in fome article or other, be found to act contrary to the plain dictates of reafon. And very manifeftly, if the enthufiafm fhall rife to fo high

high a pitch, as, in spite of all oppositions and dangers, violently to push him on to propagate his doctrines, and establish his principles upon the ruins of whatever may happen to contradict him; it is impossible but he must become notoriously guilty of many contradictions to the fixed principles of natural religion. For,

Here, certainly, so strongly agitated, and so exceeding warm and furious is a man's imagination, that, under such violent commotions and excessive heats of fancy, he will not be able to restrain himself, but must be hurried away into many open absurdities, into many wild extravagances in opinion, or practice, that will appear utterly inconsistent with the impartial reason of all mankind.

Having observed thus much concerning the spirit of enthusiasm; before I go on to consider the case of the Apostles, I will use the freedom to make this proposition, which, I am well persuaded, every honest man, every sincere lover of truth, will judge highly reasonable, and very readily comply with.

As these matters of fact, *namely*, the death, the resurrection, and ascension of *Jesus Christ*, upon the certainty whereof the truth of the Christian revelation depends, are events, neither in the nature of things impossible, nor of themselves, or, in their design and tendency, unworthy the perfections of God to be immediately concerned in them; a circumstance particularly to be regarded, and, in the whole of this argument, every where obvious: And as in my endeavouring to shew, that in the belief of these articles, or in their publishing them to the world, the Apostles were no Enthusiasts, I all along give the reasons that determine me to this opinion, so I take it to be a plain dictate of common sense, that whoever thinks otherwise, if he means

to

to promote truth among mankind, ought to produce those particular reasons whereby he came to form his judgment, that the Apostles, in such and such instances, were Enthusiasts. It is an easy matter for a fool or idiot, any the silliest creature upon earth, to make suppositions in general, and to say at random, *it may be*, or, *it might have been so and so*: But a wise man not only satisfies his own mind from the evidence of the things themselves, as far as their nature will permit him; but is willing and capable to communicate to the world those particular grounds upon which he builds his faith or opinions.

When, therefore, in any one instance wherein I endeavour to show the Apostles were no Enthusiasts, another person happens to think otherwise, I hope he will not impose upon himself by confused fancy and supposition, but stop a while, and have the courage to look into his own breast, and impartially examine what distinct particular reasons have there prevailed with him, and determined him to that fancy or supposition, wherein he differs from what I here lay before him, as supported by such and such rational considerations. This, I would fain think, is but fair dealing, common justice and equity, and ought religiously to be observed in all points of controversy whatsoever. As for example, I give my reasons why I am well assured, that, with respect to the article of the ascension, the Apostle were no Enthusiasts; and yet one may represent to himself these very men under a thousand images, wherein they will appear to him very delirious, actuated by strong fancy and delusion, that made them see visions in the air. But by what good reason am I able to justify my having conceived such an opinion of the Apostles? I consult

sult my own mind, I consider the nature and relations of things, and, I confess, I find no good reason to support me in such an imagination; so that to persist in it, would deservedly expose me to be counted full as visionary, as any man in this article can reckon the Apostles (*a*). Thus far having laid down and explained the Preliminaries I judged necessary;

SECT. XX.

The Apostles are not liable to the Charge of Enthusiasm, neither from their social Conduct, nor from their Opinions concerning the Deity and natural Religion.

I Shall now fairly examine whether, in any instance, the Apostles can reasonably be charged with Enthusiasm. And, to bring this important question within a narrow compass, and, at the same time, to handle it with some precision and distinctness, I shall here observe, there are two things in the case of the Apostles, which we must particularly consider; namely,

Their conduct and behaviour in the world, or those dispositions which, in their course of life, they expressed towards others. And then,

Those doctrines which they taught the world, 1*st*, Concerning the nature and attributes of God, and what regards natural religion: And, 2*dly*, Concerning *Jesus Christ*.

And,

(*a*) Hoc ego Philosophi non esse arbitror, testibus uti; qui aut casu veri, aut malitia falsi fictique esse possunt. Argumentis et rationibus oportet, quare quidque ita sit, docere. Cic. de Divin. lib. 2. cap. 11.

And, in one or other, or rather in all these, had the Apostles been at all actuated by such an extravagant principle, must they not have given us some plain and undeniable proofs of their Enthusiasm?

As to their conduct and behaviour in the world: After what I have explained in considering the former article of Imposture, I need here say but little upon this head. I suppose no man will seriously maintain, that they were engaged in the pursuit of any sensual or worldly passion, or that in any part of their conduct they trespassed upon the rules of universal justice and righteousness. Their appeal is certainly well founded, and it can be counted no bold presumption in them, when they call upon God and the world to witness, in all instances, the integrity of their hearts, and the unblameableness of their lives. And, indeed, the most piercing eye is able to discern, in their temper and behaviour, none of the disorders of an extravagant fancy; nothing of a clownish rusticity, or of a sullen gloom and melancholy; no instance of an imperious pride that cannot bear a contradiction; or any the least symptom of an imposing and persecuting spirit; which are all qualities inseparable from Enthusiasts, such especially as the Apostles, had they been in the power of this distemper, must have been. On the contrary, excepting some infirmities not altogether to be avoided in this state of imperfection, the whole of their deportment is an ornament to human nature, and brings them the character of great and good men. In all their several relations and capacities, they acquit themselves with honour, and discharge all the demands of sober sense and unbiassed reason. Thus there is a steady composure of mind, and a constant uniformity of of action, that shine forth in their zealous pursuit of their glorious enterprize: In their duty and devotion towards God, they always exert a regular manly elevation of soul: And in their behaviour towards their fellows, they never but exert all the feelings and sentiments of humanity; not only are they religiously just and honest, but they are kind and beneficent, courteous, meek and gentle, they are peaceable, compassionate, patient and forgiving. In a word, the Apostles are men of the most heavenly affections, of the most social and chearful, the sweetest, and the most obliging dispositions: And, in their endeavours to reform mankind, far from oppressing people's consciences, having set before them their duty in the clearest and most advantageous light, wherein they employ the finest address and insinuation (that would make us rather suspect them of what they are absolutely free from, cunning and imposture) they leave every man to his own choice, and to answer for his conduct in another world, without pretending to save men's souls by torturing their bodies.

I confess, the Apostles, particularly St. *Paul*, do value themselves highly on their character and office, and on some peculiar advantages that had fallen to their lot. And, in this, all the world must own, their judgment was governed by the nature of things: Without undervaluing other people, or expressing any neglect or contempt of them, they only do justice to themselves, in order to promote the great interests of mankind. Thus likewise *Socrates*, without exposing his character to any sort of exception, was full and large in his own commendation (*a*). So that there is nothing here that can make us suspect them of enthusiasm.

And

(*a*) Socrates introduces his self-commendation, and begs the
indulgence

Sect. XX. *Christian Revelation.* 253

And as to those doctrines which they taught the world,

of his Judges, much after the same manner with the Apostle in one of his Epistles to the Corinthians. Only the life and spirit, the handsome address of St. Paul seems to me incomparable.

Καὶ ἴσως μὲν δόξω τισὶν ὑμῶν παίζειν, εὖ μέντοι ἴστε, πᾶσαν ὑμῖν τὴν ἀλήθειαν ἐρῶ.——— κ̀ μοι, ὦ ἄνδρες Ἀθηναῖοι, μὴ θορυβήσητε μηδὲν, ἂν δόξω τι ὑμῖν μέγα λέγειν.——— τῆς γὰρ ἐμῆς, εἰ δή τις ἐςὶ σοφία κ̀ οἵα, μάρτυρα ὑμῖν παρέξομαι τὸν θεὸν τὸν ἐν Δελφοῖς.———— τί ἐν εἰμι ἄξιος παθεῖν τοιοῦτος ὤν; ἀγαθόν τι, ὦ ἄνδρες Ἀθηναῖοι, εἰ δή γε κατὰ τὴν ἀξίαν τῇ ἀληθείᾳ τιμᾶσθε· κ̀ ταῦτά γε, ἀγαθὸν τοιοῦτον ὅ, τι ἂν πρέποι ἐμοί. τί ἐν πρέπει ἀνδρὶ πένητι εὐεργέτῃ, δεομένῳ ἄγειν σχολὴν ἐπὶ τῇ ὑμετέρᾳ παρακελεύσει; ὐκ ἐσθ' ὅ, τι μᾶλλον, ὦ ἄνδρες Ἀθηναῖοι, πρέπει ὕτως, ὡς τὸν τοιοῦτον ἄνδρα ἐν Πρυτανείῳ σιτεῖσθαι.——— ἴσως ἂν ἄν τις εἴποι, σιγῶν τε κ̀ ἡσυχίαν ἄγων, ὦ Σώκρατες, ὐχ οἷος τ᾽ ἔσῃ ἡμῖν ἐξελθὼν ζῆν; τοτὶ δή ἐςι πάντων χαλεπώτατον πεῖσαί τινας ὑμῶν. ἐάν τε γὰρ λέγω ὅτι τῷ θεῷ ἀπειθεῖν τοῦτ᾽ ἐςὶ, κ̀ διὰ τοῦτ᾽ ἀδύνατον ἡσυχίαν ἄγειν, ὐ πείσεσθέ μοι ὡς εἰρωνευομένῳ. Plat. Apol. Socrat. p. 20. D. E. p. 36. D. p. 37. E.

Ὄφελον ἠνείχεσθέ μου μικρόν τι τῆς ἀφροσύνης, ἀλλὰ κ̀ ἀνέχεσθέ μου· ζηλῶ γὰρ ὑμᾶς Θεοῦ ζήλῳ.——— ἢ ἁμαρτίαν ἐποίησα ἐμαυτὸν ταπεινῶν ἵνα ὑμεῖς ὑψωθῆτε; ὅτι δωρεὰν τὸ τοῦ Θεοῦ εὐαγγέλιον εὐηγγελισάμην ὑμῖν; ——— πάλιν λέγω, μή τις με δόξῃ ἄφρονα εἶναι· εἰ δὲ μή γε, κἂν ὡς ἄφρονα δέξασθέ με, ἵνα μικρόν τι κἀγὼ καυχήσωμαι.——— οἶδα ἄνθρωπον ——— ὅτι ἡρπάγη εἰς τὸν παράδεισον.——— ὑπὲρ τοῦ τοιούτου καυχήσομαι· ὑπὲρ δὲ ἐμαυτοῦ ὐ καυχήσομαι, εἰ μὴ ἐν ταῖς ἀσθενείαις μου. ἐὰν γὰρ θελήσω καυχήσασθαι, ὐκ ἔσομαι ἄφρων· ἀλήθειαν γὰρ ἐρῶ.——— γέγονα ἄφρων καυχώμενος· ὑμεῖς με ἠναγκάσατε· ἐγὼ γὰρ ὤφελον ὑφ᾽ ὑμῶν συνίστασθαι· ὐδὲν γὰρ ὑστέρησα τῶν ὑπὲρ λίαν Ἀποστόλων, εἰ κ̀ ὐδέν εἰμι.——— τί γάρ ἐστιν ὃ ἡττήθητε ὑπὲρ τὰς λοιπὰς ἐκκλησίας, εἰ μὴ ὅτι αὐτὸς ἐγὼ ὐ κατενάρκησα ὑμῶν; χαρίσασθέ μοι τὴν ἀδικίαν ταύτην. 2 Cor. xi. 1. 2. 7. 16. xii 3.—6. 11. 13. Through the whole of this Apology, there is the genteelest wit, the finest address possible, of which no Enthusiast can be capable.

world, concerning the nature and excellencies of God, and what regards natural religion ; therein the Apostles open a new scene of things unknown before to the Heathen world, and in all their sentiments and reasoning, they are clear, regular, and sober, without the darkness, the perplexity, and extravagance of Enthusiasts. They renounce not only the false, immoral gods of the Poets, but those other imaginary deities ignorantly maintained by Philosophers, and they declare for the existence only of one God, the first Cause of all things, the sole Author of all being, life, and happiness. They clearly explain the perfections of this infinite Mind, so far as that knowledge is necessary to exalt human nature, or to promote the moral happiness of mankind: And every thinking Deist will confess, that their accounts approve themselves to the purest informations of reason. They not only teach us a general Providence upholding and governing the universe, superintending every particular system, and looking after every kingdom and every nation; but they beautifully describe a particular Providence, taking care of every individual of the human species, and concerning itself with the meanest creature, every thing existing, so that *the very hairs of our head are all numbered.* Thus it is, that in their accounts of the only true God and his Providence, a Being, according to them, of almighty power exerted in the production, the formation, and government of the world, according to the measures of infinite wisdom and goodness ; the Apostles do infinitely surpass all the learning of the Heathen world. And no less do they go beyond the greatest height of their philosophy, in their doctrines concerning a future state.

Upon

Upon this article, they express no hesitation or uncertainty, no contradictory sentiments, but are always firm and positive, always consistent and uniform. Nor do they take up with those representations of another world, that are given out by Poets and Philosophers. The future entertainments they set to view and propose to mankind, are worthy of God to bestow, and of rational minds to enjoy; they are such whose prospect necessarily tends to prevent the baseness and degeneracy, and to advance the refinement and perfection of human na- man nature. *To them, who by patient continuance in well-doing, seek for glory, and honour, and immortality;* to them *eternal life,* in those divine enjoyments, shall be awarded. *But unto them that are contentious, and do not obey the truth, but obey unrighteousness; indignation and wrath.* For *tribulation and anguish* will seize *upon every soul of man that doeth evil, of the* Jew *first, and also of the Gentile: But glory, honour, and peace* is a sure inheritance *to every man that worketh righteousness; to the* Jew *first; and also to the Gentile; for there is no respect of persons with God* (*b*). And as the Apostles do thus afford us the clearest and most rational account possible, of these two fundamental articles of natural religion, the being of God, and a future state of rewards and punishments;

So they prescribe to us a system of laws, exactly calculated to promote the glory of the great Head of the rational society, to establish order in the world, and to carry on the happiness of human nature, of personal and social life, in all instances, in every stage of existence. Such is the nature of those laws, that putting our hearts and lives under their

(*b*) Rom. ii. 7.—11.

their influence, we escape the pollutions of this world, every moral turpitude and deformity; our minds are embellished with the image of God; we become partakers of the divine nature; and here in our external actions proving the instruments of good, mutual comforts and blessings to one another, with those graces and virtues upon our souls, at the end of our Christian course, we are taken up to the beatific vision of God, in the society of an innumerable company of other happy and glorious spirits, to eternity. Nor to these purposes is the finest understanding, the purest reason, able to conceive any system of things better adapted. So that,

In the doctrines of the Gospel, the Apostles deliver the world from all idolatry and superstition, and establish among mankind *that wisdom or philosophy that is from above, which is first pure, then peaceable, gentle, easy to be intreated, full of mercy and good fruits, without partiality, and without hypocrisy. It is pure religion, and undefiled before God and the Father* (c). And this religion, which consists in the love of God, and the love of mankind, in all goodness, righteousness, and truth; of such consequence do the Apostles reckon it to the happiness of human minds, that they always represent it as indispensably necessary, in order to our being admitted into the heavenly mansions. *Though I speak,* says the Apostle, *with the tongues of men and Angels, and have not charity, I am become as sounding brass, or a tinkling cymbal. And though I have the gift of prophesy, and understand all mysteries, and all knowledge; and have not charity, I am nothing. And though I bestow all my goods to feed the poor; and though I give my body to be burned* in the cause of religion, *and have not charity,*

(c) Jam. iii. 17. i. 27.

SECT. XX. *Christian Revelation.* 257

rity; it profiteth me nothing. Charity suffereth long, and is kind, &c (*d*). How free and noble the sentiments! All this will appear manifest to every man who looks into the writings of the Apostles. And in all this do they not discover a penetration of mind, and an extent of judgment, far beyond what the learned world ever knew before, and absolutely incompatible with the visionary brain of an Enthusiast?

At the same time, how much soever the Apostles themselves are persuaded of the truth and importance of those instructions which they delivered to mankind, yet they do not pretend to impose them in the way of mere authority, or refuse to submit them to a fair and impartial examination. They consider men as reasonable creatures, and that religion does not consist in bodily motions or verbal professions, but in the sentiments and actions of the heart, arising from an inward conviction of mind; and cannot therefore enter into the human soul, but in the way of reason and argument. Hence it is, that the Apostles highly commend the *Jews* of *Berea*, and have left upon their memory a fine reputation, in recording, that *These were more noble than those in* Thessalonica, *in that they received the Word with all the readiness of mind, and searched the Scriptures daily, whether those things were so* (*e*). In short, so far were the Apostles from requiring implicit faith or blind obedience, that they command people *to prove all things, and to hold fast that which is good* (*f*): Without which, there is no observing of this other rule, wherein they enjoin their Disciples, *to be ready always to give an account to every man that asketh them a reason of the hope that is in*

VOL. II. K k *them,*

(*d*) 1 Cor. xiii. 1.—13. (*e*) Act. xvii. 11.
(*f*) 1 Thess. v. 21.

them, with meekness and fear (g), void of all intemperate heat and unbecoming treatment, which always disoblige, but never convince the gainsayers; while modesty and a respectful carriage are wonderfully engaging.

And as the Apostles encourage a rational inquiry, submitting their doctrines to a free examination; so, in the case of different opinions, either totally or in part, they conceive no angry or revengeful passions, they are heated with no spirit of persecution, an inhuman ungodly temper, contradictory to the whole evangelical institution; but they leave every man to the judgment of God (h). This is their doctrine, full of good sense and humanity: *It is the Lord that judgeth. Therefore judge nothing before the time, until the Lord come, who both will bring to light the hidden things of darkness, and will make manifest the councils of the hearts: And then shall every man have praise of God* (i). *We then, say they, that are strong, ought to bear the infirmities of the weak, and not to please ourselves. Let every one of us please his neighbour for his good to edification* (k). *For the Son of man came not to destroy men's lives, but to save them* (l).

Thus, in the doctrines of the Apostles concerning natural religion, and in the whole of their conduct, there is a nobleness of mind, with an intire command of thought; there is a clearness and extent of judgment, a purity and rectitude of manners, of which no Enthusiast was ever capable, and that cannot be equalled among mankind. And since the Apostles, thus far, were men of sound and sober heads, of composed and regular affections, and always expressed a strong, masculine piety and virtue,

---

(g) 1 Pet. iii. 15. (h) 1 Cor. v. 12, 13. Rom. xiv.
(i) 1 Cor. iv. 5. (k) Rom. xv. 1, 2. (l) Luke ix. 56.

tue, one cannot but conceive, that hitherto they are wholly free of this melancholy distemper. So that we shall proceed in our inquiry, and examine, whether any symptoms of it can be discerned in what informations they afford the world concerning their *Messiah*.

SECT. XXI.

What was taught by the Apostles in Relation to the Person and Kingdom of Jesus Christ, *can, in no Degree, expose them to the Charge of Enthusiasm.*

AND the Apostles, in the whole of their social conduct, and in all their sentiments with regard to God and natural religion, having been absolutely free from every thing wild and visionary, of necessity, the whole charge of enthusiasm against them must fall upon those doctrines which they teach us concerning *Jesus Christ*. And, indeed, as the Apostles, in every article of their doctrine, and in all the instances of their conduct in reference to both God and man, were, beyond question, steadily and uniformly governed, according to the purest informations of reason, and the noblest and most generous dictates of the sublimest piety and virtue; had they been, at the same time, only mere Enthusiasts in those doctrines they have published in relation to *Jesus Christ*, this I should have esteemed as wonderful an event as ever happened; an event, in my apprehension, in no wise consistent with the nature of things. However, we shall here inquire, whether the Apostles in those doctrines, can have this charge justly laid against them.

And,

And, for this purpose, I shall consider the accounts which they give us, concerning these several particulars that seem to be the great, fundamental articles of the Christian faith, and wherein, if in any thing, they must have been Enthusiasts, *namely*, the person of *Christ*, the nature of his kingdom, his death, and resurrection, and ascension.

But, before I enter upon this, I beg leave to remind my Reader of what I understand by an *Enthusiast*. He is one, who, in the course of his devotion, (which has always a mixture of melancholy and extravagance) comes to feel such warm and extraordinary emotions of soul, that without attending to the dictates of reason, he strongly imagines he is under the immediate influences of heaven; and therefore concludes, that those things, be they what they will, which run strongly in his mind, and are the subject-matter of his devotion, and to which these supernatural communications, as he fancies, are annexed, have the countenance and approbation of God, and are immediately impressed upon him by the divine Spirit.

Now, from hence (since the Apostles cannot possibly be suspected of enthusiasm in any point whatsoever, unless in those doctrines that relate immediately to *Jesus Christ*) it plainly follows, that the nature of *Christ*'s person and kingdom, his death, resurrection, and ascension, were so strongly settled on their fancy, in the same view wherein they are represented to us in their writings, and were so much the subject-matter of their devotion, that, in the warm contemplation thereof, they were mechanically wrought up into such extraordinary heats and fervours, that though these things were in themselves mere falsehoods, and they knew them at first to be so, yet, in the course of those raptures, they

they came at length to look upon them as most certain truths, that were miraculously confirmed and ratified to them by supernatural revelations.

This, I conceive, must have been the case with the Apostles, upon supposition that they were only visionary in these points. And it is to be remarked, that, since they are in no respect liable to this imputation before they became the Disciples of *Jesus Christ*, their enthusiasm must have been begun, and carried on in their devout contemplation of these articles. But that nothing of this nature can be laid to their charge, will manifestly appear from considering what their real and undoubted sentiments were upon these several particulars, and how they stood affected toward them, before they began, on the day of Pentecost, to propagate the Gospel to the world.

And first of all, as to the person of *Jesus Christ*: It is to be regretted, that, in the explication of their notions concerning the person of the blessed *Jesus*, some scholastic Divines have introduced such terms and phrases, as seem not only empty sounds, void of all sense and meaning, but do either tempt people to deny the truth of the Christian revelation, and to become Infidels, or betray them into such opinions as differ nothing, when narrowly looked into, from the *Sabellian*, or, which is much the same, the *Socinian* heresy, whereby they seem to deny the Lord who made and saves the world. However, I am not here to explain at large, under what ideas the Apostles in their writings represent the person of *Jesus Christ*; I shall only briefly observe, if a man will lay aside all the notions he has received, upon this great article of the Christian faith, from his education, and take his ideas of *Jesus Christ*, just as they occur to him in the New Testament, he cannot

not but apprehend him, without giving any the least shock to his own, or the common reason of mankind, as a divine person, *the only begotten Son of God* (as well as the Son of man, brought forth into the world in the fullness of the time) *by whom all things were created that are in heaven, and that are in earth, visible and invisible, whether they be thrones, or dominions, or principalities, or powers ; all things were created by him, and for him, and he is before all things, and by him all things consist, he being over all God blessed for ever.* So that the Apostles set forth *Jesus Christ* to us, not only as the Son of man, but as the Son of God, possessed of divine, infinite perfections, in which *he is the brightness of his Father's glory, and the express image of his person.* This is the account which, after the day of Pentecost, the Apostles give the world concerning the person of *Jesus Christ*. And, as to the nature of his kingdom, from the same period of time, the Apostles give us to understand what it is, not only in express declarations, and from the particular laws of his government, but from what they tell us about his design in coming into the world, and the report they make concerning the most considerable events of his Ministry; I mean his death, his resurrection, and ascension. Upon the former article of Imposture, I have already explained, that as the Apostles expressly declare, that the kingdom of *Christ is not of this world,* so they give out no laws belonging to his government, but what are purely spiritual, only affecting the souls and consciences of men, and leaving the outward frame of things, in bodies politic, to be modelled and adjusted by civil Governors. Now, still pursuing the same train of ideas, or minding only the spiritual concernments of mankind, in no other light do they set before us the design of
Christ's

Christ's appearing on earth, his submitting himself to death, his rising from the dead, and his ascending into Heaven. Thus, to give a short account of their doctrines upon these several articles concerning our Lord;

In the matter of his design in coming into this world, they expressly declare, *he was manifested to redeem us from all iniquity, and to purify unto himself a peculiar people zealous of good works.* And, particularly, with respect to his death, they take notice, that he is therein *the propitiation for the sins of the whole world,* and that *without it there is no remission of sin.* And upon his resurrection they observe, it was absolutely necessary for our justification; for, unless he had risen again from the dead, we had still continued in our sins. And as to his ascending into Heaven, this they tell us was likewise necessary, not only in order to his appearing before God with his atoning blood, thereby to purify or prepare heavenly places for our reception, but from thence to derive upon our souls the holy Ghost, or the supernatural gifts and assistances of the divine Spirit, to excite and second our hearty and constant endeavours, to promote in ourselves the great end of his death and resurrection, *the finishing the transgression, and the making an end of sin* in our hearts and lives, and *bringing in everlasting righteousness* through the whole course of our behaviour, whereby we are qualified for the purchased possession, those heavenly mansions *he is gone to prepare for us.*

And thus do the Apostles represent *Jesus Christ* to be the great Saviour of our souls, and all along set him forth in the merits and virtue of his death and resurrection, proclaiming an indemnity to the whole world; and not only thus graciously offering to admit all mankind to mercy; but giving us a perfect

perfect rule of righteousness, which particularly relates to the internal government of our minds and consciences; and promising us the inward supplies of his holy Spirit, to support us in a steady pursuit of universal holiness; at the same time, encouraging us to a continued course of piety and virtue, by proposing to us the eternal joys and felicities of heaven, as the great reward of our perseverance. So that the kingdom of *Jesus Christ*, as we are taught by the Apostles, *is not of this world*; he does not rule his subjects in the pomp of grandeur, and according to the measures of a secular Monarch, but *he is exalted to be a Prince and a Saviour, for to give repentance to* Israel, *and remission of sins*; and by the power of his Spirit secretly exerted upon our minds, to *deliver us out of the hands of* those *our enemies*, our corrupt lusts and passions, that invade the life and happiness of our souls; that *being brought from darkness to light, and from the power of Satan to God, we might serve him without fear in holiness and righteousness all the days of our lives*; and, in the end, be made happy with himself in the presence of God his Father, among Angels and Saints to eternity. Thus, I say, it appears, that the kingdom of *Christ*, as from the day of Pentecost it is all along represented, is intirely of a spiritual nature.

These are the views which the Apostles give us of *Jesus Christ* so soon as they began their public Ministry, and into which, it is supposed, they were led by enthusiasm. But how vastly different are their former apprehensions?

I will not here examine, what opinion the Apostles had concerned the person of *Jesus Christ*, before they began their public Ministry. I shall only say, upon this head, it is very obvious to me, that they did not apprehend him under that character in which

which he is reprefented to us by St. *John*, in the firft chapter of his Gofpel, and very frequently by the Apoftle *Paul* in his Epiftles.

But, as to the nature of his kingdom, certain it is, that till the day of Pentecoft, they were fo far from having any notion that *Jefus Chrift* was to eftablifh in the world a fpiritual government, that does not affect the fenfes and outward circumftances of mankind, but relates only to the redemption of their fouls, to their inward thoughts and confciences, and their future happinefs; that they were manifeftly carried away by thofe extravagant expectations, that univerfally prevailed among the *Jews*, with refpect to the kingdom of their *Meffias*; and did all along firmly believe, he was to have erected among them a fecular empire, wherein he would reign, in great pomp and magnificence, having all other nations under his dominion. And fo ftrongly did fuch things run in their minds, that they were frequently the fubject of their converfation; and never doubting but they were to be the prime Minifters of that kingdom, there fometimes arofe fuch warm difputes among them, about who fhould be preferred to the higheft pofts of that government, that, when they could not fettle the matter among themfelves, they were not afhamed to refer it immediately to *Jefus Chrift*, to be determined by his authority.

Nay, fo violently were they prepoffeffed in favour of a worldly kingdom, and that their *Meffiah* would triumph profperoufly over all oppofitions whatfoever, till he fhould raife and fettle the glory of his empire in this world; that, till it actually happened, they had not the leaft imagination he would ever fall into the hands of his enemies, and be condemned and crucified. This indeed was what they were frequently, in very exprefs terms, warned of;

but so thoroughly were they confirmed in the quite contrary expectations, that they could not possibly conceive what was to be understood when they were told plainly, *The Son of Man shall be delivered unto the Gentiles, and shall be mocked and spitefully entreated, and spitted on; and they shall scourge him, and put him to death, and the third day he shall rise again.* One would think, there is here so great plainness of speech, that the most simple cannot possibly fail to apprehend the meaning of it. But the Apostles, never in the least calling in question those notions which they had formed of the kingdom of their *Messiah*, were not able to reconcile such things to their former undoubted sentiments; and therefore were they utterly in the dark about them, and could by no means know what to make of them. Most certainly, they had not the least suspicion, that they imported that shameful death, which *Jesus Christ* suffered at *Jerusalem*. And the Apostle *Peter*, in particular, so much was he alarmed at such dreadful contradictions, as he thought, to the glory and majesty of *Christ* and his kingdom, that he openly expresseth his indignation against them, and means no less than to rebuke his Master for speaking after so odd and unaccountable a manner; *Be it far from thee; Lord, this shall not be unto thee!* And tho' *Jesus Christ*, on this occasion, did, with some vehemence, declare to his Disciples, that, in thinking and speaking at this rate, they were an offence to him, and did *not favour the things that be of God, but those that be of men*; and that *if they would be his Disciples*, and follow him, they must lay aside those thoughts of worldly power and greatness, and prepare themselves to meet with all the calamities of life in his service: Yet, so deeply was the persuasion of a worldly kingdom, to be set up by their *Messias*, rooted in their

their minds, that when their Master was on his way to *Jerusalem*, in order to suffer death, as he told them, they verily believed, notwithstanding all the representations they had had to the contrary, that *the kingdom of God would immediately appear*, *i. e.* that the *Messiah* would immediately assume his royal character, and take upon him the government of their nation, and show himself their great and triumphant Deliverer.

The Apostles, therefore, were under the strongest prejudices against the spiritual government of *Christ Jesus*, and could not, without the deepest horror, think of his death and passion. And how dreadfully must they have been confounded, when they were eye-witnesses of the captivity and crucifixion of their master, of whom they had conceived such glorious expectations! This so unexpected an event could not but wholly defeat and ruin all their hopes and confidence, and fill them with the utmost perplexities. And, indeed, during the whole of this amazing catastrophe, they were like men at their wits end, and looked upon the interest in which they had imbarked to be quite undone and ruined. —But, amidst their despair, being again revived by the resurrection of *Jesus Christ*, they immediately recover their hopes, and return to the old biass of their minds, and go on again in the same train of secular ideas, to which, before his death, they had been accustomed. So that, still full of the prospects of worldly power and grandeur for themselves and their nation, above all other persons and kingdoms upon earth, when they met together on Mount Olivet, as witnesses of the ascension of Jesus, *they then asked of him, saying, Lord, wilt thou at this time restore the kingdom to* Israel? *i. e.* Wilt thou now deliver this our nation from our present thraldom and
slavery,

slavery, and make us now to triumph over all other nations in the world? And, no doubt, they intended by this question to be informed, in what character they themselves were to act, (which they never thought would be low and mean) in bringing about this deliverance, and in raising their nation to an universal monarchy. But all the answer they received was (*m*), *It is not for you to know the times or the seasons, which the Father hath put in his own power:* whereby they were manifestly left under the full force of all their former prejudices and misapprehensions.

And therefore, upon the whole, The Apostles, till the day of Pentecost, were absolutely ignorant of the nature of *Christ*'s kingdom, and never in the least dreamed of their being put upon propagating through the world only a spiritual government, whereby their Master was to reign only in the minds and consciences of men, in order to prepare their souls for a state of future happiness. So far were they from apprehending any thing of this nature, that they were prejudiced in the most inveterate manner against it, and were intirely devoted to the expectation of a secular empire; which, they imagined, would be carried on with victory and triumph, till it should be firmly settled in the ruin and overthrow of all their enemies, and established on such sure foundations, as for ever after to be maintained with great grandeur and magnificence.

Now, the Apostles having been all along thus involved, to the very day on which they began their public Ministry; is it not manifest, that if they were Enthusiasts in the revelation of the Gospel, they must have begun their enthusiasm all at once, and upon a sudden, in those points that never

---

(*m*) Acts i. 6, 7.

were the subject-matter of their devotion, and against which, to that very moment, they had been most violently prepossessed? Which, from what I have said above, in the *first* and *second observations*, at the beginning of the *nineteenth Section*, appears plainly impossible.

And, indeed, so utterly inconsistent is such an event with the nature of things, that one may venture to challenge all the enemies of the Christian religion, to produce one single instance of a man's having acted the Enthusiast in those things, which he has not been accustomed to entertain with good liking and approbation; or upon the foundation of any other religion than that wherein he has been educated, or to which afterwards he has for some time turned his study. So that the Apostles, to the very day on which they began the propagation of the Gospel, being not only wholly unacquainted with the nature and design of Christ's kingdom and government in the world, but having entertained such notions and sentiments as were directly opposite to the whole scheme of things that was intended, it is impossible they could have been animated, in the prosecution of their Ministry, by any degree of enthusiasm; just as impossible, as it was for them to over heat their fancy with an excess of devotion, upon the death of *Jesus Christ*, the thoughts whereof they abhorred as most impious, and highly injurious to their Master; or upon his resurrection, which happened contrary to their expectation; and neither of which, as they undoubtedly thought, according to the prejudices of the *Jewish* nation, had any religious design; at least, nothing in the world like to that, which from the day of Pentecost, they all along represented them to have. And no man, I am sure, can ever be counted enthusiastic

thusiastic in those things that never were the subject-matter of his devotion, nor at any time, so much as in the lowest degree, the pleasing objects of his religious thoughts. To assert this, would indeed be extremely imaginary.

But what I am here maintaining, is, I think, put beyond dispute, from the accounts which we have of the conduct of the Apostles, in preaching the Gospel to the Heathen world. As I have already frequently observed, the *Jews* not only expected their *Messias* would have erected among them a worldly kingdom, to be supported in great pomp and glory; but that he was likewise to have triumphed over all other nations, whom they imagined he would have subdued under their dominion. So far therefore were they from apprehending, that the Gentile world were to be promoted to an equal share of the same blessings and felicities, whereof they themselves were to be possessed, that they considered them no otherwise than as men devoted to destruction, or to be reduced into a state of servitude, to maintain the grandeur of their empire. Now, in consequence of these national prejudices, and from the authority of some particular laws in the *Mosaical* constitution, whereby they were expressly forbid to have any sort of familiar intercourse with those of another nation, 'tis apparent, the Apostles were of opinion, even for some time after they understood the nature of *Christ*'s kingdom, and had been employed in the prosecution of their office, that all the Gentile world stood excluded from the covenant of grace; and that it was not lawful to admit them to a participation of the privileges of the Gospel. Upon which views of things, when they went about the world in the work of their Ministry, so scrupulously did they

observe

observe the preaching the Gospel to none, but to those of their own nation and religion, that, when the Apostle *Peter* happened to extend his Ministry to the Gentiles, this was thought to be so great a breach of his duty, that when he came up to *Jerusalem*, the rest of the Disciples openly condemned his conduct in this instance, and brought him to give an account of it in public. From hence, I say, it manifestly appears, that the Apostles were all of the opinion, that the dispensation of the Gospel was to be confined to those of their own nation, and that they were strongly prejudiced against its being extended to the Heathen world.

Now, the question is, How came it about, that they all entered into other sentiments, and pursued a clean contrary practice, while they travelled through the world, and dispensed the blessings of the Gospel, at the hazard of their lives, to all nations under the sun? And from plain matter of fact it appears, that this change of their opinion and practice, in spite of all their former prejudices, was not the effect of enthusiasm, or of a groundless imagination; that they had a command for it immediately from Heaven. For the Apostle *Peter*, in the vindication which he made of his conduct in relation to this article, proposes to the Disciples at *Jerusalem* these four considerations for their satisfaction; 1*st*, says he (*n*), " as I was in the city of *Joppa* praying, I " saw a vision, a certain vessel, as it had been a " great sheet let down from Heaven by four cor- " ners, wherein there being all sorts of beasts mixed " together, both clean and unclean, I heard a voice " saying unto me, *Arise*, Peter, *slay and eat*: But " I, struck with horror at what I had hitherto " thought so directly contrary to the law of God,
" said,

(*n*) Acts xi. 5, &c.

" said, *Not so, Lord, for nothing common or unclean*
" *hath at any time entered into my mouth.* But the
" voice answered me again from Heaven, *what God*
" *hath cleansed, that call not thou common.* And this
" was done thrice, and all was drawn up again to
" Heaven. 2*dly*, He observes, that as he was re-
" flecting what might be the meaning of this vision,
" the Spirit said unto him, *Behold three men seek*
" *thee, arise, and go with them.* 3*dly*, He takes no-
" tice, that having gone along with those three
" men to *Cesarea*, to one *Cornelius* a Centurian, who
" had called together his kinsmen and near friends,
" and were waiting his coming; as he began to
" preach to them the Gospel of Jesus Christ, *the*
" *holy Ghost fell on all them that were present, as he*
" *had done on the Apostles themselves on the day of*
" *Pentecost*; and that looking upon this as a most
" convincing evidence from Heaven, that God had
" accepted of the *Gentiles* to a participation of the
" Gospel, he had commanded them to be baptized
" in the name of the Lord. 4*thly*, Being sensible
" that the strength of his vindication lay particu-
" larly in the certainty of those miraculous effusi-
" ons of the holy Ghost, poured down from Hea-
" ven on *Cornelius* and his company, he appeals, for
" the truth of this, to the testimony of six brethren
" that were then present, and who had accompa-
" nied him from *Joppa* to *Jerusalem*."

These are the particular defences which the A-
postle *Peter* proposes to his Fellow-Disciples and A-
postles for their satisfaction. And from the force of
these considerations they are fully convinced of the
reasonableness and necessity of his conduct, and ever
after follow the same course, and propagate the Gospel
to people of all nations, without distinction. Nothing
therefore

therefore can be more manifest, than that the Apostles were no Enthusiasts, when they carried the blessings of the Gospel beyond those of there own nation and religion, and pretended they had a divine commission to dispense them to the Heathen world. And it being thus evident, that they had it revealed to them from heaven, what was the extent of *Christ*'s kingdome; we must necessarily conclude, they were after the same manner informed concerning the nature of his Government.

SECT. XXII.

The Apostles were no Enthusiasts in what they relate concerning the Death, Resurrection, and Ascension of Jesus Christ.

I SHALL now proceed to consider, in the next place, what situation of mind the Apostles were in, with respect to the death, resurrection, and ascension of *Jesus Christ*, which are the great fundamental articles of the Christian faith, and wherein, if at all, they must have been Enthusiasts. But, before I propose any thing particularly on these several articles, I beg leave to observe in general:

It would be carrying things to a strange pitch of wild extravagance to imagine, that all these events happened only, and had their existence no where else, but in the deluded fancies of the Apostles. And yet, in fair reasoning, this is what a man will be forced to, if he alledges they were visionary in any one of them. So that by this way of reckoning, " the death of *Christ* with all its particular cir-
" cumstances, was a tragedy acted only in the i-
" magination of the Apostles: And when they tell

"us, that on such a particular day they went up in company with *Jesus* himself to Mount *Olivet*; that he was there openly among them; and that after he had discoursed for some time familiarly with them, he was sensibly lifted up, and in the view of all present ascended into Heaven; and that they immediately after this returned full of joy in company with many others to *Jerusalem* ——This was all a waking dream, there was nothing of truth or reality in it, it was pure fancy and illusion in all the particular parts of it." For, I say, if we judge the Apostles visionary in one point, must they not necessarily fall under the same imputation in all? Why truly, since these things are all matters or fact, whereof one's senses are competent judges, and the Apostles were equally capable of understanding the certainty of every one of them; if there be not some particular reasons (which I am quite ignorant of, and shall be glad to learn from any hand) that affect the testimony of the Apostles in one article, more than in another, I am apt to think, we must, according to justice, suppose them visionary either in none, or in all.

And therefore, if it was by mere enthusiasm, that they saw *Christ* among them on Mount *Olivet*; that they heard him discoursing with them; and beheld him going up from thence into Heaven; what can hinder us from being persuaded, that it was only in the same manner, by mere enthusiasm, that they were at that place, among such persons, and that they came down, and returned to *Jerusalem?* Were they not fully as capable of know whether *Jesus Christ* was there and then present among them, and whether he left them, and went upwards; as whether they themselves, or any body else were there, and whether they parted from one another, and
came

came down in great companies to return every man to his own home? I shall be glad to know what greater evidence there is upon one side, than there is upon the other. And if the Apostles must needs be reckoned visionary in the resurrection and ascension of *Jesus Christ,* why not likewise in his being apprehended, and condemned, and crucified, and buried, and in all the particulars that accompanied these several events? It is not in the power of all the enemies of the Christian religion to show, that they were more competent judges of the latter than of the former, or that their testimony is more to be depended on, in what relates to the crucifixion, than in what relates to the resurrection and ascension. And to charge them with enthusiasm in one article, and not in another, wherein they are manifestly equally obnoxious, is against all the principles of what can deserve the name of Freethinking, and most certainly, can come from nothing but such prejudices, as miserably entangle the mind, and deprive it of all freedom of thought. I am at no loss to conceive what treatment I should meet with in the world, should I assert, " that *Julius Cæsar,* in " making his escape from the Island of *Pharus,* was " drowned, and did not save himself by swimming, " as is confidently reported; for that all the Histo- " rians who give this account of him, were led in- " to it by strong fancy, and some kind of enthusi- " asm." And, in the mean time, no Infidel will find it possible to show the contrary of this wild enough assertion, without the assistance of those principles, which regarding all characters concerned, will necessarily prove the truth of the resurrection of *Jesus,* and consequently, that the Apostles were no Enthusiasts.

But

But let us now particularly consider, what impressions the Apostles were under, with respect to the death, resurrection, and ascension of their *Messiah*.

As to the death of *Christ*, this is an event, wherein, if there was no more to be said of it, but that it happened at *Jerusalem* about 1700 years ago, there is no man that would judge himself in the least concerned. But it being set forth to us as the only propitiatory sacrifice, on the consideration whereof, we have the offer of mercy and forgiveness of sins; it is, in this view, of the last consequence, and of infinite concern to all mankind. I have already observed, that the Apostles, in offering their crucified Master in this light to the world, were no Enthusiasts. And let some of our modern Infidels, whose wild contradictious spirit is of late mightily improved, think what they will concerning the reality of the death of our Lord upon the cross, it can never be counted a meer groundless conceit of the Apostles, flowing from an over-heated imagination. It was certainly so contradictory to all their expectations, and they were so violently prepossessed against the probability, or rather possibility of the event, and they all along rejected the thoughts of it with so much aversion and abhorrence, that they could never be induced to entertain any the least suspicion, that it would ever happen. Of necessity, therefore, it must have been the strongest evidence imaginable, no less than ocular demonstration, that convinced them, and made them publish every where through the world, that *Christ* suffered death at *Jerusalem*. And therefore,

To come, in the next place, to the resurrection of *Jesus Christ*: This likewise is a matter of fact, that fell under the cognizance of their senses, and of the certainty

tainty whereof the Apostles had all possible opportunities to be fully satisfied. And, as I have already hinted, if they are not to be credited on this article, why do we admit their testimony in the former: It is by no means to be said, that it is not the evidence of the Apostles, but that of other Historians who have taken notice of, and handed down the history of the crucifixion, which ought to induce the world to believe the truth of this event. For what is it in the case of the Apostles, that can make us reject their testimony, while that of others, who are not Christians, is admitted.

I will take the liberty to observe to our Gentlemen Freethinkers, there are none of those Writers upon whose credit they receive the truth of the crucifixion, that were eye-witnesses of this matter of fact; and therefore they must have had it only from the information of others. But what do they know concerning those others? Can they tell us their character and circumstances, that we may understand how far they are to be depended on? As for the Apostles, who were themselves eye-witnesses, we know every thing of them, that can be thought necessary to enable us to form a true judgment of the value of their evidence. And though they had had it only at second hand, yet wherein is their credit inferior to that of those Heathen Authors, from a regard to whose reputation, such as deny the resurrection, do nevertheless believe the crucifixion? For my own part, I am fully satisfied, that the testimony of the Apostles in this article, is, on many accounts, far preferable to that of all others whatsoever. To instance in one particular proof for this purpose, it is manifest, to any considerate man, that the Apostles were under the power of such violent prejudices against the death of *Jesus Christ*, and were

so

so fully poffeffed of the firm belief, that *he would live for ever* (a), at leaft till he fhould triumph over all the enemies of their nation, and eftablifh the glory of their empire upon fuch fure foundations as fhould never be fhaken, that unlefs they had been upon the fpot, and with their eyes had feen his crucifixion, or at leaft, had had all the ftrongeft evidence that the nature of things was able to afford them, they would never have been prevailed on to believe, that fuch a death had befallen him. Upon which I will venture to fay, the man who refufes to give credit to the teftimony of the Apoftles in this article, muft at the fame time overturn all the foundations of moral certainty, and run the world into the greateft fcepticifm and confufion. And I make not the leaft fcruple to affirm, that if their evidence is good (as unqueftionably it is) upon the crucifixion, it is no lefs valuable upon the refurrection; nor is there any the leaft fhadow of reafon (upon attending to all the circumftances of thofe events) to difbelieve them in one, and to give credit to them in the other. But what good reafon we have to depend on the teftimony of the Apoftles, with refpect to this great article of the Chriftian faith, will appear from confidering, how once in their life they ftood affected towards it.

It is very obvious, that never were men upon earth lefs in a condition to work up their imagination into any delirious or enthufiaftic ravings, than the Apoftles were at the time when the refurrection is faid to have happened. For the fad misfortune that juft now had befallen them, the crucifixion of their Mafter; the fatal overthrow of that perfon from whom they expected fo much glory and triumph,

---

(a) John xii 34.

umph, had so intirely broken and confounded all that fine scheme of thoughts, which they had hitherto so fondly indulged, had sunk them into so helpless and desperate a condition, alarming their souls with the most dreadful apprehensions of impending dangers, that in such unhappy circumstances, they could not possibly enjoy any composure of mind, to form themselves into any frame of devotion, but were certainly overwhelmed in the deepest inward convulsions, and the greatest and most distracting perplexities; a situation of mind in no sort susceptible of enthusiasm.

Besides, that the Apostles, during the life of *Jesus Christ*, having never once suffered his death to enter into their thoughts as that which they imagined would ever happen, they could not be accustomed to entertain any the least prospect or belief of his resurrection, so as thereby to be prepared, from any bias of mind, to have such a conceit to settle upon their fancy, or to admit the truth of the fact, upon slight grounds, or without full and convincing evidence: On the contrary, from the natural connection of our ideas, one cannot but conclude, that the way to the resurrection, the death of their Lord, being so very shocking, and that which they so violently abhorred and rejected, they could not but have, while *Jesus* was alive, as great an aversion to the one, as to the other; at which rate, by no means were they in the way to become Enthusiasts.

And therefore, there being so small a distance of time betwixt the crucifixion and the resurrection, if the Apostles were only so many wild visionaries with regard to this article, it is plain, their enthusiasm must have been begun, carried on, and screwed up to the highest pitch that ever madness or frenzy

frenzy was raised to, within the compass of but a few hours, and that in spite of the most stubborn prejudices, in which they were all along involved; nay, whilst they were under all the agonies and distractions of mind, wherewith all the most dreadful and confounding disappointments could oppress them: Which, from considering the nature of things, according to what I have formerly observed, must be esteemed absolutely impossible.

I have just now hinted, that the Apostles, during the life of *Jesus Christ*, were so far from having any notion of his resurrection, that they were rather very strongly prejudiced against it. And it does not appear, that, after his death, they were in any better situation; nor, when one considers their circumstances, was it really possible it could be so. For, not to speak of that terrible disappointment they had met withal, which had totally dashed their hopes, and put an end to all their expectations; and how they were thereby reduced to so melancholy a pass, that, at least, full of confusion and perplexity, they knew not what to think; we may reasonably conceive, that *Christ*'s falling a sacrifice to the malice and revenge of his enemies, being an event utterly destructive of all the notions they ever had of their *Messiah* and his kingdom, they could have no good reason to induce them to look for his resurrection. For, besides the strangeness of the thing itself, *viz.* A man's raising himself from the dead (which they might here think impossible; for they do not as yet seem to have had any notion of his divinity) the Apostles being still tenacious of the expectation of a worldly kingdom under their *Messias*, they could imagine to themselves no end, for which he would come back from the dead again, that he might not have compassed much more honourably,

nourably, while he was alive among them.' And for *Jesus Christ* wholly to neglect the end for which, as they conceived, he appeared, and which, while he was on earth, might have been accomplished more to his own glory, and the credit of his friends; and shamefully to suffer death, and to rise again, with a view of doing no more, but to pursue the same very end which formerly he had intended: This they thought, as it really is, most absurd and unaccountable. Upon all which, one cannot but conclude, that the Apostles must have been strongly fortified in their prejudices against the resurrection of *Jesus*; and that they certainly gave up all for lost, upon his crucifixion, and had no hopes of his ever returning to life again, but rashly considered him as a person in whom they had been sadly deceived or disappointed (*b*).

What I have hitherto said upon this article is taken from the principles of human nature, as they would operate upon people of the same notions, or in the same situation and circumstances with the Apostles. And, in fact, we have a very good confirmation of all that is here advanced, from the account which St. *Mark* gives us of their behaviour on the third day after the crucifixion.

This Evangelist tells us (*c*), that on that very day, on which, in the judgment of our Saviour (*d*), they ought to have been joyfully expecting the resurrection, according as it had been foretold them, they were together, imparting their sorrows to one another,

---

(*b*) Ἔδοξε γὰρ ἂν αὐτοῖς, εἰ μὴ ἀνέστη, ἀπατεὼν εἶναί τις ᾖ εἴρων. Chrysost. in 1 Cor. i. 31. p. 270. And in this light must they not have apprehended him, while they had no hopes of his rising to life again? So that the English of Chrysostom's language, in the former edition, needed not to have given so much offence.

(*c*) Mark xvi. 10, 11. (*d*) Vid. Joh. xiv. 28.

another, and like so many poor, hopeless creatures, weeping over their sad misfortunes and disappointments, which they thought to be so far beyond remedy, that they could not believe *Mary Magdalene*, and other women, who came and told them, that *Jesus was risen*, and that they had seen him; but looked upon all the accounts which they had of this extraordinary event; as so many *idle tales* (*e*), and which therefore they rejected, as the effects of mere fancy and delusion.

And indeed they were all of them so far from being forward in admitting for a truth, this essential point of the Christian religion, that it should rather seem, they were most unreasonably incredulous, and strangely obstinate in the prejudices they had against it. For, do they not absolutely refuse to give credit to one another in this article? Indeed, they renounce all human testimony; they will not trust to the relations which they have of it from any of their own company, though ever so well vouched; but continue unbelievers, till they are forced to yield to the testimony of their own senses. Nay, one of them in particular judged it a matter so extremely incredible, that he rejected the testimony of ten Apostles, and of other Disciples, though they gave it concerning what they had themselves seen distinctly; and declares openly, that nothing under the highest and fullest evidence, even that of seeing with his own eyes, and feeling with his own hands, and narrowly examining into the truth of the fact, as far as (not one, but) all his senses, that were capable of discerning, would carry him, should be able to persuade and convince him. From which I am apt to think, that this Apostle, especially, looked upon *Jesus Christ* as one, by whose means they had been
led

(*e*) Luke xxiv. 11.

led into the vainest and most delusive expectations. But that they were all thus under the strongest prejudices, and had no hopes of the resurrection, will manifestly appear from the plain account which we have of their conduct, on this occasion; which I shall relate in the following manner:

"*Mary Magdalene*, and some other women, who
"had conceived a very tender esteem towards *Je-*
"*sus Christ*, having attended his funerals, and taken
"particular notice of the place where the corps
"was laid, return home, and prepare spices and o-
"ther materials, with a design to anoint the dead
"body on the third day after, the immediately fol-
"lowing being the *Jewish* Sabbath. And for this
"purpose, very early in the morning of the first
"day of the week, having come to the place where
"the corps had been laid, they are mightily alarm-
"ed, when they find the stone rolled away from
"the door of the sepulchre, (for they had been say-
"ing among themselves, as they were coming, *who*
"*shall roll us away the stone from the door of the se-*
"*pulchre?* (for it was very great) and having no
"imagination of any thing, but that the dead body
"was stolen away, they are greatly perplexed, and
"know not what to do; while, in the mean time,
"*Mary Magdalene* hastes back to the Apostles *Pe-*
"*ter* and *John*, and with the deepest concern ac-
"quaints them, that they had taken the Lord out
"of the sepulchre, and, say they, *we know not where*
"*they have laid him*.

"Upon this, these two Apostles, greatly sur-
"prized at the relation, run immediately to the se-
"pulchre, and having both of them gone down in-
"to the cave, they find the body gone, but saw the
"linen cloaths lying, and the napkin that was a-
"bout his head, wrapped together and laid in a
"place

"place by itself. The Apostle *John* was, from
this, led into the same opinion with the women,
and *believed* with them, that *they had taken away
the Lord out of the sepulchre.* But the Apostle
Peter is struck with wonder and amazement at
this which had come to pass; and though he had
certainly, on this occasion, many different reflections, yet it does not appear, that it ever once
entered into his thoughts, that *Jesus* was risen.
So that both of them returned, one apprehending,
that the body had been by some people secretly
conveyed away; (for as yet (*f*), as he owns
himself, *they knew not the Scripture*, i. e. the plain
declarations of the Old Testament concerning the
death of the *Messias*, and *that he must rise again
from the dead*) and the other wondering within
himself at that which had happened.

"But, as to *Mary Magdalene*, her anxious concern not suffering her to return, she stays behind,
and hangs on about the sepulchre, that, if possible,
she might, some how or other, get intelligence
whither the dead body was conveyed. And as
she is in great distress, weeping with a good deal
of anxiety, she sees an Angel sitting upon the
stone that was rolled away from the door of the
sepulchre, who said unto her and the rest of the
women that were with her; *Fear not ye, for I
know that ye seek* Jesus *which was crucified; he is
not here, for he is risen as he said; come see the place
where the Lord lay; and go quickly, and tell his Disciples that he is risen from the dead.* Upon which
Mary Magdalene, in obedience to the Angel,
stooping down, and looking into the sepulchre,
she seeth two other Angels in white, sitting, the
one at the head, and the other at the feet, where
"the

(*f*) Joh. xx. 9.

" the body of *Jesus* had lain; and they say unto
" her, *Woman, why weepest thou?* She, it would seem,
" not giving much credit to what the other Angel
" had told her, saith to them, *because they have ta-*
" *ken away my Lord, and I know not where they have*
" *laid him.* To which the Angels again answered,
" *Why seek ye the living among the dead? he is not*
" *here, but is risen; remember how he spake unto you*
" *when he was yet in Galilee, saying, the Son of man*
" *must be delivered into the hands of sinful men, and*
" *be crucified, and the third day rise again.*

" These apparitions of Angels made *Mary* and
" her company greatly afraid; while at the same
" time, the repeated assurances they had from them
" of the resurrection filled them with great joy.
" But, so far were they from expecting so extraordi-
" nary an event, and so little did they understand
" what to make of this great fundamental article of
" the Christian faith, that the testimony of three
" Angels was not able to put them beyond doubt,
" and to give them full satisfaction: For, as they
" are coming away in great haste from the sepul-
" chre, in order to inform the Disciples of what
" had happened, *Jesus* himself appears to them,
" and saith unto *Mary Magdalene, Woman, why*
" *weepest thou? whom seekest thou?* She, supposing
" him to be the Gardener, and her heart still mis-
" giving her concerning the resurrection, saith un-
" to him, with no little concern upon her spirit,
" *Sir, if thou hast bore him hence, tell me where thou*
" *hast laid him, and I will take him away.* Jesus,
" saith unto her, *Mary*; she in a suprize, turneth
" herself, and saith unto him, *Rabboni!* and im-
" mediately falling down, clings about his feet.
" But *Jesus* saith unto her, *Do not spend time in thus*
" *fondly embracing me, you will have occasion to see*
" *me*

" me afterwards, for I am not yet afcended to my Fa-
" ther, being to ftay for fome time upon earth; but
" go to my Brethren, and fay unto them, I am alive,
" and in the way to afcend unto my Father and your
" Father, and to my God, and your God. Where-
" upon *Mary Magdalene*, and the other women,
" having no room to doubt any longer, but, now
" that they had feen *Jefus* himfelf, being fully per-
" fuaded of the truth of the refurrection, immedi-
" ately hafte away to the Apoftles and other Dif-
" ciples, whom they found together in a hopelefs
" manner, all weeping and mourning for thofe fad
" difappointments that had befallen them. And
" though they affured them, from the teftimony of
" three Angels, and that of their own fenfes, that
" *Jefus* was rifen, yet they believed them not,
" but continued to indulge their own melancholy
" prejudices, and looked upon all the accounts
" which the women gave them, as mere idle re-
" ports not to be regarded.

" The fame day, as two of the Difciples were
" going from *Jerufalem* to *Emmaus*, and were talk-
" ing together by the way of all thofe things which
" had happened, *Jefus* came up to them, and ha-
" ving inquired of them, what they might be dif-
" courfing on, that made them look fo fad and
" melancholy; one of them, whofe name was *Cleo-*
" *pas*, faid unto him, *Art thou only a ftranger in*
" *Jerufalem, and haft not known the things which have*
" *come to pafs there in thefe days?* And he faid unto
" them, *What things?* And they faid unto him, *con-*
" *cerning Jefus of Nazareth, who was a Prophet mighty*
" *in deed and word before God, and all the people; and*
" *how the chief Priefts and our Rulers delivered him to be*
" *condemned to death, and have crucified him*: *but we*
" *trufted that it had been he who would have re-*
" deemed

" deemed *Israel*. And besides all this, this is the
" third day since these things were done. *Yea*, and
" certain women also of our company made us astonish-
" ed, who were early at the sepulchre, and when they
" found not his body, they came, saying, that they had
" also seen a vision of Angels, which said that he was
" alive. And certain of them who were with us, went
" to the sepulchre, and found it even so as the women
" had said, but him they saw not. In which, with a
" beautiful simplicity, that distinctly speaks the up-
" rightness and ingenuity of their hearts, they ma-
" nifestly express a great deal of concern and an-
" guish of mind, and strongly insinuate how much
" they were disappointed, and what little hopes
" they had of the resurrection.

" Upon which, *Jesus Christ*, in order to prepare
" their minds for that discovery he was about to
" make them, cites and expounds to them those
" passages of the Old Testament, that relate to
" the death and resurrection of the *Messiah*. And
" having gone along with them into the village,
" as they sat at meat, their eyes being fixed on
" him, they knew who he was, upon which he
" unexpectedly withdrew, and they saw him no
" more. The two Disciples are exceedingly struck
" with this so unexpected a discovery, and with
" great surprize and joy returned that same hour
" to *Jerusalem*, and informed the Apostles and o-
" ther disciples, who were all assembled together
" in some secret place for fear of the *Jews*, of what
" things were done in the way, as they were go-
" ing to *Emmaus*, and how he was known of them
" in breaking of bread. But the Apostles, as it
" should seem, and the rest of their company, being
" still under the power of their prejudices, and ha-
                                                    " ving

"ving no notion of any such event, would not believe what was thus attested to them.

"In the interim, as they are discoursing of these extraordinary occurrences, *Jesus* himself, comes suddenly among them, and faith unto them, *Peace be unto you*. But they were all terrified and affrighted, and supposed they had seen a spirit. And therefore *Jesus Christ*, in order to compose their minds, that they might be in a condition coolly and impartially to judge for themselves, said unto them, *Why are ye troubled, and why do doubtful thoughts arise in your hearts? Behold my hands and my feet, that it is I myself; handle me and see, for a spirit hath not flesh and bones as ye see me have*. And when he had thus spoken, and at the same time rebuked them for their unbelief and hardness of heart, in rejecting the evidences they had already received for his resurrection, he shewed them his hands and his feet. But this was an event so unexpected and surprising, which naturally raised such high tides of different passions within them, and which, all at once, crouded their minds with such various images of the hopeless melancholy condition wherein they had been involved, and of the great deliverance and happiness of which they were now possessed, so disproportioned to the inward sense of their own merit, (which, by the by, is far too modest and humble for Enthusiasts) and so much beyond, nay, contrary to their expectations, that they could not believe for joy, but stood all wondering and gazing, and did not well know how to give credit to their own senses, but seem rather to be enchanted into some golden dream, or pleasing delusion (*g*).

"Whereupon,

(*g*) Much after the same manner, were the states of Greece and

" Whereupon, *Jesus Christ*, giving them time to
" recollect themselves, that he might convince
" them fully of the truth of his resurrection, and
" put them beyond all possible doubt as to the
" reality of this appearance, said unto them,
" *Have ye here any meat?* And they gave him a
" a piece of broiled fish, and of an honey-comb.
" And he took it, and did eat before them. And
" he said unto them, *These things are the accomplish-*
" *ing of the words which I spake unto you, while I*
" *was yet with you, that the Son of man must be cru-*
" *cified, and the third day rise again, and that all*
" *things must be fulfilled which were written in the*
" *law of* Moses, *and in the Prophets, and in the*
" *Psalms concerning me.* Upon which, they could
" no longer refuse the evidences they had of the
" resurrection, but, as in reason they were bound,
" gave full credit to the truth thereof.

" But, all this having been transacted in the ab-
" sence of the Apostle *Thomas*; when the other
" Disciples informed him of what had happened,
" and how they were now all fully satisfied, as to
" the truth and certainty of the resurrection; for
" that they had seen the Lord his pierced hands
" and

and Asia affected, upon their being surprized with a proclamation from the Roman Herauld, declaring them all free, and at liberty to use their own laws.

Audita voce Præconis, majus gaudium fuit, quam quod universum homines caperent. Vix satis credere se quisquam audiisse. Alii alios intueri mirabundi, velut somnii vanam speciem. Quod ad quenquam pertineret, suarum aurium fidei minimum credentes, proximos interrogabant. Revocatus Præco. Cum unusquisque non audire, sed videre libertatis nuntium averet: iterum pronuntiaret eadem. Tum ab certo jam gaudio tantus cum clamore plausus est ortus, totiesque repetitus, ut facile appareret, nihil omnium bonorum multitudini gratius, quam libertatem esse. Liv. lib. 33, 35.

"and feet, and had for some time conversed with him; so little did this Apostle regard their information, that, still retaining a quick sense of those dreadful disappointments they had met withal, in relation to this *Jesus*, while they trusted that it had been he who should have redeemed *Israel*; and still looking upon his resurrection, after he had been so shamefully put to death, to be beyond all credibility; he openly rejects all the proofs they were able to afford him, and obstinately declares, he will never be brought over to believe the truth of it, unless he should himself see and examine the body of *Jesus*, in such a a manner, as he might have the fullest demonstration, without a possibility of having a cheat put upon him, which he seems all along to have violently suspected: *Except*, says he, *I shall see in his hands the print of the nails, and put my finger into the print of the nails, and thrust my hand into his side, I will not believe.* This indeed was very brisk, and at an infinite distance from the least degree of credulity, and most certainly would have exposed the whole matter, had it been an imposture, or had it been only founded on enthusiasm, one of which this Apostle seems to have apprehended. Nor was any thing able to overcome his obstinacy, till he had actually seen *Jesus*, which happened about eight days after. For when his Disciples were again within, and *Thomas* with them, then came *Jesus*, and stood in the midst, and said, *Peace be unto you.* Then saith he to *Thomas, 'Reach hither thy finger, and behold my hands, and reach hither thy hand, and thrust it into my side; and be not faithless but believing.* And *Thomas* answered and said unto him, My Lord, and my God!"

This

This is a plain account of the behaviour of the Apostles, and other Disciples, with respect to the resurrection of *Jesus*. And wherein does the Enthusiast appear? I dare be bold to say, 'tis impossible to fix upon any one instance of their conduct upon this occasion, from which one may fetch a charge of enthusiasm against them. On the contrary, they were unreasonably headstrong in the disbelief of this article, and all along betrayed a surprising dulness and stupidity of heart; which can be accounted for, no otherwise than by supposing them, as they really were, under the grossest mistakes concerning the nature of *Christ*'s kingdom, which involved them in the most inveterate prejudices against his death and resurrection, and so miserably entangled their minds, that they knew not the Scriptures, nor what to make of those plain words of *Jesus Christ*, when he distinctly told them, that *he must rise again from the dead.* And I may here be allowed to observe, had there been any degree of enthusiasm in this article among the Disciples, it would have certainly broken out among those fond, compassionate women who went first to the sepulchre. But, amidst all their fondness, so far are those religious women from having a strong fancy in favour of the resurrection, that it is the thing in the world they have the least thought or apprehension of: And therefore do they act with so much natural simplicity, according to their pious design of anointing the dead body, and the undoubted persuasion they had of its being stolen away.

Thus were the Apostles, all of them, forced out of their infidelity by the irresistible testimony of their own senses; and necessarily determined to admit the truth of the resurrection; in the certain belief of which they were further established by frequent

frequent appearances, which *Jesus Christ* afterwards, before his ascension, made to them, wherein he wrought miracles, and conversed familiarly with them, while in an open and friendly manner they sat and eat together. Among those appearances, the most public and solemn of all, were those two that happened, the one at a mountain in *Galilee*, where our Lord had most of his Disciples; the other at *Bethany*, from whence he went up into heaven. And, in his account of the first of these, see the manly composure of mind, and the sincere honesty of the sacred Historian! St. *Matthew* tells us, that *when the Disciples saw* Jesus *they worshipped him, but some doubted* (*h*). Some doubted! with what high contempt would an Enthusiast, in the heat of his imagination, have mentioned this circumstance! and, with what caution would an Impostor have avoided every thing like it. The telling the world of such a circumstance, without in the least offering to show it was groundless, or that the persons who doubted came to be satisfied, is a strong proof, that not only the Writer himself was absolutely certain of the truth of the resurrection, but that he regarded the matter of fact, as supported by the most incontestable evidence, to be wholly beyond question, and universally believed, or that it was not capable of being contradicted. Whether it was at this appearance in *Galilee*, or at the other at *Bethany*, that *Jesus* was seen of above five hundred brethren at once, cannot well be determined; but this is certain, that more than twenty years after this, St. *Paul* publicly declares before the world (*i*) that the greater part of those Discipes, who

(*h*) Matth. xxviii. 17.
(*i*) 1 Cor. xv. 6.

who had thus seen *Jesus Christ*, were then still alive. So that any man, even after so long a time, had it in his power to satisfy himself as to the truth of the resurrection, from several hundreds of people who were eye-witnesses, and whose testimony cannot be doubted, since it is given for a matter of fact, of the certainty whereof they were competent judges; and which they themselves obstinately rejected, till they were downright constrained to yield by the force of those evidences, whereby a man that is reading this page is under a necessity to own, that it is a piece of paper all over regularly marked, from top to bottom, with various words and sentences.

And, indeed, the way how the Priests and leading men among the *Jews*, managed on this occasion, carries a strong conviction along with it of the certainty of the resurrection. For, though all their worldly concernments, and their keenest passions exasperated to the highest pitch, did, questionless, violently prompt them to ruin the credit of this extraordinary event, and to make it pass for a mere forgery of wicked Impostors, or the groundless fancy of a few deluded visionaries (which they might have done easily, had it been so) yet all their wit, malice, and power, could advance only a stupid, ridiculous story, wherein they impudently affront the common sense of mankind, and leave an imputation upon their own memory, of the blackest villany that can possibly be conceived. Say they, *While the soldiers that were set to guard him were asleep, his Disciples came by night and stole him away;* for which they never pretended any other evidence than the testimony of the sleeping soldiers. And, tho' this was openly published against them, in the Gospel of St. *Matthew,* within a few years afterward,

ward, with the addition of the execrable guilt of bribery, whereby they perſuaded the ſoldiers to ſpread abroad this moſt ſenſeleſs ſtory, againſt the plain dictates of their own conſciences, and contrary to the expreſs declarations which they had made in preſence of thoſe ſage Gentlemen; yet they never once attempted to confute theſe heavy charges, or to vindicate themſelves from ſuch horrid imputations, which manifeſtly tended to render them exceeding vile and infamous, in the view of all mankind. And this, I ſay, is a farther demonſtration of the truth of the reſurrection.

For, ſince they were ſenſible, that the belief of the reſurrection, ſhould it come to take among the people, would be of far more dangerous conſequence to all their valuable enjoyments, than any thing that had yet happened; and therefore uſed all poſſible precautions to prevent a cheat in the matter, by rolling a great ſtone to the door of the ſepulchre, and ſealing it, and ſetting a watch or guard, which they obtained, by a ſolemn addreſs, from *Pilate* the *Roman* Governor; I ſay, ſince they were thus precautious, in uſing all poſſible endeavours to prevent a cheat in the matter of the reſurrection, which they foreſaw would be intirely deſtructive of all their intereſts; 'tis utterly inconſiſtent with the nature of things, that theſe men would have neglected any poſſible method, whereby to diſprove the fact, when it was talked that *Jeſus* was riſen; and to lay open the impoſture, or to expoſe the deluſion to the world; which, with great eaſe, they might have effected, had it been nothing elſe but an invention, or a groundleſs fancy of the Apoſtles. And, foraſmuch as they did nothing this way, but endeavoured only to diſguiſe the matter by a poor ſilly ſtory that deſtroys itſelf; this, in my opinion,

is

is a sufficient demonstration (which carries as great certainty along with it as any proposition in *Euclid*,) that they themselves believed the report which they had at first from the soldiers, or that they saw the matter of fact to be supported by such incontestible evidences, that it was impossible for them to insist upon one single circumstance, that could incline people to believe or suspect the contrary. Indeed, those wise and great Rabbies, who had malice, revenge, and pride enough to quicken their wit, power, and activity, must have certainly been reduced to a very low pass, when they fled to downright nonsense and absurdity as their only refuge, whereby to protect all their highest and most valuable concernments, from the dreadful influence of a plain matter of fact, which might have been laid open from the bottom, and, had it been a cheat, or a delusion, made to appear so, to the full conviction of all mankind. But what can people say or do, when they are outfacing the Sun at noon-day?

Now, from this conduct of the Rulers, among the *Jews* on one hand, and that of the Apostles on the other, with regard to the article of the Christian faith; I will venture to say, there are such degrees of evidence as are sufficient to command the assent of every impartial man to the truth of the resurrection, and to put him beyond doubt, that the Apostles, in this particular, were no Enthusiasts.

As to the third great article of the Christian faith which I mentioned, namely, the ascension of *Jesus Christ* into heaven; I do likewise contend, that 'tis altogether impossible that this could be only an imaginary conceit of the Apostles. For, not to insist upon their being persons by no means of a credulous turn of mind; (which, methinks, evidently

dently appears from what I have above obferved) as this was nothing but that, which, after the refurrection, they had been frequently forewarned of; fo the particular day and place were appointed when and where it fhould happen. Befides, that it was done in broad day-light, with great deliberation, and in the prefence of a great number of people: And, in fuch circumftances, there is manifeftly no room for mere fancy and imagination. The plain hiftory is this:

" *Jefus Chrift* having commanded his Apoftles to
" repair on fuch a day to *Bethany*, from which he
" told them he intended to go up to heaven; they
" acquainted the reft of the Difciples of what was
" to happen. When they therefore were come
" together on the day and place that were appointed, the Apoftles, who had attended our
" Lord from *Jerufalem*, being as yet wholly ignorant of the nature of *Chrift*'s government, and
" not knowing what part they were now to act
" upon earth, after he fhould have left them, or
" what was now to become of that kingdom,
" which they thought he came to eftablifh in the
" world; they judged this was a proper feafon to
" be informed, and to receive their inftructions in
" fuch inftances; and therefore did they afk of
" him, *Lord*, fay they, *wilt thou at this time re-*
" *ftore again the kingdom unto Ifrael?* But he faid
" unto them, *It is not for you to know the times*
" *and the feafons, which the Father hath put in his*
" *own power.* And, having told them, that all
" power in heaven and earth was lodged in his
" hands, he gives a commiffion to his Difciples, to
" go and teach all nations in his name: And reminding them of the promife, which, before his
" death, he had made to them of the Holy Ghoft,
" whom

"whom he said he would send down to them from the Father in heaven; he lets them know, what great wonders and miracles they should be impowered to work, and enjoins them to stay at *Jerusalem* till this promise should be accomplished. And having thus given them what information and instructions he thought necessary at this juncture, he lift up his hands in a solemn manner and blessed them; and, it came to pass while he blessed them, *he was parted from them, and carried up into heaven.* And they worshipped him, and returned to *Jerusalem* with great joy."

This is a plain simple account of a very extraordinary event, that speaks the relators plain honest men, who were utter strangers to the extravagant conceits of a wild raving fancy, or visionary brain, (which most certainly, on this occasion, would have been worked up into the most fantastic or pompous images) and who had no plot but to tell naked truth, which does not want, like fiction and imposture, to be coloured over, and set off with studied embellishments.

And indeed as this was an event, of the certainty whereof a man's senses were competent judges; so it can never reasonably be supposed, that these very men, who were so hard to be gained over to a belief of the resurrection, were, in this point, wholly visionary. Nor is possible that men, of but common sense and prudence, could ever have, at any rate, represented to the whole world, that upwards of five hundred persons, as well as themselves, had been eye-witnesses of a plain matter of fact, the resurrection or ascension of *Jesus*, if it had not been really so; and, more than twenty years afterwards, be openly appealing to above two hundred and fifty of them (the reſt being dead) for the truth of what they aſſerted.

But that which convincingly ſhows us, that the aſcenſion was no imaginary conceit, or ſtrong fancy of the Apoſtles, and gives us a full demonſtration of its undoubted truth and certainty, is, the amazing influence, which, within a few days after it happened, it had upon the Apoſtles. *Jeſus Chriſt had, frequently before his death, promiſed to his Diſciples the extraordinary gifts of the holy Ghoſt; but at the ſame time he acquainted them, that, before this promiſe could be accompliſhed, he muſt neceſſarily go up into heaven; for that it was from the Father that he was to derive thoſe miraculous influences upon them.* When therefore he was about to aſcend into heaven, ſtill mindful of his promiſe, and conſcious of his power to perform it, he expreſsly commands his Apoſtles to tarry at *Jeruſalem*, till they ſhould thus be *endowed with power from on high*.

Accordingly, the Apoſtles, in expectation of the fulfilling of this promiſe, waiting in *Jeruſalem*; as they were all aſſembled together in one place on the day of Pentecoſt, a few days after the aſcenſion: BEHOLD! *on a ſudden, there came a ſound from heaven as of a ruſhing mighty wind, and it filled all the houſe where they were ſitting: And there appeared unto them cloven tongues like as a fire, and it ſat upon each of them: And they were all filled with the holy Ghoſt; and began to ſpeak with other tongues, as the Spirit gave them utterance. And there dwelled at Jeruſalem Jews, devout men out of every nation under heaven. Now when this was noiſed abroad, the multitude came together, and were confounded, becauſe that every man heard them ſpeak in his own language. And they were all amazed, and marvelled, ſaying one to another, Behold,*

hold, are not all these which speak, Galileans? And how hear we every man in our own tongue, wherein we were born?. Parthians, and Medes, and Elamites, and the dwellers in Mesopotamia, and in Judea, and Cappadocia, and Pontus, and Asia, Phrygia, and Pamphylia, in Egypt, and in the parts of Lydia about Cyrene, and strangers of Rome, Jews and proselytes, Cretes and Arabians, we do hear them speak in our own tongues, the wonderful works of God. And they were all amazed, and were in doubt, saying one to another, What meaneth this (k)?

These are occurrences very uncommon, and may be thought to portend something very extraordinary. And it was on this day, and upon this event, that the Apostles began their public ministry; in the prosecution whereof, by virtue of this power, which now they had received from on high, they not only published to people of all languages the doctrines of *Jesus*, but, in his name, they, every where through the world, not in dark corners, but in the most public places, openly and in the face and view of all orders of men, amazingly wrought, for a tract of years, many thousands of wonders and miracles; such as, *restoring sight to the blind, making the deaf and dumb to hear and speak, and the lame to walk, healing all kinds of diseases, and raising the dead to life again.* And this gift of tongues, and power of working miracles they derived to others; who thus sharing with the Apostles, were likewise enabled to preach the Gospel to all nations, and every where to convince mankind of the superiority of the Christian institution, infinitely above every thing wherein any man could pretend to rival it. And to derive such a power to other people, is, I suppose, a piece of

virtue

(k) Act. ii.

virtue that cannot be equalled by any thing of the like nature in the Heathen world (*l*); how much soever, in order to lessen the credit of those mighty works that were done by *Jesus Christ* and his Disciples, some people may poorly insist upon the reputed miracles of *Apollonius* and others (*m*).

And

(*l*) I must here be so fair as to observe, that Empedocles, Epimenides, and Abaris, are said to have had the power of working miracles from Pythagoras; who, they say, had his again from Pherecydes. And here is an instance of their miracles in the case of Abaris, of whom it is reported, ὅτι ἄρα οἰστῷ τῷ ἐν Ὑπερβορέοις Ἀπόλλωνος δωρηθέντι αὐτῷ ἐποχούμενος, ποταμούς τε ἢ πελάγη, ἢ τὰ ἄβατα διέβαινεν, ἀεροβατῶν τρόπον τινά. The like miracle was performed also by Pythagoras. Porph. de Vit. Pythag. § 27. 29.

Whether the Church of Rome were aware of such miracles, and thought it necessary to counterbalance them, I know not; but, in their Breviary, they represent the Apostles, with terrible rapidity flying in the air from all quarters of the world, and, in a moment of time, assembling at Jerusalem, in order to assist at what they call the *Dormition of the blessed Virgin*: Tempore gloriosæ dormitionis beatæ Virginis, universi quidem sancti Apostoli, qui orbem terræ ad salutem gentium peragrabant, momento temporis in sublime elati, convenerunt Ierosolymis. Fest. Aug. 18.

(*m*) Euphrates, a Philosopher of great reputation, (Vid. Plin. lib. i. epist. 10. Arrian. Epict. lib. iii. cap. 15.) and who, as he was his contemporary, and of his acquaintance, had easy access to know the truth of his character, represents Apollonius as an Impostor. (Vid. Euseb. contra Hierocl. p. 530. 533.) And Arnobius, a learned Heathen, who turned Christian, is not only of opinion, that Apollonius, and those others they talk of, wrought no miracles; but stands amazed at the power that derives such a virtue to frail mortals.—— He thinks it a power far above the reach of that God whom he formerly counted supreme.

Quid dicitis, o mentes incredulæ, difficiles, duræ! Alicuine mortalium Jupiter ille Capitolinus, hujusmodi potestatem dedit? Curionem, aut Pontificem maximum, quinimmo Dialem, quod ejus est, flaminem isto jure donavit? Non dicam, ut mortuos excitaret, non ut cœcis restitueret lucem, non ut membrorum situm

enervatis

SECT. XXII. *Christian Revelation.* 301

And from those astonishing effects, which, after the ascension of our Lord, were, according to his promise, produced in the Apostles themselves, and, by their means, in other people; one must judge it convincingly manifest, that in the belief of this article, the Apostles were no Enthusiasts. And indeed, that man's fancy must be excessively wild, and, beyond measure, extravagant, who can imagine, that their speaking in so many various tongues, and their doing so many wonders and miracles, was only a continuation of the enthusiasm; ridiculously pretending, that it was by the mere strength of their over-heated and deluded imagination, that at first, all on a sudden, they acquired the faculty of discoursing to so many different nations in those languages, which they never learned or understood before; and that it was no otherwise that they came, at first, to give eyes to the blind, health to the sick, and life to the dead. A most wonderful species of enthusiasm this, which betrayed not only the Apostles into a mighty conceit of their working miracles; but even the deaf and dumb, the blind and the lame,

---

enervatis redderet et dissolutis: Sed ut pustulam, reduviam, papulam, aut vocis imperio, aut manus contrectatione comprimeret. Ergo illud humanum fuit, aut ex ore terrenis stercoribus inutrito tale potuit jus dari, talis licentia proficisci, et non divinum, et sacrum? Aut, si aliquam superlationem res capit, plus quam divinum et sacrum? Nam si facias ipse quod possis, et quod tuis sit viribus potentatuique conveniens, admiratio non habet quod exclamet: Id enim quod potueris, feceris, et quod præstare debuerit vis tua, ut operis esset una, et ipsius qui operaretur, qualitas. Transcribere posse in hominem jus tuum, et quod facere solus possis, fragilissimæ rei donare, et participare faciendum, supra omnia sitæ est potestatis, continentisque sub sese est rerum omnium causas, et rationum facultatumque naturas.——Neque quidquam est ab illo (Christo) gestum, per admirationem stupentibus cunctis, quod non omne donaverit faciendum parvulis illis et rusticis, et eorum subjecerit potestati. Arnob. lib. i. p. 18.

lame, into an undoubted perfuasion of their being perfectly cured, every way found and intire; nay, the dead themselves, into a ſtrong belief of their having come back to life again! But let us conſider:

As the higheſt, or the only infallible evidence we can have of our own being or exiſtence, is the conſciouſneſs of our exerting ſuch particular powers and faculties, ſo, after this manner, or by this inward conſciouſneſs of ſuch certain, undoubted powers producing their proper effects, were the Apoſtles ſenſible of their having a power of ſpeaking languages, and healing diſeaſes: And thus likewiſe did the blind, the lame, &c. from their inward feelings of the real change produced in the ſtate of their bodies, as they came under the apoſtolical influence, perceive themſelves cured. In their belief therefore of the reſurrection and aſcenſion of *Jeſus*, grounded on ſuch evidence, the Apoſtles, and all thoſe upon whom they exerted their healing power, muſt have been as certain of their being void of all enthuſiaſm, as they were ſure of their own exiſtence: And as the men of that age, who were eye-witneſſes, could not but be induced; ſo, we, at this diſtance of time, from our being ſatisfied as to the truth and certainty of thoſe facts, the real effects of real powers, fairly confeſſed, as I have explained in the firſt *Section*, by the earlieſt oppoſers of Chriſtianity, are inevitably led, with as little heſitation, to pronounce, *The Apoſtles were no Enthuſiaſts*.

Upon the whole: From all theſe particulars laid together, I have given, what, in my apprehenſion, is a full and clear, a convincing proof, that the Apoſtles, in none of thoſe great articles of the Chriſtian faith, wherein, it may be thought, they ſtand moſt expoſed to have ſuch a charge laid againſt them, can at any rate be counted Enthuſiaſts. And
whereas

whereas they are, manifeftly, in no fort liable to this imputation in thofe fundamental articles of the Chriftian revelation; with no fhew of reafon can it be alledged, that enthufiafm was the great fpring that fet them a-going, and fupported them in the propagation of the Gofpel. For, according to what I have laid down in the *Third General Obfervation, Sect.* XIX. had they been actuated in the manner they were, by any fuch mad, extravagant principle, of neceffity, the diftemper muft have been derived to other parts of their conduct, either in opinion or in practice, efpecially in thofe particulars, wherein it was moft eafy and natural for their imagination to rave and grow delirious, fuch as are the refurrection and afcenfion: In the belief of which articles, they appear at an infinite diftance from the fmalleft degree of enthufiafm.

No man, therefore, who attends to the nature of things, and is not led away by mere fancy and felf-delufion, but thinks without biafs, and hearkens to the dictates of reafon, can fuffer himfelf to apprehend, that the Apoftles were a company of poor, deluded creatures, going about the world under the power of enthufiafm, and foolifhly expofing themfelves to all kinds of miferies, having no commiffion from heaven, as they pretended, to propagate the Gofpel among mankind, which was the only thing that involved them in all their hardfhips and calamities. I cannot but flatter myfelf, that, from what I have been difcourfing hitherto, every impartial man will conclude quite the contrary. And the guilt and fhame of being found fcandaloufly partial in judging of characters, ought to engage our Freethinkers, in particular, to come with all readinefs into this conclufion. For what opinion have
thofe

those Gentlemen concerning that man, who, as *Cicero* alledges, *first fetched Philosophy from heaven?*

SECT. XXIII.

By what Arguments the Deists can vindicate Socrates *from Enthusiasm; by the same must they justify the Apostles.*

I Confess, indeed, that for any particular man or company of men, absolutely to neglect all their own private interests in this life, and intirely to devote themselves to the spiritual good, the moral improvement of other people; for the sake of this service to forego all their present ease and quiet, to suffer poverty, and all other hardships, even death itself, under a persuasion, that in all this they are acting in obedience to the will of God: This is an instance of so much self-denial, of such high beneficence towards mankind; it is an event so uncommon and extraordinary, so widely different from the way of the world, and from any dispositions that we ourselves are conscious of, that people are strongly tempted to suspect, that the persons thus employed are out of their sober senses; that they are far gone in the visionary way, and can be government by nothing but enthusiasm. It is upon their taking such a general heedless view of the conduct of the Apostles, I am apt to conjecture, that the Deists, otherwise strongly prejudiced, have unhappily come into their dangerous mistake about the character of those first Publishers of the Gospel, and to regard them as so many poor deluded Enthusiasts, who, instead of the notice and reverence, deserve the pity and compassion of the sober, and thinking part of mankind. But, I say, I would gladly know of our Deists, What character, in matters of religion, does *Socrates* bear among them whom, in concert with Lord *Shaftesbury*, they willingly confess "the greatest of Philosophers, the very founder of philosophy itself?"

This divine man, the divinest, as the noble Author assures us, who had ever appeared in the Heathen world, abandoning his worldly ease, and totally neglecting all his own private affairs, did, for many years, employ all his thought and care in promoting the spiritual good, the moral improvement of his fellow citizens. Nor did he leave it to people's pleasure to attend his instructions, but he went about intruding himself, as the world would now reckon it, upon the repose or business of other people; and in this manner, making up to rich and poor, to citizen and stranger, to all men, without distinction, warmly recommended to them the love and practice of virtue (*a*). At the same time, so zealous

---

(*a*) We have a specimen of Socrates's way in the case of Xenophon.

Τȣτον ἐκ ξενωπῶ, φασὶν, ἀπαντήσαντα Σωκράτει, διατεῖναι τὴν βακτηρίαν ᾗ κωλύειν παριέναι, πυνθανόμενον ποῖ πιτράσκοιτο τῶν προσφερομένων ἕκαςον· ἀποκρινομένȣ δὲ, πάλιν πυθέσθαι, Πȣ δὲ καλοὶ κἀγαθοὶ γίνονται; ἀπορήσαντος δὲ, Ἕπȣ τοίνυν, φάναι, ᾗ μάνθανε, ᾗ τȣντεῦθεν ἀκροατὴς Σωκράτȣς ἦν. D. Laert. in Xenoph.

Should a man now take upon him to use the same freedom with our young Gentlemen, which Socrates did with those of his time, what character would he bear? Socrates's whole life was such a constant series of what the world now calls impertinent meddling, troublesome cant, or wild enthusiasm, that one cannot help observing, if the Deists are not shamefully ignorant of this Philosopher's course of life, they are notoriously guilty of respect of persons, in their judgment about the Apostles.

zealous was he in the discharge of this service, that, for the sake thereof, he chearfully suffered poverty, and reproach, and death: Nothing, in a word, was able to overcome the obstinacy of his concern for the spiritual good of mankind. And, let our Infidels speak impartially, has not all this very much the appearance of rank enthusiasm?

Nay, *Socrates* takes upon him boldly to tell his Judges, " They might acquit or condemn him, it
" was indifferent to him; for his part, he was ab-
" solutely determined, was he even often to suffer
" death, never to change his course of life, but al-
" ways to persist in using his best endeavours to do
" all the good he was able to the souls of men;
" openly avowing he could no otherwise approve
" himself to God, who had charged him with that
" service, and whose authority he would obey ra-
" ther than that of man." Thus we are still kept in view of what the world may be apt to think, a bold resolute Enthusiast.

And, to compleat the character, *Socrates* may seem to express a great deal of enthusiastic pride and vanity: Says he, before his Judges, " As to the
" integrity of my life, I will yield to no man.
" And indeed the consciousness of my having al-
" ways lived in the constant exercise of holiness
" and righteousness, affords to me the most
" pleasing reflections; and it mightily adds to my
" joy, that my companions think the same of me.
" So that your condemning me will prove more
" hurtful to yourselves than to me: For death, in
" my case, can never possibly be an evil. It is not
" therefore for my own sake, but for yours, that I
" am making this defence; that, if possible, I may
" prevent your giving judgment against me, where-
" in you would become guilty, not only of con-
" demning

"demning an innocent man, but of rejecting the
"gift which God hath bestowed upon you; a gift,
"the best you could receive, and of such conse-
"quence to your well-being, that putting an end
"to my Ministry, by condemning me to death,
"you will sleep on in your wickedness, unless God
"shall be pleased, out of his concern for you, to
"send you some other Instructor. Nay, I will ven-
"ture to prophesy, that heavier judgments than
"any death you can inflict upon me, shall soon o-
"vertake you (*b*)."

Such

(*b*) All these particulars in the conduct of Socrates, are reported, in his Apology, by Plato and Xenophon. And, for the satisfaction of the Reader, or to save him some trouble, I shall here transcribe them:

Καὶ ἐγὼ οἶμαι ὐδὲν πω ὑμῖν μεῖζον ἀγαθὸν γενέσθαι ἐν τῇ πόλει, ἢ τὴν ἐμὴν τῷ θεῷ ὑπηρεσίαν, ὐδὲν γὰρ ἄλλο πράτθων ἐγὼ περιέρχομαι ἢ πείθων ὑμῶν ᵹ νεωτέρυς ᵹ πρεσβυτέρυς μήτε σωμάτων ἐπιμελεῖσθαι μήτε χρημάτων πρότερον, μήτε ἄλλυ τινὸς ὕτω σφόδρα, ὡς τῆς ψυχῆς, ὅπως ὡς ἀρίςη ἔςαι. ―――
ὦ ἄνδρες Ἀθηναῖοι, ἢ πείθεσθε Ἀνύτῳ, ἢ μὴ ᵹ ἢ ἀφίετέ με, ἢ μὴ ὡς ἐμῦ ὐκ ἂν ποιήσοντος ἄλλα ὐδ' εἰ μέλλω πολλάκις τεθνάναι. ―――
εὖ γὰρ ἴςε ἐὰν ἐμὲ ἀποκτείνητε τοιῦτον ὄντα οἷον ἐγὼ λέγω, ὐκ ἐμὲ μεῖζω βλάψετε ἢ ὑμᾶς αὐτὸς. ἐμὲ μὲν γὰρ ὐδὲν βλάψει, ὔτε Μέλιτος, ὔτε Ἄνυτὸς. ὐδὲ γὰρ ἂν δύναιντο. ―――
νῦν ὖν, ὦ ἄνδρες Ἀθηναῖοι, πολλῦ δέω ἐγὼ ὑπὲρ ἐμαυτῦ ἀπολογεῖσθαι ὥς τις ἂν οἴοιτο, ἀλλ' ὑπὲρ ὑμῶν, μὴ ἐξαμάρτητε περὶ τὴν τῦ θεῦ δόσιν ὑμῖν, ἐμῦ καταψηφισάμενοι. ἐὰν γάρ με ἀποκτείνητε ὐ ῥᾳδίως ἄλλον τοιῦτον εὑρήσετε, ἀτεχνῶς εἰ ᵹ γολοιότερον εἰπεῖν, προσκείμενον τῇ πόλει ὑπὸ τῦ θεῦ, ὥσπερ ἵππῳ μεγάλῳ μὲν ᵹ γενναίῳ, ὑπὸ μεγέθυς δὲ νωθροτέρῳ, ᵹ δεομένῳ, ἐγείρεσθαι ὑπὸ μύωπός τινος. οἷον δέ μοι δοκεῖ ὁ θεὸς ἐμὲ τῇ πόλει προστεθεικέναι τοιῦτόν τινα, ὃς ὑμᾶς ἐγείρων ᵹ πείθων, ᵹ ὀνειδίζων ἕνα ἕκαςον, ὐδὲν παύομαι τὴν ἡμέραν ὅλην πανταχῦ προσκαθίζων. τοιῦτος ὖν ἄλλος ὐ ῥᾳδίως ὑμῖν γενήσεται,

Such was the conduct of *Socrates*: And if, all this notwithstanding, the Deists are positive, as I think they have good reason to be, that *Socrates* was no Enthusiast, as *Melitus*, in his charge, seems to ridicule

ται, ὦ ἄνδρες. ἀλλ᾽ ἐὰν ἐμοὶ πείθησθε, φείσεσθέ μȣ, ὑμεῖς δ᾽ ἴσως τάχ᾽ ἂν ἀχθόμενοι, ὥσπερ οἱ νυςάζοντες ἐγειρόμενοι, κρȣ́σαντες ἄν με, πειθόμενοι Ἀνύτῳ, ῥᾳδίως ἂν ἀποκτείνητε. εἶτα τὸν λοιπὸν χρόνον καθεύδοντες διατελοῖτε ἄν, εἰ μή τινα ἄλλον ὑμῖν ὁ θεὸς ἐπιπέμψειε, κηδόμενος ὑμῶν. ὅτι δ᾽ ἐγὼ τυγχάνω ὢν τοιȣ́τος οἷος ὑπὸ τȣ̃ θεȣ̃ τῇ πόλει δεδόσθαι, κλ. The rest is transcribed above, near the end of Sect. xvi. See likewise the other two quotations which there follow from Plato:

Εἴ μοι πρὸς ταῦτα εἴποιτε, ὦ Σώκρατες, νῦν μὲν Ἀνύτῳ ȣ᾽ πεισομέθα, ἀλλ᾽ ἀφίεμέν σε ἐπὶ τȣ́τῳ μέν τοι ἐφ᾽ ᾧτε μηκέτι ἐν ταύτῃ τῇ ζητήσει διατρίβειν μηδὲ φιλοσοφεῖν. ἐὰν δὲ ἁλῷς ἔτι τȣ̃το πράτ]ων, ἀποθάνῃ. εἰ ȣ̃ν με, ὅπερ εἶπον, ἐπὶ τȣ́τοις ἀφίοιτε, εἴποιμ᾽ ἂν ὑμῖν, ὅτι ἐγὼ ὑμᾶς, ὦ ἄνδρες Ἀθηναῖοι, ἀσπάζομαι μὲν κ̀ φιλῶ, πείσομαι δὲ τῷ θεῷ μᾶλλον ἢ ὑμῖν, κ̀ ἕωσπερ ἂν ἐμπνέω κ̀ οἷός τε ὦ, ȣ᾽ μὴ παύσομαι φιλοσοφῶν, κ̀ ὑμῖν παρακελευόμενός τε κ̀ ἐνδεικνύμενος, ὅτῳ ἂν ἀεὶ ἐντυγχάνω ὑμῶν, λέγων ἷάπερ ἔιωθα. κλ. Plat. APol. Socrat. p 29. C.

Ὀυκ οἶσθα, ὅτι μέχρι μὲν τȣ̃δε ȣ̓δενὶ ἀνθρώπων ὑφείμην βέλτιον ἐμȣ̃ βεβιωκέναι; ὅπερ γὰρ ἥδιςόν ἐςιν ἥδειν, ὁσίως μοι καὶ δικαίως ἅπαντα τὸν βίον βεβιωμένον· ὥςε ἰσχυρῶς ἀγάμενος ἐμαυτὸν, ταυτὰ ἕυρισκον τὰ τȣ̀ς ἐμοὶ συγγινομένȣς γιγνώσκοντας περὶ ἐμȣ̃. Xenoph. Apol. Socrat. p. 702. vid. p. 704.

Τὸ δὲ δὴ μετὰ τȣ̃το ἐπιθυμῶ ὑμῖν χρησμωδῆσαι, ὦ καταψηφισάμενοί μȣ. κ̀ γάρ εἰμι ἤδη ἐνταῦθα ἐν ᾧ μάλις᾽ ἄνθρωποι χρησμωδȣ̃σιν, ὅταν μέλλωσιν ἀποθανεῖσθαι. φημὶ γὰρ, ὦ ἄνδρες, ἔι με ἀποκτενεῖτε, τιμωρίαν ὑμῖν ἥξειν ἐυθὺς μετὰ τὸν ἐμὸν θάνατον, πολὺ χαλεπωτέραν νὴ Δία ἢ ὅιαν ἐμὲ ἀπεκτείνατε. Plat. ub. sup. p. 39. C. Vid. Argument. Busirid. apud Isocrat. Upon all which, let me subjoin Cicero's opinion:

His

ridicule him (c); must not one stand amazed, what it is they have discovered in the conduct of the Apostles, upon which they can ground against them such an imputation! There is so great a likeness of characters, that, if they think freely, one cannot but judge it impossible for them, not to be, at least, equally forward in justifying the Apostles. As Lord *Shaftesbury* calls him, the *philosophical Patriarch*'s penetration, his wonderful good sense and extent of judgment, the command he had of his thoughts and sentiments, the substantial truths, the noble instructions he proposed to mankind, his address and insinuation, his constant chearfulness of mind, the universal rectitude of his manners; all these, the Deists will confess, are convincing proofs of a clear head and a sober heart, void of all the ravings, of all the gloom, the madness, and extravagance of enthusiasm. But which of these qualities do the Deists find wanting in the character of the Apostles? Is it not much rather *here*, that a good eye perceives them, shining in their greatest lustre? I have often wondered, how the same men could so much admire *Socrates*, and yet bear in their minds so great a contempt of the Apostles.

But I begin now to foresee, that what I have observed in relation to *Socrates*, upon these two articles of imposture and enthusiasm, some people may be apt to apprehend, I mean to raise the character of that Philosopher too high, and would maintain
that

His et talibus [concerning the immortality of the soul] adductus Socrates, nec patronum quæsivit ad judicium capitis, nec judicibus supplex fuit, adhibuitque liberam contumaciam, a magnitudine animi ductam, non a superbia. Tuscul. lib. 1. cap. 29.

(c) Μοὶ θεῖόν τι ϰ̀ δαιμόνιον γίγνεται φωνή. ὃ δὴ ϰ̀ ἐν τῇ γραφῇ ἐπικωμῳδῶν Μέλιτος ἐγράψατο. Plat. ub. supr. p. 31. D.

that *Socrates*, tho' not in the same ample manner, yet as truly as the Apostles, was commissioned from Heaven to instruct mankind. And I would fain hope, there is no heresy, nothing contradictory to any article of the Christian faith, in my professing, I am strongly inclined to think there was in *Socrates*'s case something supernatural. I confess, there are some doctrines and practices, such as, the divinity of the heavenly bodies, and the paying them religious worship, said to be taught and observed by *Socrates*, wherein a man instructed and guided by Heaven, cannot well be thought capable of having any concern. But I violently suspect, we have no sincere genuine history of this great Philosopher; and that doctrines and actions are imputed to him, which he never thought or did. And, indeed, we are told, that *Socrates* himself complained of *Plato*, for making him hold sentiments which had never entered into his mind. *Xenophon*'s account of his doctrines seems to be much purer than what we have from *Plato*: And one may reasonably conjecture, that had they been transmitted to us without all mixture, they would have been found, in every article, far more agreeable to what one might expect from a man immediately employed by Heaven to reform the world, or, as I have elsewhere expressed it, who was raised up by the special Providence of God, to bear witness to the glorious truths of natural religion. And that *Socrates*'s Disciples mixed their own prejudices with their Master's doctrines, cannot be much wondered at, when one reflects, that the same would have happened to the doctrines of the blessed *Jesus*, had his Apostles been likewise left to themselves in explaining them to mankind.

If other people, however, are of opinion, that from those heavenly doctrines which *Socrates* certainly

SECT. XXIII. *Christian Revelation.* 311

tainly taught, and the divine part he really acted (for what can be more divine, than to deny one's self, and take up one's crofs, and follow God in the caufe of virtue and religion?) one cannot conclude the truth of his having had a fupernatural voice, commonly called his *Dæmon*, conftantly to attend him (*d*); or of his having been by dreams, and every other way whereby the Deity reveals himfelf to mortals, commanded of God to undertake the inftructing of mankind (*e*); yet furely they will acknowledge, that in this man's character, there is fomething moft uncommon and inexplicable. And fince the Deifts do maintain, that *Socrates* was quite free as well of enthufiafm as impofture, may not thofe who think not fo highly of this extraordinary man, bear with other people in this article, and employ what I have obferved from his conduct, in order to juftify the Apoftles from each of thofe imputations, as an *argumentum ad hominem?* One fhould think, if the Deifts fhall once be brought to judge as impartially, or with as unbiaffed difpofitions, about the Apoftles, as they do about *Socrates*, whofe characters, in fome very confiderable articles, do fo nearly refemble one another, they will be in a fair way of becoming profelytes of the Gofpel. In the mean while, I would here prefume to beg of our Freethinkers, as they are perfuaded of the integrity

(*d*) Ἐμοῦ πολλάκις ἀκηκόατε πολλαχοῦ λέγοντος, ὅτι μοι θεῖόν τι καὶ δαιμόνιον γίγνεται φωνή. Plat. APol. Socrat. p. 31. C.

(*e*) Ἐμοὶ δὲ τοῦτο, ὡς ἐγώ φημι, προστέτακται ὑπὸ τοῦ θεοῦ πράττειν, ᾗ ἐκ μαντειῶν, ᾗ ἐξ ἐνυπνίων, ᾗ παντὶ τρόπῳ ᾧπέρ τις ποτὲ ἄλλη θεία μοῖρα ἀνθρώπῳ ᾗ ὁτιοῦν προσέταξε πράττειν. ταῦτα, ὦ ἄνδρες Ἀθηναῖοι, ᾗ ἀληθῆ ἐστι, ᾗ εὐεξέλεγκτα. Id. ibid. p. 33. C.

grity of *Socrates*'s character, to consider these two or three reflections:

SECT. XXIV.

Socrates claims a divine Mission, and, in his Case, Providence seems to have taught the World, that to introduce true Religion and establish it among Mankind, unassisted Reason is quite insufficient.

SO far was *Socrates* from judging supernatural revelation absolutely needless, that he himself pretended a commission from Heaven to instruct mankind; and tell his *Athenians*, that, if after his death, God did not send them some other such Instructor, they would continue ignorant and wicked, and die in their sins (*a*). And as in this pretension, and in these sentiments, *Socrates* is approved of by *Plato* and *Xenophon*, and the most renowned among the Antients; may not one use the freedom to ask, for what good reason do the Deists, whilst they so much admire *Socrates*, *Plato*, *Xenophon*, &c. give themselves the strange liberty to ridicule the Apostles for pretending the same thing, and professing the same sentiments? I say, what matter of falshood, what subject of ridicule, do the Deists find in these passages of the Gospel? *God who at sundry times and in divers manners, spake in time past unto*

(*a*) Not only does *Socrates* condemn the principles of our modern Freethinkers, in his pretending to revelation himself; but in his professing (as one would think) that a fuller revelation than any he could pretend to, was still necessary, particularly to ascertain the immortality of human souls, and to teach mankind to pray. Vid. Plat. in Phæd. p. 85. C. Alcibiad. 2. p. 150. C.

Sect. XXIV. *Christian Revelation.*

to the Fathers by the Prophets, hath in these last days spoken unto us by his Son (b). *Now then we are ambassadors for Christ, as though God did beseech you by us; we pray you in Christ's stead, Be ye reconciled to God* (c). *O Jerusalem, Jerusalem, thou that killest the Prophets, and stonest them which are sent unto thee, how often would I have gathered thy children together, even as a hen gathereth her chickens under her wings, but ye would not! Behold, your house is left unto you desolate. For I say unto you, ye shall not see me henceforth, till ye shall say, Blessed is he that cometh in the name of the Lord.* (d).

In the next place, Socrates having been employed by the special Providence of God, to recover the interest of religion and virtue in the world, or to bring about the reformation of mankind, in the way of mere reasoning, or, as bare argument should be able to determine human faculties, without the assistance of miracles, or the concurrence of supernatural influences upon people's minds: Herein God, as if he thereby meant to prepare the world for the reception of the Christian revelation, seems to have given us a proof in fact, how very little is to be expected from mankind left to themselves, committed wholly to the conduct of their own understanding; or that the unassisted powers of human nature, in matters of religion, are not available to human happiness. For, notwithstanding all the powerful reasoning, all the zeal and labour, the winning address and insinuation, which Socrates daily employed among all sorts of men, to gain proselytes; yet, how few, how very few did he prevail on? And, as even those few, together with his

Vol. II.   R r

(b) Heb. i, 1. 2.
(c) 2 Cor. v. 20.
(d) Matth. xxiii. 37, 38, 39.

his doctrines while he was alive, did all of them retain some of the common principles of idolatry and superstition, *e. g.* confessing the divinity of sun, moon, and stars; and paying them religious worship; so, after his death, the very foundation of religion itself, the belief of the being of God, came very soon totally to be extinguished. So that,

In the *last* place, this experiment, if I may so call it, by mere reasoning to recover men to religion, presuming upon the innate strength of their unassisted faculties, soon failing intirely: If God shall be pleased to make any future attempt to reform the world, may not one reasonably expect, that those supernatural helps, for the want of which *Socrates*'s scheme proved ineffectual, shall be interposed? And do we not find those helps concurring in the Christian revelation?

Supposing *Socrates* to have taught no doctrines, but what in every article were pure and divine; yet working no miracles, (unless it be alledged, that his foretelling some particular events, that actually came to pass (*e*), may be counted of that nature) and his doctrines being attended with no supernatural influences on the minds of men; (unless one shall think otherwise, from *Plato*'s seeming to report, that the success of his instructions depended on the concurrence and influence of the Dæmon who was always with him (*f*)) he made but

few

(*e*) Vid. Plat. in Theag. p. 128. D. 129. Cic. de Divinat. lib. i. cap. 54.

(*f*) The passage is so remarkable, and so naturally brings to one's mind some texts of Scripture, such as Mark vi. 5. and others, which some people are pleased to make merry with, that I cannot but chuse to transcribe it:

Ταῦτα

few proselytes: And, his most intimate Disciples not being quite freed from all their prejudices, but still retaining some of their idolatrous principles; as, by this means, his instructions, in the minds of his Disciples, during his life, came to be mixed and adulterated; so, no provision having been made for recovering, after his death, the purity of his doctrines, and to propagate and preserve them to the world; those fundamental articles of religion, which he taught, and which directly overthrew all idolatry and superstition, could not be secured from falling into a total and absolute neglect. Thus it fared with the doctrines of *Socrates*, in the hands of men still universally famous for learning and philosophy,

Ταῦτα δὴ πάντα εἴρηκά σοι, ὅτι ἡ δύναμις αὕτη τῦ δαιμονίυ τύτυ ᾗ εἰς τὰς συνυσίας τῶν μετ᾽ ἐμῦ συνδιατριβόντων τὸ ἅπαν δύναται. πολλοῖς μὲν γὰρ ἐναντιῦται, ᾗ ὐκ ἔςι τύτοις ὠφεληϑῆναι μετ᾽ ἐμῦ διατρίβυσιν. ὥςε᾽ὑχ οἷόν τέ μοι τύτοις συνδιατρίβειν· πολλοῖς δὲ συνεῖναι μὲν ὐ διακωλύει, ὠφελῦνται δὲ ὐδὲν συνόντες· οἷς δ᾽ ἂν συλλάβηται τῆς συνυσίας ἡ τῦ δαιμονίυ δύναμις, ὑτοί εἰσιν ὧν ᾗ σὺ ᾔσϑησαι. ταχὺ γὰρ παραχρῆμα ἐπιδιδόασι· ᾗ τύτων αὖ τῶν ἐπιδιδόντων, οἱ μὲν ᾗ βέβαιον ἔχυσι ᾗ παραμόνιμον τὴν ὠφέλειαν· πολλοὶ δὲ ὅσον ἂν μετ᾽ ἐμῦ χρόνον ὧσι, ϑαυμάσιον ἐπιδιδόασιν· ἐπειδὰν δὲ μυ ἀπόχωνται, πάλιν ὐδὲν διαφέρυσιν ὁτυῦν.——ἔςιν ὖν, ὦ Θέαγες, τοιαύτη ἡ ἡμετέρα συνυσία· ἐὰν μὲν τῷ Θεῷ φίλον ᾖ πάνυ πολὺ ἐπιδώσεις ᾗ ταχύ· εἰ δὲ μὴ, ὐ. Plat. in Theag. p. 129. E. This last sentence, and what follows a few lines after, viz. αὐτὸ τὸ ϑεῖον τὸ σοὶ γιγνόμενον πειρασόμεϑα παραμυϑεῖσϑαι εὐχαῖσί τε ᾗ ϑυσίαις, seem to me to confirm Simmias's opinion in Plutarch, or to put it beyond question, that this ϑεῖον τι ᾗ δαιμόνιον, which constantly attended Socrates, cannot be construed *his own mind*, as some people imagine; but must be understood, as it was believed by those of his own age, and by many eminent Authors of after-ages, *something supernatural*, or a *divine intelligence*.

losophy, acting only upon the strength of their natural faculties. And,

In like manner, had the Apostles, even after the resurrection of our Saviour, been left to their own understanding, in reporting and explaining the doctrines of their Master: As we should have been ignorant of some important truths of the Gospel; so others would have been corrupted by a gross mixture of absurd opinions and prejudices; and hardly any thing of the evangelical institution could have long subsisted. But, by a supernatural interposition, all along from the day of Pentecost, the Apostles came to be wholly cleared of all their prejudices; their minds were opened to recollect, and to conceive a just and full understanding of the doctrines of our Lord (g); they were enabled to work miracles; and their instructions were seconded, as I shall explain afterward, by supernatural influences upon the minds of their hearers: And that, after their death, the pure doctrines they had received, might not, in any age, be lost or neglected, they not only faithfully committed them to writing, but they every where set a-part public Teachers, to explain and recommend them in religious assemblies, frequently to be held for that purpose; and they appointed, that a succession of men in that character or office should be continued to the end of the world.

Thus, I say, upon the total failure of *Socrates*'s scheme to reform the world from idolatry and superstition, and from vice and impiety; or to establish a system

---

(g) "These things, says our Lord, have I spoken unto you, being yet present with you. But the Comforter, which is the holy Ghost, whom the Father will send in my name, he shall teach you all things and bring all things to your remembrance, whatsoever I have said unto you. john xiv. 25, 26."

system of true religion among mankind, by the mere force of reason and argument, applied to the unassisted powers of human nature; the Deists may see, that what other things might be judged necessary, in any future attempt, to accomplish such a gracious design of Providence, were particularly employed by *Jesus Christ*, in the Christian institution: So that, according to the judgment of *Xenophon*, Christians are the men in the world, who, with good reason, may be deemed the happiest of mortals; since they are the men, beyond all question, blessed with an Instructor infinitely better than *Socrates* (*h*). But, I now come to explain our general conclusion.

SECT. XXV.

The general CONCLUSION *deduced and illustrated.*

FROM the principles of human nature, I have above observed, That it is as certain as any mathematical truth, that the Apostles, in the propagation of the Gospel, were animated with the prospect of some good or happiness, which, by means of that Ministry, they hoped to arrive at. And since I have, permit me to say, fully demonstrated, That the good they had in view was none of the enjoyments of *this* world; it must, of necessity, have been of *another* world, and, as they publish themselves, that consummate happiness which is at God's right-hand to eternity. It is true, people may be honest and sincere, and yet be imposed upon

---

(*h*) Εἰ δέ τις τῶν ἀρετῶν ἐφιεμένων ὠφελιμωτέρῳ τινὶ Σωκράτους συνεγένετο, ἐκεῖνον ἐγὼ τὸν ἄνδρα ἀξιομακαριστότατον νομίζω. Xenoph. Apol. Socrat. in fin.

upon or mistaken in their apprehensions of this nature:

But I have likewise, I hope, put it beyond all reasonable dispute, That, in their assured prospect of of a glorious immortality as the reward of their Ministry, the Apostles were clear and distinct, well founded, and in no measure governed by the strength of groundless fancy and imagination.

And having thus made it, as I think, unquestionably evident, that while the Apostles openly professed, that, in propagating the Gospel to mankind, they acted in obedience to the command of God, and under the prevailing hopes of a *crown of righteousness eternal in the heavens*, they were neither Impostors nor Enthusiasts, neither deluded themselves, nor deceiving other people; is not this conclusion unavoidable and infallibly certain? *viz.*

The great Father of spirits, after an extraordinary and supernatural manner, laying open to the minds of the Apostles the happiness or glories of heaven, as the sure reward of their propagating the Gospel of *Jesus Christ* to the world, and still continuing to apply this commanding motive to their active faculties, was thereby pleased to derive so constant and prevailing an impulse to their passions, the immediate springs of action, that in spite of all the most frightful oppositions and discouragements that every where befel them, they were made, with the greatest zeal and steadiness, still to exert themselves in the prosecution of that service wherein they had the honour of being employed.

This is a rational account of the conduct of the Apostles, which after no other manner can be made consistent with the essential principles of human nature, as they are universally known to operate in all sorts of men, whether Impostors or Enthusiasts, or
whether

Sect. XXV. *Christian Revelation.*

whether honest or wise men, with all their senses and reason strong, clear and regular about them. And, indeed, the character given *Sallust* as an Author, upon much stronger evidence, from their writings, belongs to the Apostles, of whom it may be truly said, they had " a nobleness of mind that made " them incapable of imposing on the world, and a " sedateness and extent of judgment that would not " suffer a cheat to pass upon itself." But because, for the truth of this argument, I all along mean to appeal to the inward sense and feeling, or to the consciousness of every man of common understanding, that will be at the pains to look into his own breast, or to consider what part he himself, assuming any determined character, would have acted in such particular circumstances; I hope the Reader will give me leave me to illustrate this conclusion, in briefly explaining human nature as it is governed by *Fears* and *Hopes*, the mighty springs of every arduous undertaking.

In the conclusion to which we have been necessarily led, it is insinuated, that the Apostles were under the power of a thorough strong conviction, that should they not pursue the propagation of the Gospel, and prove faithful in that service, they would certainly fall under the displeasure of almighty God, and come to be involved in all the miseries of another world. And the Apostles being absolutely free from all imposture, as well as enthusiasm, nothing can be more apparent than that this was really their case.

By an invincible necessity of nature, human minds do constantly bear an irreconcileable aversion to mere *pain:* Nor is it possible for any man to bring himself to that pass, as to make choice of pain purely as such, without any other consideration.

tion. It is true, there are daily instances wherein we see people voluntarily submitting themselves to certain degrees of pain; but, in all such cases, the patient must be supposed to consider his *pain* as a *good*, or as a promising means whereby to prevent some other pain, which, in his apprehension, would be more oppressive to his nature, or afflict him with greater uneasiness. In no instance, however, will a prudent man deliberately exchange pleasure for pain, without being well assured, as far as is possible, that no otherwise he can avoid some more terrible evil. And as those miseries which we mean to escape, must appear to us so much the more dreadful and insufferable, as the miseries to which we chuse to expose ourselves, in order to prevent them, are hard and severe; so the greater certainty will we endeavour to have, that these our present afflictions will effectually secure us against those other more frightful threatened calamities. So that if a wise man, under no sort of external force, with thought and deliberation, knowingly involves himself in any great hardships or miseries; this certainly is with a view to keep off some other more terrible disasters, which, he is well persuaded, would fall upon him and oppress him: And, if he undauntedly sustains those miseries he submits to, and goes on still under them, with inward chearfulness and triumph; this makes it manifest, that he heartily approves the choice he has made, and is in no doubt, so far as he is capable of judging, but it will answer his expectation, and have success attending it.

When we therefore come to understand, in fact, that the Apostles, having no prospect of better treatment in this life, and being compelled to it by no worldly or bodily force, did willingly, and with great chearfulness, undergo all the most dreadful ca-

Sect. XXV.   *Christian Revelation.*   321

lamities of this world, the cruellest persecutions and deaths; in propagating the Gospel of *Jesus Christ*; is not this an infallible proof, that they clearly foresaw, and were well satisfied in their own minds, that all the woes and miseries of another world would most certainly overtake them, if they did not heartily engage, and prove faithful in the Ministry of the Gospel; whilst their zealously attending that service would effectually protect them from those future pains and agonies? I cannot but think I shall have the inward conviction of every man, who looks into his own breast, and considers the movements of human nature, to go along with me in affirming; that no man of common sense, of any degree of reflection, being absolutely free from the influence of every worldly consideration, can deliberately chuse to expose himself to all the miseries of this life, without being thereto determined, from an undoubted, thorough persuasion, that no other way is left him, whereby to prevent his being for ever overwhelmed in all the gloomy horrors of another world. Thus it is that the Apostles must be understood to be under a necessity to preach and propagate the Gospel of *Jesus Christ*, as they hoped to escape eternal ruin. And what we have here concluded, from the general conduct of the Apostles, is, in so many words, expressly declared by themselves: *Though I preach the Gospel*, says the Apostle Paul, *I have nothing to glory of; for necessity is laid upon me; yea, wo is unto me, if I preach not the Gospel* (i). So that, I say, the Apostles were under the power of a strong conviction, that should they not pursue the propagation of the Gospel, and prove faithful in that service, they would

Vol. II.   S f

(i) 1 Cor. ix. 16.

would certainly fall under the displeasure of Almighty God, and come to be involved in all the miseries of another world.

And as the Apostles were well assured, that their escaping the being undone for ever, depended on their being faithful in discharging the Ministry of the Gospel; so they were no less persuaded, that they could no otherwise gain heaven, or attain to the enjoyment of future happiness. This necessarily follows from what I have just now explained. And, according to the principles of human nature, from which I have been arguing, it is apparent,

No man will chuse to part with any of his present possessions which he conceives necessary to the happiness of life, but upon the prospect of his thereby acquiring others, which he has reason to think will render his condition more easy and comfortable. The common principle of self-preservation, inseparable from the human constitution, necessarily prompts us to defend ourselves against all attacks, that would rob us of any of those comforts and conveniences, whereof we have the enjoyment: Nor, without extinguishing this principle, or directly contradicting its main power and influence, both which are impossible, can we chuse to forego those particular objects, in which we apprehend, is included our greatest good and happiness. Indeed, a man, as I have just now hinted, may willingly forfeit some lower delights, which now make up his present happiness, that he may attain to the possession of other things he has in prospect, which, on several accounts, he reckons more valuable: And to this, the principle of self-preservation, under the government of reason and prudence, will necessarily oblige us. But, at the same time, it must be confessed, that were it possible for us to keep what we

at

at present have, so as not to lose that which is in prospect, and which we regard as more necessary to our well-being, we would never chuse to quit the things already in our hand. No man, I am sure, would ever give up his estate to preserve or regain his liberty, nor would he willingly renounce all his worldly comforts for the sake of future felicities, had he it in his power to secure himself in the possession of all those valuable blessings, without their interfering with one another. So that we chuse to part with our present enjoyments, because we are well assured (for a man of any prudence will never act at random in such circumstances) that our keeping them would prove an unlucky bar to our attaining to those objects, that are of higher value, and which, we conceive, are of far greater importance to our safety and happiness.

Thus, if by my own deliberate choice, I chearfully forego all my present most valuable possessions, my safety and quiet, my reputation and fortune, my nearest and dearest friends and relations, and quit all regard to life itself, showing an ambition to lay it down, while I daily expose it to mortal dangers; as this evidently shews, I am certainly engaged in the eager pursuit of some other happiness ; so it serves sufficiently to prove, that beyond doubt I am persuaded, that the happiness I have in view can never be acquired, while I continue in the possession of my present enjoyments: For, did I see there is no inconsistency betwixt my retaining the good things now in my hands, and my arriving at those at a distance, which I judge far more eligible, such sort of conduct could be compatible to no one, but to an arrant fool or downright madman. And when the Apostles, without any the least regard or attachment to any earthly thing whatsoever, do in a
chearful

chearful and triumphant manner, deliberately abandon and forsake all and every thing that can be counted near and dear and comfortable to men in this world; must not this be esteemed full and clear evidence, that they were under the strongest convictions possible, they could no otherwise gain heaven, or attain to the fruition of eternal happiness? This conclusion, necessarily arising from the general conduct of the Apostles, as they must have been determined from the essential principles of human nature, shews itself distinctly in some of their express, particular declarations.

The Apostles indeed, had no ample possessions to forfeit for the sake of the Gospel; but they had enjoyments wherein they found life easy and comfortable. And as a smaller fortune is of as great consequence to a man that has no more, as the most opulent estate can be to the rich proprietor; so the Apostles, guided by the indispensable laws of our constitution, did not part with what they had, but upon the prospect of having something better in exchange. *Behold,* say they to our Saviour, *we have forsaken all and followed thee. What shall we have therefor?* And to this demand, so natural and reasonable in itself, our blessed Saviour, far from checking it as mercenary, is pleased to return this answer: *And Jesus said unto them, Verily, I say unto you, that ye which have followed me in the regeneration, when the Son of man shall sit in the throne of his glory, ye shall also sit upon twelve thrones, judging the twelve tribes of Israel. And every one that hath forsaken houses, or brethren, or sisters, or father, or mother, or wife, or children, or lands, for my name's sake, shall receive an hundred fold here,* in blessings incomparably more valuable, *and shall inherit everlast-*

ing life hereafter (k). So that the Apostles, in propagating the Gospel of *Jesus Christ*, did chearfully forego all their worldly enjoyments, having the assured hopes, that, in exchange, they should come to the lasting possession of a glorious immortality. *I am now ready to be offered*, says the Apostle Paul, *and the time of my departure is at hand. I have fought a good fight, I have finished my course, I have kept the faith. Henceforth there is laid up for me a crown of righteousness, which the Lord, the righteous Judge, shall give me at that day* (l).

Now these hopes and fears, whereby the Apostles were steadily governed in the prosecution of their enterprise, being, without question, sincere and rational, not pretended, nor yet arising from enthusiasm, they must have been derived to their minds immediately from heaven. And thus the great Disposer of our futurity, having been pleased to excite, *i. e.* to command the Apostles to pursue the propagation of the Gospel, by supernaturally affording them the certain prospect of future rewards and punishments, that should severally befal them according to their behaviour, there is no avoiding of this conclusion, namely, " As the Apostles were
" commanded from heaven to propagate the Gospel of *Jesus Christ*, so the great power, or the
" commanding motive, that animated them in the
" prosecution of their office, was a vigorous, lively
" persuasion impressed upon their minds from a-
" bove, that their eternal happiness depended on
" the faithful and zealous discharge of their duty
" in this particular (m): Upon which we cannot
" but

(k) Matth. xix. 27, 28, 29.   (l) 2 Tim iv. 6, 7, 8.
(m) Μὴ γὰρ ἐξεπλήεισαν, ὥςε τοιῦτόν τι λογίσασθαι ἁπλῶς

" but rest satisfied, that all the parts of their
" conduct, with relation to the Gospel of *Jesus*
" *Christ*, all the doctrines they taught, and all
" the miracles they wrought, in a word, *the*
" *whole of their Ministry is of God*, and *has a*
" *divine original.*" And this conclusion, already
so manifest, shews itself further supported, in a
strong, additional evidence, arising from the wonderful success that attended the first publication
of the Gospel.

SECT.

ἢ εἰκῆ; ἢ γὰρ ὑπερβάλλει πᾶσαν μανίαν τὸ προσδοκῆσαι ἄνευ
θείας χάριτος τοσούτου περιγενέσθαι πράγματος. πῶς αὐτὸ κατώρθωσαν μαινόμενοι ἢ ἐξεστηκότες; εἰ δὲ ἐσωφρόνουν, ὥσπερ οὖν
ἢ τὰ πράγματα ἔδειξε, πῶς ἄνευ τοῦ λαβεῖν ἐνέχυρα ἀξιόπιστα
ἐκ τῶν οὐρανῶν ἢ τῆς ἄνωθεν ἀπολαῦσαι ῥοπῆς, ὑπέμενον πρὸς
τοιούτους ἐξελθεῖν πολέμους, ἢ γῆς ἢ θαλάττης κατατολμῆσαι,
καὶ πρὸς μεταβολὴν τῶν τῆς οἰκουμένης ἁπάσης ἐθῶν τῶν ἐν
χρόνῳ τοσούτῳ παγέντων ἄνθρωποι δώδεκα ἀποδύσασθαι, ἢ στῆναι γενναίως ὅτῳ;—— εἰ δὲ ἢ προσεδόκων κρατῆσαι, ποίαις
ἐλπίσι τοσούτους ἀνεδέχοντο κινδύνους, εἰ μὴ πρὸς τὰ μέλλοντα
ἑώρων; Chrysost. in 1 Cor. i. 31. p. 270. The reflections that
follow, and those which Chrysostom had before made, after ver.
17. and 25. seem unanswerably to prove, that the Apostles
themselves were under the influences of heaven, and that their
instructions were likewise seconded by a divine power.

SECT. XXVI.

That the Apostles were commissioned from Heaven to propagate the Gospel to Mankind, is strongly confirmed from the divine Efficacy, that appears in the amazing Success of their Ministry.

A Few particular persons, by the special direction of the supreme Governor of the world, having been employed to instruct mankind in the great truths and articles of religion and virtue, it seems reasonable to expect, that one will find the instructions of those few powerfully seconded by the extraordinary favour and influences of the same kind Being, in whose name they carry on their Ministry. Indeed, had Providence pursued the measures which human prudence now finds necessary; I mean, since, for the conveniency of civil government, or the more commodious administration of civil justice, all the several states and kingdoms of the world have happened always to be divided in greater and smaller districts, had Providence, in each of these smaller divisions, qualified and raised up one or more public Teachers, and committed to their care, as 'tis now the course in Christian countries, the instruction of a competent number of people; it is possible, that human care and industry, without any supernatural interposition, might have been attended with some tolerable good success. But, for twelve mean and obscure persons, to have it in command to *go and teach all nations, baptizing them in the name of the Father, and of the Son, and of the Holy Ghost, teaching them to observe all things whatsoever Jesus had commanded*

commanded them (a). This is a scheme for reforming the world, which, supported by no means but human industry, must necessarily prove abortive. Such a number of Teachers, in a course of years, might have come to make some proselytes in some small districts; but how do the labours of twelve persons seem proportioned to the task of converting all nations? The undertaking, without the immediate concurrence of Heaven, with respect to any measure of success, is far too romantic to bear the face of probability. And yet, we learn from the history of the Apostles, that, by their Ministry, an universal spiritual kingdom was intended every where to be erected, that should stand against all the powers of hell, and last to the end of the world. So that, I say, only twelve persons having been sent abroad to found and propagate this universal kingdom among all nations, one may reasonably expect to find their instructions attended with some extraordinary influences from Heaven. And that it so happened, is put beyond question from undoubted matters of fact. But, to explain this article distinctly, we must consider the moral circumstances of mankind, at the time when the Gospel was first published.

The *Jews*, whose sacred Writings instructed them in the knowledge of the true God, of the designs of his mercy towards mankind, and of that religious service, those instances of duty, enforced by proper sanctions, which he would accept of, came nevertheless to entertain very gross and absurd notions, with respect to almost every article of religion and virtue. Tho' the whole of their temple-service, all the sacrifices, rites and ceremonies instituted in their

---

(a) Matth. xxviii. 19, 20.

their law, being only *a shadow of good things to come*, were therefore to disappear in the greater light of the Gospel; yet they held them to be of perpetual obligation; and, in those types and shadows, without regarding the real things intended, made the main of religion to consist. So far were they from imagining, that any of those temporary ceremonial institutions could be abolished, that they conceived it no less than blasphemy to propose it. This was the charge that was brought against St. *Stephen*, when, in preaching of the Gospel, he touched upon abrogating their temple-service, and other legal rites and ceremonies: *This man, say they, ceaseth not to speak blasphemous words against this holy place and the law; for, we have heard him say, that this Jesus of Nazareth shall destroy this place, and shall change the customs which Moses delivered us* (b). And,

As it is common among mankind, for people to abate of their concern for the substantial points of religion, as their zeal for outward ceremonies happens to increase; so it shamefully came to pass in the case of the *Jews*. They had got a set of men among them for their public Teachers, who, by their false glosses, and interpretations (mostly founded on oral traditions, which, instead of coming from God, as was pretended, were all mere forgery) had so strangely perverted and disguised the sense and meaning of the eternal laws of righteousness, that thereby they made void the commandments of God, and rendered people quite insensible to their force and obligation. So that outward rites and ceremonies, coming to be substituted in the room of the weightier matters of the law; that inward

(b) Act. vi. 13, 14.

purity and rectitude of foul, wherein religion particularly confifts, fell under a total neglect, and the exercife of judgment, mercy and faith had no reputation, in comparifon with the paying of tithes of mint, annife, and cummin. And thus people's minds being wholly withdrawn from all attention to moral duties, to the love of God and the love of mankind; and being taught to regard form and ceremony, fome ritual obfervances, as the moft important and neceffary duties, they muft have been intirely over-run with fuperftition, and quite loft to all fenfe of true piety and virtue. Nor was it only thofe doctrines of the Pharifees that perverted people's fentiments, and debauched their morals; there was another fet of doctrines taught by the Sadducees no lefs pernicious to religion. Thefe men openly profeffed, there is no fuch thing as Angel or Spirit, no fuch thing as a refurrection from the dead, no rewards or punifhments in another world. And, as fuch principles feem to afford very confiderable relief to the guilty confciences of wicked men, who cannot think of parting with their impieties; there is reafon to apprehend, that they were gladly embraced by not a few of the *Jewifh* nation.

Such were the religious fentiments that prevailed among the *Jews*, and in all their fuperftition and bigotry, they were ftrongly fortified by the notions they entertained about their *Meffiah*. Inftead of that fpiritual redemption, which their Scriptures taught them to expect for themfelves and the reft of mankind, they had all their hopes fettled in a temporal deliverance, that fhould free them from every public or national calamity. In their views of the *Meffiah*, they fondly conceived a great worldly monarch, who, by the fuccefs of his arms, was to

recover

recover the freedom and independency of their state; to extend their dominions, and to establish their government, in the overthrow of all other states and kingdoms: So that, upon the coming of their *Messiah*, whom they confidently expected about the time that *Jesus* appeared, the *Jews* flattered themselves, the yoke of their oppressors should be broken; and the world being subdued under them, their nation should for ever triumph, and possess the glory of an universal empire: In which happy situation, it was past doubt with them, the whole of their constitution, particulary their temple-service, all their religious rites and ceremonies, should be sacredly maintained, observed with pomp and lustre greater than ever; and, in time to come, stand firm and secure above the danger of any future shock or invasion. After this manner were the *Jews* affected with respect to matters of religion; and such were their expectations concerning the *Messiah*.

As for the Heathen world, so far as history can inform us, 'tis pretty certain, that, at the time when the Gospel was first published, learning and knowledge was farther diffused, and more universal than it had been at any former period whatsoever. But, notwithstanding all the improvements to which the Heathen had attained, they were still grossly ignorant and wholly in the dark, with respect to the essential articles of religion. There was no where to be found the knowledge of the one, only living and true God (*z*). Their best and greatest

(*c*) Zenoni, et reliquis fere Stoicis, Æther videtur summus Deus, mente præditus, qua omnia regantur. Cleanthes, qui quasi majorum est gentium Stoicus, Zenonis auditor, Solem dominari et rerum potiri putat. Itaque cogimur, dissensione sapientum, Dominum nostrum ignorare: Quippe qui nesciamus, Soli an Ætheri serviamus. Cic. Acad. 2. lib. iv. cap. 41.

greatest Philosophers, in all their inquiries and reasoning, went no higher in their notions of a supreme God, the great Author of all being, life, and good, than a material soul animating the universe; and they so firmly believed the divinity of sun, moon, and stars, that they judged it impious and destructive of religion to think otherwise (*d*).

And, as the Heathens were intirely destitute of the knowledge of God; so they were equally ignorant about a future state of existence. Those Philosophers, who professed the immortality of the soul, were able to propose no rational certainty:

Amidst

(*d*) What a wretched account does Arnobius give of himself, before he embraced Christianity! And, upon his change, how infinitely more manly does he appear? From his own experience, he justifies the character of Jesus, and vindicates the credit of his Gospel.

Venerabar, says he, o cœcitas! nuper simulacra modo ex fornacibus prompta, in incudibus deos et ex malleis fabricatos, elephantorum ossa, picturas, veternosis in arboribus tænias: Si quando conspexeram lubricatum lapidem, et ex olivi unguine ordinatum, tanquam inesset vis præsens, adulabar, affabar, et beneficia poscebam, nihil sentiente de trunco: Et eos ipsos divos quos esse mihi persuaseram, afficiebam contumeliis gravibus; cum eos esse credebam ligna, lapides, atque ossa, aut in hujusmodi rerum habitare materia. Nunc, Doctore tanto, in vias veritatis inductus, omnia ista, quæ sint, scio: digna de dignis sentio, contumeliam nomini nullam facio divino; et quid cuique debeatur, vel personæ, vel capiti, inconfusis gradibus atque autoritatibus tribuo. Ita ergo Christus non habeatur a nobis Deus? Nec qui omnium alioquin vel maximus potest excogitari, divinitatis afficiatur cultu; a quo jamdudum tanta et accepimus dona viventes, et expectamus, dies cum venerit, ampliora? Sed patibulo affixus interiit. Quid istud ad causam? Neque enim qualitas et deformitas mortis, dicta ejus immutat aut facta; aut eo minor videbitur disciplinarum ejus autoritas, quia vinculis corporis non naturali dissolutione digressus est, sed vi illata decessit.———Similiter Socrates civitatis suæ judicio damnatus, 'capitali affectus est pœna: numquid irrita facta sunt, quæ sunt ab eo de moribus, virtutibus, et officiis disputata, quia injuria expulsus e vita est? Adversus Gentes, lib. i. p. 13.

SECT. XXVI. *Christian Revelation.*

Amidſt the continual doubting and heſitation which they every-where betray, they all ſeem to hold a tranſmigration: And the Stoics, who were reckoned the moſt knowing and zealous in the matters of virtue, do, in this article, go along with Atheiſts, and maintain a final extinction of all human ſouls whatſoever.

Thus, nothing but groſs ignorance reigning among Philoſophers, what can one expect to meet with among the bulk of mankind? The common Heathen, ſuch of them, I mean, as were not Atheiſts, not only firmly believed the divinity of the luminaries of heaven, but they acknowledged that world of gods and goddeſſes, they entertained thoſe notions concerning them, and they paid them that worſhip and devotion, which their Poets particularly have repreſented as the common popular religion (*e*). And, as

---

(*e*) In the queſtion concerning the gods, Velleius proceeds thus: Expoſui fere non Philoſophorum judicia, ſed delirantium ſomnia. Nec enim multo abſurdiora ſunt ea; quæ, Poetarum vocibus fuſa, ipſa ſuavitate nocuerant: Qui et irâ inflammatos, et libidine furentes induxerunt deos; feceruntque, ut eorum bella, pugnas, prælia, vulnera, videremus; odia præterea, diſſidia, diſcordias, ortus, interitus, querelas, lamentationes, effuſos in omni intemperantia libidines, adulteria, vincula, cum humano genere concubitus, mortaleſque ex immortali procreatos. Cic. de Nat. Deor. lib i. 16.

  Idibus eſt Annæ feſtum geniale Perennæ
   Haud procul a ripis, advena Tibri, tuis.
  Plebs venit, ac virides paſſim disjecta per herbas
   Potat, et accumbit cum pare quiſque ſua.
  Sub Jove pars durat: Pauci tentoria ponunt:
   Sunt, quibus e ramo frondea facta caſa eſt;
  Pars ibi pro rigidis calamos ſtatuêre columnis:
   Deſuper extentas impoſuêre togas.
  Sole tamen vinoque calent: annoſque precantur,
   Quot ſumant cyathos; ad numerumque bibunt.
  Invenies illic, qui Neſtoris ebibat annos:
   Quæ ſit per calices facta Sibylla ſuos.

Illic

as to another world, they knew nothing of it, but what we learn from the extravagant accounts; which the same Poets have been pleased to afford us. So that the Heathen world was utterly ignorant of those fundamental articles, upon which alone religion and virtue can subsist; and the gods they professed, and the worship they paid them, only flattered the corruptions of human nature, and encouraged vice, lewdness and impiety (*f*). Their gods were brought upon the stage, and acted the most criminal characters (*g*).

Such, in general, was the state of religion among mankind in the days of the Apostles; and what stronger bar can one possibly imagine to oppose and hinder the progress of the Gospel? Both *Jews* and Gentiles, from their earliest days, having been trained up to a sacred regard of their several religious sentiments, absolutely repugnant to the evangelical institution; by the whole bias of their minds,

    Illic et cantant, quidquid didicêre theatris,
      Et jactant faciles ad sua verba manus :
    Et ducunt posito duras cratere choreas,
      Cultaque diffusis saltat amica comis.
    Cum redeant, titubant, et sunt spectacula vulgo :
      Et fortunatos obvia turba vocant.
    Occurri nuper : Visa est mihi digna relatu
      Pompa : Senem potum pota trahebat anus.
                      Ovid. Fast. lib. iii. ver. 523.

(*f*) Quid aliud est vitia nostra incendere, quam Auctores illis inscribere deos, et dare morbo, exemplo divinitatis, excusatam licentiam? Senec. de Brevit. Vit. cap. 16.

Πᾶς γὰρ ἑαυτῷ συγνώμην ἕξει κακῷ ὄντι, πεισθεὶς ὡς ἄρα τοιαῦτα πράτ]υσί τε κ̓ ἔπρατ]ον κ̓ οἱ θεῶν ἀγχίσποροι, Ζηνὸς ἐγγύς. Plat. de Repub. lib. iii.

(*g*) The God Mercury, who has likewise a great share in the comedy, speaks the prologue, and tells the audience of Jupiter, the hero of the play; Is amare occepit Alcumenam clam virum, usuramque ejus corporis cepit sibi : Et gravidam fecit is eam compressu suo. Plaut. Amphit.

minds, they muſt have been led zealouſly to retain them; wherein they would inſiſt with the greater eagerneſs, as thoſe ſentiments gave countenance to their corrupt inclinations. And, if to this we add, that their ſeveral religions made a conſiderable part of the civil conſtitution, and were under the protection of public authority, which ſeldom fails to oppreſs people's minds and bodies in favour of the eſtabliſhed orthodoxy; 'tis eaſy to conceive that the Goſpel of *Jeſus* could not poſſibly take place, and prevail among mankind, without overcoming the fierceſt oppoſition, not only the inveteracy of long confirmed habits, but the violence of all ſort of perſecution. And what oppoſition, in the common courſe of things, muſt have ariſen to the progreſs of the Goſpel, from people's vitious habits, one may learn from looking a little into their nature.

Certain it is, that, as in contracting any habit, which is done by particular acts frequently repeated, the mind grows up under a continued propenſion towards the object about which it is converſant; ſo this propenſion, in proportion to the frequency of thoſe acts, neceſſarily becomes ſtronger; and, if long continued, comes to be the inſeparable caſt or turn of the mind, and ſo is wrought into its very nature; a truth long ſince obſerved in this common ſaying we have among us, *Cuſtom is a ſecond nature*. And this I take to be the caſe of all finite ſpirits, even thoſe that are independent of all matter or body, with reſpect to thoſe habits they may have acquired.

But then, there ſeems to be an additional ſtrength in thoſe habits that belong to the human mind, ariſing from the particular make of our bodies. The fact itſelf is inconteſtable; and therefore it imports us very little, whether one can account for it philosophically: I only mean, in a few words, which may well enough be done upon the common hypothesis, to help the Reader to conceive, that, some some way or other, the passions or habits of the mind are mightily strengthened by the temper or disposition of the body. And,

Since soul and body, in the human constitution, do mutually depend on one another, and reciprocally affect each other in all the actions of life; one may imagine, that in apprehending any objects, about which our desires or aversions are employed, there is a certain motion or direction which the mind derives to the course of the animal spirits, answering to such particular affections, or that disposes the body to avoid such particular objects, or to pursue and enjoy them. Now, this motion of the animal spirits, while we are contracting any habit, being for some time frequently repeated, these parts of the body along which they flow, coming thereby to be so affected, that without any sort of resistance, they yield to their current, the mind has obtained a ready instrument to follow its thoughts, or to assist or promote its inclinations. And whereas the smallest circumstance or incident that can relate to those objects, to which we have been accustomed, is very apt to bring them to our thoughts, and those thoughts do immediately give a motion to our animal spirits, that cannot but naturally flow along those parts of the body, through which, by the frequency of their current, they have traced out for themselves a free and open course; hence it comes to pass, that the mind is strongly led away, and is almost continually bending towards them. And when one considers, that such particular parts of the body, by their having been long yielding to
such

such a certain motion of the animal spirits, do at length contract so great a firmness in such a particular position, or so strong a bent towards it, that it is almost impossible for them to receive any other; this gives us to understand, that the mind comes under a sort of necessity to pursue those objects, to which the mechanism of the body, its great instrument of acting, is almost unalterably turned and adapted. So that, I say, the particular temper and constitution of the body, which we acquire in the contracting of habits, strongly fortifies the dispositions of the mind, and renders our habits exceeding obstinate, and near the matter, wholly impregnable.

In the mean while, if our habits be vicious; as they are then more easily and speedily acquired; so they are by far stronger and more obstinate. For as the depravity of human nature, universally felt and complained of in all ages, has a constant unhappy influence upon our minds, perpetually bending us towards sensual and worldly objects, which by their presence make a deep impression on our hearts, while things at a distance very slightly affect us; and as the corrupt examples about us, and other powerful snares and temptations, are very frequent and numerous; so all those things conspiring together, to prompt us to the pursuit of sensual gratifications; the growth of our vicious habits must be very quick, and the root they take in our minds, deep and strong: Whereas, the same very things violently opposing us in the acquisition, and frequently besetting us in the exercise of any good or virtuous habits, this renders their growth very slow, and their continuance or stability not so very sure or certain; so that vicious habits are of all o-

ther the strongest, and consequently the hardest to be shaken off. But,

How stubborn must they be, when they are fortified by a persuasion, that, in indulging them, we have the favour and protection of that Being, to whom we pay our religious worship, and in whose hands is the disposal of our futurity: In this case, no checks of conscience, as if we were therein acting against our duty and interest, can disturb our criminal pursuits, or interrupt us in following the swing of our corrupt hearts. On the contrary, the conceit of our having the approbation of God to conspire with the bent of our inclinations, will derive such an impulse to our passions, as will make us go on amain in the course of our vicious habits; being now favoured as it were, *both by wind and tide*, and out of the reach of all restraint whatsoever. And what other was the condition, either of the *Jewish* or of the Heathen world?

The *Jews* were justified, as they thought, by the authority of Heaven, while they were firm in the expectation of a great secular prince for their *Messiah*; while they were settled in the persuasion of the perpetuity of their ceremonial law, and paid an equal, in many instances a greater regard to their traditions, than they did to the commandments of God. And as for the Heathen; in a suitableness to the nature and example of their gods, they could look upon them no otherwise than as patrons and protectors of impiety (*h*). And vicious

---

(*h*) Τί δ' ἂν εἴποις περὶ ἠδικῶ μέρος αὐτῶν; πόθεν, ᾗ ἐκ τίνων ὁρμώμενοι, ᾗ τίσι χρώμενοι λόγοις, πλάτ]ειν αὐτὺς εἰς ἀρετὴν δυνήσονται, ᾗ πλείσυ ποιεῖν ἀξίυς ταῖς παραινεσέσιν; —— ὓς γὰρ ᾗ δίχα τῶν εἰς τὸ χεῖρον ἑλκόντων χαλεπὸν μεταθεῖναι

ous habits thus universally supported, could not but prove every where most stubborn and inveterate.

Besides, that a man being always prone to regard those vicious habits, whereby he has been long governed, as so many undoubted maxims or first principles, not to be questioned or contradicted; from hence it comes to pass, that when any thing happens to be proposed to him, that would overthrow these settled principles; so far is he from giving it a fair hearing, or making it the matter of his serious inquiry, that forthwith he rejects it, without examination; and with contempt and scorn will express his prejudice against it. And must not this still keep him at the greatest distance from receiving any impressions, that can contribute to his conversion or reformation? Nay,

Tho' a man should go about to examine into those things, that are contrary to his settled and prevailing appetites, yet his mind, as to its notions of moral truths, being sadly involved in very great darkness and confusion, will not be able to discern the beauty and excellency, or the justness and reasonableness of those things that stand opposed to his vicious habits. For of a long time, having had no correspondence with such divine objects, they are none of his acquaintance, and therefore, when laid before him,

τα θεῖναι κακίας, ἢ πρὸς τὴν κρείσσω μεταςῆσαι μοῖραν ἀπὸ τῆς χείρονος, τύτυς τίς ἂν πείσειεν ἡμέρυς εἶναι ἢ καθεκτύς, θεοῖς χρωμένυς ὁδηγοῖς τῶν παθῶν ἢ προςάταις; ἔνθα τὸ κακὸν εἶναι, ἢ τίμιον, ὡς θεῶν τινα προϊςάμενον ὃ τὸ πάθος ἐςὶ. βωμοῖς τε ἢ θυσίαις τιμώμενον, ἢ παῤῥησίαν εἰληφὸς ἔννομον. τῦτο γὰρ τὸ δεινότατον, ὅτι ἃ τοῖς νόμοις κολάζεται, ταῦτα ὡς θεῖα σέβεται. τοσαύτη τις ὑμῖν τῆς ἀδικίας ἡ περιυσία. Greg. Nazian. Adver. julian. Orat. 3. p. 107. A. Ego homuncio hoc non facerem? Teren. Eunuch. act. 3. sc. 5.

him, he can make no judgment of them; only, in general, understanding they contradict his darling principles, and oppose that to which he is vehemently inclined, he is strongly prepossessed against them, and looks on them with so evil an eye, that whatever can be said in their favour, appears to him mean and contemptible; whilst the least objection that starts up to their disadvantage, is, in his conceit, mighty and considerable. At the same time, those objects which have been long familiar to his mind, intruding themselves almost continually upon his thoughts; his attention cannot but be very much broken and interrupted, which must of course prevent his pursuing any argument that leans not to the side of his commanding bias, with that measure of steadiness, that is necessary to conviction. And thus will he still continue under the power of his vicious habits.

Nay, suppose a man under the prevalency of such habits, to be able to lend so much attention, as shall not only discover to him the beauty and advantage of those things that are proposed to him, in opposition to those sentiments and customs to which he has been hitherto habituated; I say, suppose a vicious man's attention should not only make him sensible of the beauty and advantage of religion and virtue, but further engage him to purpose, for the future, steadily to embrace those contrary principles, and to govern himself by them in every instance of his after conduct; still I cannot but apprehended, it is a thousand to one if he shall continue any time of the same mind, or ever come to put his design in execution. The matter is, his vicious habits still exerting their influence over him, and exciting in his mind those thoughts and passions to which he has been long accustomed, this will darken en and confound all the reasonable notions he had acquired; and thus making him lose all sight of the beauty and excellency of religion, will put a stop to his pursuing the virtuous course he had intended, and bring him back again to the old bias of his corrupt mind.

In a word, a man, in crossing his vicious habits, necessarily undergoes no little pain and uneasiness: 'Tis manifestly against the grain, and cannot possibly be done without offering violence to one's nature. Experience may teach us, 'tis like the *cutting off of the right-hand*, or the *plucking out of the right-eye*, an operation there is no body but will make a thousand shifts to have prevented. When we therefore consider how utterly averse human nature is to every thing painful, and always strongly inclines to be undisturbed and easy, indulging to itself its own pleasures and gratifications, one may easily apprehend, that the conquering any vicious habit, is a matter of the greatest difficulty. On many accounts, it requires that labour and application, that watchfulness and circumspection, and that firmness and resolution, which, in this state of humanity, very few are capable of. At any rate, it is a work not possible to be effected all on a sudden, or without the assistance of a great deal of time and exercise.

Such is the nature of those habits, whereby *Jews* and Heathens, at the first promulgation of the Gospel, were absolutely governed. And when we reflect, that all their vicious habits, in their own nature very stubborn, were, amidst numberless bad examples, and all other snares and temptations, continually cherished and supported by the natural

depravity

depravity of their corrupt minds;——That they were further strongly fortified by a firm perfuafion, that the indulging them was acceptable to God, or to the feveral objects of their religious worfhip;——That they were regarded as fo many firft principles, and would therefore caufe every thing propofed of a contrary nature to be rejected without examination;——That they fo darkened the mind and broke its attention, that, fhould a man have gone about to examine into the doctrines of the Apoftles, he would not have been able to difcern their beauty and excellency, or to purfue the argument with that fteadinefs that is neceffary to conviction;——That they had taken fuch deep root in the foul, that tho' one fhould have come to perceive the excellency of the Gofpel, and to refolve to obey it, yet, by frequently exerting their influence, they would again confound all his apprehenfions, and thereby fully reftore the uncontrolled prevalency of his old biafs;——That the croffing one's vicious habits is always attended with pain, which being greater or lefs, in proportion to their ftrength, a man muft have been wholly averfe to the fubduing of thofe habits, which he could not but feel moft ftubborn and inveterate; I fay, when we reflect on all thefe particulars, one may judge, how very ftrongly both *Jews* and Heathens muft have been guarded againft any impreffions that could be made on them by the Gofpel of *Jefus Chrift*. And, indeed, what can we conceive capable of engaging them to endure the pain of conquering their vicious habits, and to forego the pleafure of indulging them, when, in giving up themfelves to their influence, they apprehended, they had the favour and approbation of their feveral
Deities?

SECT. XXVI. *Christian Revelation.*

Deities (*i*)? In the common course of things, one should think it impossible that any such persons, without

(*i*) From the following remarkable story, one clearly perceives, what sort of notions the Heathen had concerning their gods; and how powerfully the lewd and intemperate passions of human nature must have been thereby encouraged. Mundus, desperately in love with Paulina, not being able to overcome her impregnable chastity, bribes the Priests of Isis, to whose worship that Lady was greatly devoted; and, by their perfidy, obtains the gratification of his infamous passion; whilst the unfortunate Lady verily believed she was all night in the embraces of the god Anubis. Those impious flagitious Priests having agreed upon the reward of their villany.

Αὐτῶν ὁ γεραίτατος ὡς τὴν Παυλίναν ὡσάμενος γενομένων εἰσόδων, καταμόνας τε διὰ λόγων ἐλθεῖν ἠξίε· ᾗ συγχωρηθέν, πεμπτὸς ἔλεγεν ἥκειν ὑπὸ τῦ Ἀνὑβιδος, ἔρωτι αὐτῆς ἡσσημένε τῦ Θεῦ, κελεύοντος τε ὡς αὐτὸν ἐλθεῖν· τῇ δὲ ἑυκτὸς ὁ λόγος ἦν, ᾗ ταῖς τε φίλαις ἐνεκαλλωπίζετο τῇ ἐπὶ τῦτοις ἀξιώσει τῦ Ἀνὑβιδος, ᾗ φράζει πρὸς τὸν ἄνδρα, δεῖπνον τε αὐτῇ ᾗ εὐνὴν τῦ Ἀνὑβιδος εἰσηγγέλθαι· συνεχώρει δ' ἐκεῖνος, τὴν σωφροσύνην τῆς γυναικὸς ἐξεπισάμενος. χωρεῖ ἐν εἰς τὸ τέμενος, ᾗ δειπνήσασα, ὡς ὕπνε καιρὸς ἦν, κλεισθεισῶν τῶν θυρῶν ὑπὸ τῦ ἱερέως, ἔνδον ἐν τῷ ναῷ ᾗ τὰ λύχνα ἐκποδὼν ἦν· ᾗ ὁ Μῦνδος, προεκέκρυπτο γὰρ τῇδε, ἐχ ἡμάρτανεν ὁμιλιῶν τῶν πρὸς αὐτήν. παννύχιόν τε αὐτῷ διεκονήσατο, ὑπειληφυῖα Θεὸν εἶναι· ᾗ ἀπελθόντος πρότερον ἢ κίνησιν ἄρξασθαι τῶν ἱερέων, οἳ τὴν ἐπιβελὴν ἐκ ᾔδεσαν, ἡ Παυλίνα πρωὶ ὡς τὸν ἄνδρα ἐλθῦσα, τὴν ἐπιφάνειαν ἐκδιηγεῖται τῦ Ἀνὑβιδος, ᾗ πρὸς τὰς φίλας ἐνελαμπρύνετο λόγοις τοῖς ἐπ' αὐτῷ. Joseph. Antiq. lib. 18. cap. 3. § 4.

To this I cannot but add a passage in Lucian, concerning that Impostor Alexander, wherein we see the same notions prevailing: Only, instead of the God, here we have the Priest. Ἦν μέγα, ᾗ εὐκτὸν ἑκάστῳ, εἴ τινος γυναικὶ προσβλέψειεν (Ἀλέξανδρος) εἰ δὲ ᾗ φιλήματος ἀξιώσειεν, ἀθρόαν τὴν ἀγαθὴν τύχην ᾤετο ἕκαστος εἰς τὴν οἰκίαν αὐτῷ εἰσρυήσεσθαι· πολλαὶ δὲ ᾗ ἐξ αὐτῦ τετοκέναι παρ' αὐτῦ, ᾗ οἱ ἄνδρες ἐπεμαρτύρυν ὅτι ἀληθῶς λέγυσιν. Lucian. in Pseudomant. p. 772. Amphitryon

without having a great deal of pains and labour beſtowed on them, could ever come to ſubmit themſelves to the Chriſtian faith.

So that, on finding, that ſeveral thouſands of thoſe very perſons, one may ſay, infinite multitudes, every where thro' the world, without any previous endeavours to break the power of their vicious habits, did, all on a ſudden, chearfully embrace the Goſpel, and, with heart and hand, reſign themſelves univerſally to all its doctrines and precepts, this one cannot but regard as an event the moſt aſtoniſhing.——And ſtill more amazing muſt it prove, when one conſiders this very powerful temptation they all had to the contrary:

A main condition, on which a man was admitted into the profeſſion of the Chriſtian faith, was *his denying himſelf*, his renouncing the world in all its pleaſures and riches and honours; it was *his forſaking all* and *his taking up his croſs daily and following Chriſt*. Now, this was not a condition, of which the primitive Chriſtians had no proſpect of ever being put upon performing, nor yet what they could look upon as a thing at a great diſtance, that could not overtake them but at the end of ſo many years; on the contrary, it very ſoon happened, that a man was not then able to caſt his eyes about him in the world, but he was every where met by the moſt diſmal objects of miſery, cruelly oppreſſed for the ſake of the Goſpel; that gave him to underſtand, what dreadful ſufferings he muſt reſolve to undergo, from the moment he ſhould embrace that new religion. Nay, the Apoſtles

---

phitryon was not ill pleaſed that Jupiter had ſhared with him in his wife Alcumena. Pol me haud pœnitet, ſcilicet boni dividuum mihi dividere cum jove. Plaut. Amphit. Act. v. ſc. 1.

postles themselves took pains to inform people of those immediate dangers, that attended the profession of Christianity. And one should think, that St. *Paul*'s publishing his case to the world, was but a sorry way to gain proselytes, or to tempt a man to turn Christian. " He was in labours abundant, " in stripes above measure, in prisons frequent, in " deaths oft. Of the *Jews* (says he) five times " received I forty stripes save one; thrice was I " beaten with rods, once was I stoned, thrice I " suffered shipwreck, a night and a day I have been " in the deep: In journeying often, in perils of " waters, in perils of robbers, in perils by mine " own country-men, in perils by the Heathen, in " perils in the city, in perils in the wilderness, in " perils in the sea, in perils among false brethren; " in weariness and painfulness, in watchings of- " ten, in hunger and thirst, in fastings often, in " cold and nakedness, &c. (k)" Such was the miserable condition of the Apostle *Paul*; and every man who had the courage to espouse the same cause, for which he was thus suffering, was sure to be involved in the like calamities. The matter of fact is beyond question; Christians, in those days, stript wholly naked of all the comforts and conveniencies of life, had, for their common lot, *contempt, poverty, persecution*, every sort and every degree of misery, that the most cruel and revengeful passions could inflict upon them; nor could any man turning Christian then hope to escape those frightful dangers. So that, in embracing the Gospel of *Jesus Christ*, people, in those days, must have been alarmed and terrified, with all the most dreadful images of certain ruin and destruction.

Vol. II.   X x   Thus

(k) 2 Cor. xi. 23, &c.

Thus the *inward* principles and fentiments; the *inward* paffions and appetites; the *inward* confirmed habits of thofe who became profelytes; the *outward* cruelties and perfecutions of the Civil Magiftrate, of revengeful Priefts, and of enraged mobs; contempt, poverty, mifery of every fort and of every fhape, barbarous deaths; all thefe, the fierceft and moft violent oppofitions, arifing from all quarters, with united force, ftood in the way of the progrefs of the Gofpel (*l*). And, in fuch circumftances, what can one expect fhall be its fate?——If we judge of the event from the nature of things, or upon human appearances, muft not one totally defpair of fuccefs? 'Tis the opinion of one of our moft learned Infidels, that where there is no old revelation on which the new can be grafted (which was certainly the cafe of the Heathen world with refpect to the evangelical inftitution, and feems likewife to have been the cafe of the *Jews,* among whom the old revelation may be faid to have been intirely loft, as in the underftanding of the whole nation it had obtained a meaning quite contradictory to that which it originally bore: I fay, 'tis the opinion of one of our moft noted Freethinkers, that in fuch circumftances) it is hard, if not impoffible, to perfuade men to abandon their old principles: " If we con-
" fider (fays he) the nature of things, we fhall
" find, that it muft be difficult, if not impoffible,
" to

(*l*) Ἔτι δὲ Χριστιανοῖς ἡ Ῥωμαίων σύγκλητος βυλὴ, ᾗ οἱ κατὰ καιρὸν βασιλεῖς, ᾗ τὰ ϛρατιωτικὰ, ᾗ οἱ δῆμοι, ᾗ οἱ τῶν πιϛευόντων συγγενεῖς, προσπολεμήσαντες τῷ λόγῳ, ἐκώλυσάν ἄν, αὐτὸν νικηθέντα ὑπὸ τῆς τῶν τοσούτων ἐπιβυλῆς, εἰ μὴ θείᾳ δυνάμει ὑπερέκυψε ᾗ ὑπερανέβη, ὡς νικῆσαι ὅλον κόσμον αὐτῷ ἐπιβυλεύοντα. Orig. contra Celf. lib. i. p. 6.

" to introduce among men (who in all civilized
" countries are bred up in the belief of some re-
" vealed religion) a revealed religion wholly new,
" or such as have no reference to a preceeding one,
" for that would be to combat all men in too ma-
" ny respects, and not to proceed on a sufficient
" number of principles necessary to be assented to
" by those, on whom the first impressions of a new
" religion are proposed to be made (*m*)." But, in
spite of all opposition whatsoever, how gloriously did
the Gospel of *Jesus* every-where prevail?

Notwithstanding all their strong prejudices, and
the most forbidding and frightful discouragements;
upon the hearing of one single discourse, a vast number of *Jews* were so sensibly touched, *pricked at the
heart*, for their having crucified *Jesus Christ*, and
opposed his Gospel, that they were made to cry out
to the twelve Apostles, *Men and Brethren, what
shall we do?* And, by no less sudden and wonderful a
turn, when the Apostles directed them to *repent and receive Baptism in the name of Jesus Christ*, do they immediately, to the number of about three thousand souls,
embrace the Gospel with gladness, how contrary soever to their former confirmed notions and customs,
and submit themselves universally to all its particular doctrines (*n*). On another occasion, we have
an account of about five thousand more, who all at
once too, renouncing the opinions in which they
had been bred and educated, and wherein, by long custom and practice, they had been quite settled and established, joyfully embraced the truths of the Gospel,
and yielded themselves wholly up to its power and
influence (*o*). But, besides these two amazing instances of the success of the Gospel,

We

(*m*) Grounds of the Christian religion, p. 23.
(*n*) Acts ii. 41.   (*o*) Acts iv. 4.

We are told, that *the word of God increased*, that *the number of the Disciples multiplied in Jerusalem greatly*, and that *a great company of the Priests became obedient to the faith* (o). In a word, such vast multitudes, *both of men and women, were added to the Lord*; and people came flocking together in such crowds to the Christian profession, that the *Chief-Priest, and those that were with him*, were so much alarmed at this extraordinary event, which was like totally to overthrow the whole of their constitution, that, *filled with indignation, they laid their hands on the Apostles, and put them in common prison*, in order to prevent the spreading of this new religion (p). But, so far was the success of the Christian revelation from being put to a stand, that, in a short space of time, even in that very place where every measure was taken to prevent it, the number of Disciples amounted to several myriads (q). Nor did this mighty progress of the Gospel among the *Jews*, stop at *Jerusalem* or the land of *Judea*, it went on and spread itself all over those parts of the world where the *Jews* happened to be dispersed.

The Apostle *James* directs his Epistle to *the twelve Tribes that are scattered abroad*, and comforts them under those persecutions they were suffering for the sake of the Gospel. And the Apostle *Peter* writes his two Epistles to *the Strangers*, *i. e.* to the *Jews* scattered throughout *Pontus, Galatia, Cappadocia, Asia,* and *Bythinia*; wherein he speaks to them, as being formed into particular churches of *Christ*; for he exhorts the Elders that were among them,

---

(o) Act. vi. 7.
(p) Act v. 14, &c.
(q) Θεωρεῖς ἀδελφὲ, πόσαι μυριάδες εἰσὶν Ἰουδαίων τῶν πεπιστευκότων. Act. xxi. 20.

SECT. XXVI. *Christian Revelation.* 349

them, to be faithful in difcharging the feveral duties of that public office, with which they were invefted in the Chriftian church: And, in general, he recommends to all of them, *not to think it ftrange concerning the fiery trial they were enduring, as though fome ftrange thing had happened unto them; but to rejoice, in as much as they were partakers of the fufferings of Chrift, that when his glory fhould be revealed, they might be glad alfo with exceeding joy.* And, nce,
to preach the Gofpel to the *Jews*, one fhould think, that, from thofe two inftances juft now mentioned, of the fuccefs of the Gofpel in his hands, one may reafonably apprehend, that, in the courfe of his Miniftry, he gained over vaft numbers of profelytes to the Chriftian faith.

So that, altho' the whole of the *Jewifh* nation, was far from being converted to the profeffion of Chriftianity; there being, at this day, fcattered through the world, an infinite number of thofe people, whom, one is tempted to fufpect, a miraculous providence ftill keeps unmixed, wholly diftinct from the reft of mankind, as living witneffes of an ancient revelation; as ftanding monuments of the fulfilling of fome prophecies of the Gofpel; and as certain pledges for the accomplifhing of others, when the deftined time fhall come : I fay, tho' the whole *Jewifh* nation was far from being converted to the Chriftian faith, yet the fuccefs of the Gofpel, in fpite of all the mortal dangers that attended its profeffion; and, notwithftanding its being directly oppofite, clean contradictory to all thofe facred principles and practices, which, by long cuftom and habit, had taken deep root in their minds, and to which, beyond meafure, they were obftinately obstinately devoted, was, among them, most certainly very considerable.

But, how successful soever the Gospel was among the *Jews*, it was much more so among the Gentiles. Within the compass of a few years, so mightily grew the word of God and multiplied, that as we learn from the Epistles of St. *Paul*, not only at *Corinth* and several other places, but at *Rome* itself, there were churches, frequent assemblies of Christians, of very considerable note. And, indeed, the Professors of Christianity came soon to overspread all the *Roman* provinces. Not to speak of the banishment of the Disciples of *Christ* from *Rome*, which, a few years after the crucifixion happened under the Emperor *Claudius* (*r*). I shall only observe (what shews us the daily, or the continued success of the Gospel, and that hard or cruel treatment was not able to prevent its influences); That, soon after this, in the days of *Nero*, so numerous were the proselytes of the Gospel, so great a figure did they make, and so much were they distinguished by the public hatred, that, as if the world about them had held them capable of any whatever wickedness, when that Tyrant would have thrown off the odium from himself, he laid the burning of *Rome* upon the Christians, and, under pretence of that guilt, exercised, for several months, a violent persecution against them, wherein, not only the Apostles St. *Paul* and St. *Peter* suffered martyrdom, but a vast multitude of other Christians were put to the cruellest and most barbarous deaths (*s*). But all the inhumanities

---

(*r*) Vid. Sect. i. marg.

(*s*) Non ope humana, non largitionibus principis, aut Deum placamentis, decedebat infamia, quin jussum incendium crederetur. Ergo abolendo rumori Nero subdidit reos, et quæsitissimis pœnis

ties of *Nero* notwithstanding, and the cruel attempt which *Domitian*, not long after, made, to suppress and extinguish the Gospel every-where in the *Roman* empire, yet still it prevailed, and its prevalency was so great, that, before the death of St. *John*, the last of the Apostles, it had filled towns and villages, and all other inhabited places; so that Heathen temples were almost every-where quite forsaken and deserted (*t*). Thus, no opposition whatever was able

to

pœnis afficit, quos per flagitia invisos vulgus Christianos appellabat. Auctor nominis ejus Christus, Tiberio imperitante per Procuratorem Pontium Pilatum supplicio affectus erat. Repressaque in presens exitiabilis superstitio rursus erumpebat, non modo per Judæam originem ejus mali, sed per urbem etiam quo cuncta undique atrocia aut pudenda confluunt, celebranturque. Igitur, primo correpti, qui fatebantur, deinde indicio eorum multitudo ingens, haud perinde in crimine incendii, quam odio humani generis conjuncti sunt. Et pereuntibus addita ludibria, ut ferarum tergis contecti, laniatu canum interirent, aut crucibus affixi, aut flammandi, atque ubi defecisset dies in usum nocturni luminis urerentur. Tacit. Annal. lib. xv. cap. 44. This persecution is mentioned more briefly by Sueton: Afflicti suppliciis Christiani, genus hominum superstitionis novæ ac maleficæ. Suet. in Nero. cap. 16. " And says Lactantius:" Cum animadverteret Nero, non modo Romæ, sed ubique quotidie magnam multitudinem deficere a cultu idolorum, et ad religionem novam damnata vetustate transire; ut erat execrabilis ac nocens tyrannus, profilivit ad exscindendum cœleste templum, delendumque justitiam; et primus omnium persecutus Dei servos, Petrum cruci affixit, et Paulum interfecit. Lactant de mortib. persecut. cap. 2.

(*t*) Multi enim omnis ætatis, omnis ordinis, utriusque sexus etiam vocantur in periculum, et vocabuntur. Neque enim civitates tantum, sed vicos etiam atque agros superstitionis istius contagio pervagata est, quæ videtur sisti et corrigi posse. Certe satis constat prope jam desolata templa cepisse celebrari, et sacra solennia diu intermissa repeti; passimque venire victimas, quarum adhuc rarissimus emptor inveniebatur. Ex quo facile est opinari, quæ turba hominum emendari possit, si sit pœnitentiæ locus. Plin Epist. 97. lib. 10. Not long after Pliny, Justin Martyr and Tertullian give us this account of the progress of the Gospel:

to give a check to the progress of the Gospel; but great numbers of people of every age, and of every quality, in contradiction to their long confirmed habits, and the established bias of their minds, did every where abandon their idolatry and superstition, and, renouncing the worship of those Gods that patronized sensual gratifications, came to acknowledge only one supreme Being of infinite purity and rectitude, and, under the assured persuasion of a future state of rewards and punishments, submitted themselves chearfully to his holy and righteous laws: And all this they did, whilst they had the certain prospect of their being thereby involved in the greatest calamities, as to every article of their present enjoyments; even of exposing themselves to the cruellest deaths. With great truth, therefore, does the

---

Ὀδε ἓν γὰρ ὅλως ἐςὶ τὸ γένος ἀνθρώπων, εἴτε βαρβάρον, εἴτε Ἑλλήνων, εἴτε ἁπλῶς ὡτινιῶν ὀνόματι προσαγορευομένων, ἐν οἷς μὴ διὰ τῦ ὀνόματος τῦ ςαυρωθέντος Ἰησῦ εὐχαὶ ᾗ εὐχαριςίαι τῷ πατρὶ ᾗ ποιητῇ τῶν ὅλων γίνωνται. Just. M. Dial. p. 345.

Hesterni sumus, et vestra omnia implevimus, urbes, insulas, castella, municipia, conciliabula, castra ipsa, tribus, decurias, palatium, senatum, forum. Sola vobis relinquimus templa. Tertul. Apologet. cap. 37. "More fully elsewhere:" Inquem enim alium universæ gentes crediderunt, nisi in Christum qui jam venit? Cui enim et aliæ gentes crediderunt, Parthi, Medi, Elamitæ, et qui inhabitant Mesopotamiam, Armeniam, Phrygiam, Cappadociam, et incolentes Pontum, et Asiam, et Pamphiliam: Immorantes Egyptum, et regionem Africæ quæ est trans Cyrenen inhabitantes, Romani et incolæ: Tunc et in Hierusalem Judæi et cæteræ gentes: Ut jam Getulorum varietates, et Maurorum multi fines, Hispanorum omnes termini, et Galliarum diversæ nationes, et Britannorum inaccessa Romanis loca, Christo vero subdita: Et Sarmatarum, et Dacorum, et Germanorum, et Scytharum, et abditarum multarum gentium, et provinciarum, et insularum multarum nobis ignotarum, et quæ enumerare minus possumus, in quibus omnibus locis Christi nomen, qui jam venit, regnat. Tert. adv. Judæos. cap. 7.

the Apostle observe, that *the weapons of their warfare,* the measures they employed in propagating the Gospel, *were not weak, but powerful and mighty to the pulling down of strong holds, casting down imaginations, and every high thing that exalteth itself against the knowledge of God, and bringing into captivity every thought to the obedience of the Gospel of Christ* (*u*).

Now, this rapid progress of the Gospel, this wonderful success, which among *Jews* and Heathens, every where attended its first promulgation, seems, I say, to have something in it more than human.

Those infinite numbers of people, who, during the short time of the Ministry of the Apostles, throughout *Asia, Africa,* and *Europe,* in all the parts of the known world (*x*), rejected their idolatry and superstition, and embraced the Gospel of *Jesus Christ,* were not taken one by one, and convinced separately, or in small classes or companies, of the pernicious errors, the destructive courses they were following; nor were they trained up by easy degrees, and, as it were, by piece-meal in the knowledge of the truths of the Gospel: And yet this way of managing, one should think, was absolutely necessary, in order to have prevailed with those who were under the power of the most obstinate and stubborn prejudices; sure I am, that now-a-days we should find it so, were we going about to persuade the world into a religion wholly repugnant to that to which they are intirely devoted: I say, it was not by easy steps, by slow and gentle degrees, that people were gained over to the belief and profession of the Gospel: No, the Apostles generally propounded their doctrines to vast confluences of people all at once, and, in the name of

(*u*) 2 Cor. x. 4, 5.
(*x*) Colos. i. vi.

God, giving them the certain prospect of an after-judgment, a future state of rewards and punishments, earnestly beseeched and warmly pressed their obedience. So that barely upon such representations, without any more ado, thousands of people have all at once, in spite of their most inveterate prejudices, and in defiance of the most threatening dangers, on a sudden, totally quit all their errors and their lusts, and, at the manifest hazard of every worldly enjoyment, of life itself, resolutely declared for the Christian faith. And, in recollecting what powerful influence any habit whatsoever, particularly those that are vitious, never fail to have on human minds, more especially, when the indulging one's habits is attended with safety, and the altering one's course would expose us to every degree of misery; must not such a revolution be counted extremely wonderful?

What more astonishing, than great multitudes of people, under the power of the most stubborn habits and prejudices, all along from their infancy, up to this very moment, sticking to such principles of religion, as flattered their proud and vicious habits, and indulged and protected them in all their sensual pleasures and gratifications; at the same time, with respect to both worlds, living undisturbed, enjoying all the sweets and comforts of a peaceful life; I say, what can a man conceive more astonishing, than many thousands of such persons, all of a sudden, bidding defiance to their most inveterate prejudices, chearfully renouncing all their present ease and quiet, and every thing else that could make them happy in this world, and immediately turning over to a religion, clean contradictory to their former confirmed principles, and undoubted

undoubted interests; upon the embracing of which they observed the most dreadful miseries hanging over their heads, and threatening every moment to swallow them up! This is a revolution that is indeed full of wonder, and cannot but appear so to every considerate man. But, how an event so astonishing, could possibly have happened, without the interposition of some supernatural power, immediately exerted on the minds of men, is, I confess, beyond my comprehension.

'Tis very certain, as things are now constituted, no man can have immediate access to the mind of another, so as to convey to him what thoughts and impressions he could wish him to be inspired with. Our senses are the only avenues, by which our minds are accessible to our fellow-men; and these are so much in our own power, and so closely follow the direction of the mind, that we open or shut them to whatever applications are made to us, as we ourselves, in our secret thoughts, are disposed or chuse to be employed. They may, indeed, appear to stand open to those addresses that are made to us, and whereby it is designed we should be so and so affected: But our minds in the mean while, may be turned quite another way, and amusing themselves only with their own entertainments. Or, if we be not thus wholly taken off, and otherwise employed, our attention may be very much broken, and in great confusion; or it may be very slight and superficial, or not all lasting and durable. And while our attention is thus scattered or superficial, and not steddy and permanent, what signify the most lively and vigorous addresses that mortal man can make to us? The clearest demonstrations, and most forcible arguments, either not being perceived, or making

king no lasting impression on the mind, shall not be able to convince and determine us. So that, in such circumstances, we shall certainly hold out against the warmest and strongest representations wherewithal we can be attacked, how much soever our complying with them might contribute to our true honour and interest. And therefore,

Without a man has a power to arrest our attention, to make it close and penetrating, and of so permanent a nature, that it shall abide with us, till we be thoroughly convinced and determined, as the considerations laid before us are naturally fit to sway and direct us; he shall find it quite impossible to alter the course of our thoughts and actions, or to gain us over to a steady and hearty pursuit of our duty and interest. But, by what means shall a man acquire so great a command over human minds? I have above observed, that, under the prevalency of vicious habits, we are not ourselves able to command our attention, to keep it steady, and still awake in our minds: And, since no man has immediate access to our inward thoughts, which must be first engaged, before we feel a conviction that may come to determine us; he may discourse to us from one day to another, on matters of the highest consequence; he may urge them upon us with all possible distinctness, and in the most moving and passionate manner, and yet, all the while, he shall be doing nothing, but beating the air only. We are strongly guarded against all the efforts he can use to affect us, and will stupidly stand the shock of his most vigorous addresses; for, as I have already said, till our attention be once fixed, and made permanent, (which, in the present case, is neither in his power, nor in our own), it can never possibly happen,

happen, that any thorough converſion ſhould be wrought on us.

I confeſs it a thing poſſible (and this is really all that can be ſaid for it) for one man to gain over another, who has been long under the prevailing power of vicious habits, to the love and practice of piety and virtue. And, if we will try the experiment, we ſhall ſoon find what a tedious and difficult taſk we have undertaken; what art and ſkill, what addreſs and inſinuation, we muſt neceſſarily employ, ere one can bring him to any tolerable degree of attention; and what pains and labour it will coſt us to improve and ſtrengthen this attention, and to keep it ſteady upon his mind, till we get him confirmed in all goodneſs. From the nature of vicious habits it ſeems neceſſarily to ariſe, that this event is next to impoſſible. *Can the Ethiopian change his ſkin, or the leopard his ſpots? Then may ye alſo do good that are accuſtomed to do evil.* No wonder then, for one ſucceſsful attempt of this nature, we ſhall meet with a thouſand diſappointments.

But, if it be a matter of the greateſt difficulty, and next to a miracle, even by a tedious courſe of the moſt inſinuating endeavours, to make a man a proſelyte to virtue, in whom vicious habits have taken deep root, and have been long confirmed, it muſt undoubtedly be altogether impoſſible, to bring about a compleat and thorough change all on a ſudden. For, in order to effect this ſudden converſion on a man hardened in ſin, and wholly in the power of ſenſual appetites, is it not abſolutely neceſſary, that, all at once, his mind be quite cleared of all that darkneſs and confuſion in which he is involved? That thoſe impertinent thoughts, that would be always crowding in upon him, from thoſe objects to which he has been habituated, be kept off

and

and debarred? That his attention be awakened and kept steddy; whilst his mind is opened to the truth and excellency of those things that are laid before him, till they effectually engage his affections on the side of virtue and religion? And that, from those things, such powerful impressions be at the same time conveyed to him, as shall totally break the force of his vicious habits, and give him a quite other cast and turn of mind, that will make him always attentive for the future, in the steddy and resolute pursuit of his real duty and interest? Besides, that, if this new turn of mind, and change of life, is manifestly the high way to expose a man to great persecutions and miseries, not to be avoided; is it not further absolutely necessary, that the superior advantages and happiness of persisting in this state of conversion, be set before him in very deep and affecting colours, so as to give him lasting impressions thereof, that will over-balance all the losses he may happen to suffer, and fortify him against all the temptations he may have to revolt? Such are the particular influences, which, in the case of a sudden change from vicious habits, to the contrary dispositions, must all at once, and of the sudden, immediately be exerted on human minds. And, to effect any such conversion on one single person, not to speak of great multitudes of people together; can this at any rate be pretended to lie within the reach of any human power whatsoever? It seems impossible to avoid apprehending, that the bringing about so sudden a conversion, must be the work of a Being, who has immediate access to our minds, who knows and sees all the most secret thoughts and motions of the heart, who has a power to dispose of them, and is able to make what impressions on us he shall judge best adapted to compass his purposes. So that, if
this

SECT. XXVI. *Christian Revelation.* 359

this sudden conversion be wrought, not on a single person only, but on thousands of people, all at once; must not the same be the work of a Being, who is intimately present to such numbers of different persons, all at the same time; who has thousands of human minds, all in one view, lying fully open and naked before him; who perfectly understands all the different biasses, that are hanging on every one of them; who distinctly perceives the infinite variety of thoughts, which, according to their several tempers, may be continually arising within them; and who, in all circumstances, can turn human hearts, without encroaching on human liberty, as the rivers of water, whithersoever he will? How one can judge otherwise, I am not able to conceive. And whether this does not directly point out to us that great Being, who is every-where present, before whom all things are naked and manifest in one simple view, whose goodness is beyond measure, and whose power is infinite, is what I leave the Reader to determine (y). For my part, I cannot but apprehend,

(y) Ὀυκ ἔστιν ἀνθρώπῳ ψιλῷ τοσαύτην ἐν βραχεῖ καιρῷ περιελθεῖν οἰκουμένην ᾗ γῆν ᾗ θάλατταν, ᾗ ἐπὶ τούτοις καλεῖν πράγμασιν οὕτω, ᾗ ταῦτα ὑπὸ ἀτόπου συνηθείας προκατειλημμένους ἀνθρώπους, μᾶλλον δὲ ὑπὸ τοσαύτης κακίας κατεχομένους. ᾗ ὅμως ἴσχυσε τούτων πάντων τὸ τῶν ἀνθρώπων γένος ἐλευθερῶσαι, οὐχὶ Ῥωμαίους μόνον ἀλλὰ ᾗ Πέρσας, ᾗ ἁπλῶς τὰ τῶν βαρβάρων γένη. ᾗ ταῦτα κατώρθωσεν, οὐχ ὅπλοις χρώμενος, ο χρήματα δαπανῶν, ο στρατόπεδα κινῶν, ο πολέμους ἀναρριπίζων, ἀλλὰ δι' ἕνδεκα ἀνθρώπων τὴν ἀρχὴν ἀσήμων, εὐτελῶν, ἀμαθῶν, ἰδιωτῶν, πενήτων, γυμνῶν, ἀόπλων, ἀνυποδέτων, μονοχιτώνων. τί λέγω κατώρθωστε; πεῖσαι ἠδυνήθη τοσαῦτα φῦλα ἀνθρώπων, ο περὶ τῶν παρόντων μόνον, ἀλλὰ ᾗ περὶ τῶν μελλόντων [namely, περὶ ἀθανασίας, ᾗ περὶ ἀναστάσεως,

prehend, that those sudden thorough conversions, which, beyond question, were effected by the Ministry of the Apostles, are rather more miraculous, than healing the sick and raising the dead by a word only, which every body will own, are the effects of a power superior to the established laws of nature, and that can dispose of Beings in both worlds (z).

Thus,

σεως, ἢ τῶν ἀποῤῥήτων ἀγαθῶν.] φιλοσοφεῖν, ἢ νόμως πατρῴως ἀνασπᾶσαι, ἢ παλαια ἔθη τοσούτω ῥιζωθέντα χρόνω ἐκ ῥιζῶν ἀνελεῖν, ἢ ἕτερα ἀντιφυτεῦσαι, ἢ τῶν εὐκόλων ἀπαγαγόντα εἰς τὰ δύσκολα ἐμβάλειν τὰ αὐτοῦ. Chrysost. Demonst. Quod Christus sit Deus. p. 622. Oper. tom. vi. Chrysostom's reflections from p. 634. to the end of this Discourse, are so very pertinent, so much to the purpose of our present argument, that I could wish the Reader to take a view of them. The edition I use is that of Savil. an. 1612. Etonæ.

Ο δ' οἱ σώματα πολλὰ κάμνοντα θεραπεύοντες, ἀθεεὶ τυγχάνουσι τοῦ κατὰ τὴν ὑγίειαν τῶν σωμάτων τέλους· εἰ δὲ ἢ ψυχάς τις δύναιτο ἀπαλλάττειν τῆς κατὰ τὴν κακίαν χύσεως, ἢ ἀκολησημάτων, ἢ ἀδικοπραγημάτων, ἢ τῆς περὶ τὸ θεῖον καταφρονήσεως, ἢ δεῖξιν διδοίη τοῦ τοιούτου ἔργου, βελτιωθέντας τὸν ἀριθμὸν ἑκατὸν, ἔσω γὰρ ἐπὶ τοσούτων ὁ λόγος· οὐδὲ τοῦτον ἂν εὐλόγως φήσαί τις ἀθεεὶ λόγον τοσούτων κακῶν ἀπαλλακτικὸν ἐμπεποιηκέναι τοῖς ἑκατόν.—— ἐξετάζων δέ τις τὰ πράγματα, ὄψεται ὅτι μεῖζον τῆς ἀνθρωπίνης φύσεως ἐτόλμησεν ὁ Ἰησοῦς, ἢ τολμήσας ἤνυσε. Orig. contra Cels. lib. i. p. 21.

(z) Origen seems to judge rightly, when he apprehends, that, without the working of miracles, the Apostles would have failed in converting the world. But to assign miracles as the cause of those extraordinary conversions, would be very injudicious. It should seem, that some such sudden conversions happened in Origen's time, and he ascribes them to the influence of a certain spirit. The passage deserves the Reader's attention. He concludes it thus: Ἀλλὰ γὰρ Θεὸς μάρτυς τοῦ ἡμετέρου συνειδότος, βουλομένου οὐ διὰ ψευδῶν ἀπαγγελιῶν, ἀλλὰ διά τινος ἐναργείας ποικίλης συνιστάνειν τὴν Ἰησοῦ θείαν διδασκαλίαν. Orig. contra Cels. lib. i. p. 34, 35.

SECT. XXVI. *Christian Revelation.*

Thus, the speedy rapid success, that every-where attended the Gospel when first published, seems sufficient to satisfy every free-thinking and considerate man, that, as one might reasonably have expected, the instructions of those few who were employed to open the eyes of mankind, and *to turn them from darkness to light, and from the power of Satan unto God,* were powerfully seconded by the extraordinary favour and influences of Heaven, immediately exerted on human minds (*a*). Nor am I able to imagine, what can shake a man in the belief of this article? Some people, indeed, in order to break the credit

---

(*a*) Nonne vel hæc saltem fidem vobis faciunt argumenta credendi, quod jam per omnes terras in tam brevi tempore et parvo, immensi hujus sacramenta diffusa sunt? Quod nulla jam natio est tam barbari moris, et mansuetudinem nesciens, quæ non ejus amore versa, molliverit asperitatem suam, et in placidos sensus assumpta tranquillitate migraverit? Quod tam magnis ingeniis præditi, Oratores, Grammatici, Rhetores, Consulti juris, ac Medici, philosophiæ etiam secreta rimantes, magisteria hæc expetunt, spretis quibus paulo ante fidebant?———Quod cum genera pœnarum tanta sint a vobis proposita religionis hujus sequentibus leges, augeatur res magis, et contra omnes minas interdicta formidinum, animosius populus obnitatur, et ad credendi studium prohibitionis ipsius stimulis excitetur? Numquid hæc fieri passim et inaniter creditis, fortuitis incursibus adsumi has mentes? Itane istud non divinum et sacrum est, aut sine Deo eorum tantas animorum fieri conversiones, aut cum carnificis unci, aliique innumeri cruciatus impendeant crediturus, veluti quodam dulcedine atque amore correpti, cognitas accipiant rationes, atque mundi omnibus rebus præponant amicitias Christi? Nisi forte obtusi et fatui videntur hi vobis, qui per orbem jam totum conspirant, et coëunt in istius credulitatis assensum. Quid ergo? Vos soli sapientia conditi, atque intelligentiæ vi mera nescio quid aliud videtis et profundum? Soli esse nugas intelligitis hæc omnia? Soli verba et pueriles ineptias, ea quæ nobis promittimus principali ab rege ventura? Unde, quæso, est vobis tantum sapientiæ traditum? Unde acuminis, et vivacitatis tantum? Vel ex quibus scientiæ disciplinis tantum cordis assumere, divinationis tantum potuistis haurire? Arnob. lib. ii. p. 26.

credit of this argument, are pleased to take notice of the speedy and sudden propagation of Mahometism. Upon which I would beg leave to make this supposition, which, I hope, will not be judged extravagant.

A sober and learned Mathematician is discoursing of Sir *Isaac Newton*'s *Principia*, to a rude ignorant multitude, who do not so much as understand the first Rudiments of Geometry. Now, while he is thus entertaining them with things they are utterly unacquainted with; some of them are quite heedless and unconcerned, amusing themselves secretly in their own thoughts with those objects that are most familiar to their minds; and others stand gazing, having their senses only struck with figures and sounds, of which the mind, in thick darkness, has no understanding. But behold, all on a sudden, without the influence of any visible cause, the attention of the whole multitude is closely fixed, and their minds are all opened to the whole series of his demonstrations; so that they are quite ravished with those amazing truths that are laid before them, and become so much enamoured with such glorious discoveries, that ever after they pursue that kind of study, and, to the utmost of their power, propagate those principles to mankind. But,

By a melancholy turn of Providence, there starts up, some time after this, a cunning ambitious Sophist, who, having got together an armed force, goes about the world as an open usurper; and, with the sword at their throats, proposes to whatever number he gets in his power, to renounce all those principles, and to embrace the clean contrary. The poor creatures, quite confounded at this impending hazard of their lives, for their own preservation, are

forced

forced to comply: And this force still hanging over them, they continue in the profession of those new doctrines, till they have totally lost the sense of all their former principles: And their posterity being trained up in the same absurdities, they at length become the choice of a whole nation, tho' at first they had nothing to recommend or support them, but mere brutal force and violence.

I need make no reflections on these two very different events. Every body will allow, that the means whereby the latter was brought about, were most impious and execrable, plainly contradictory to the nature both of God and man: Whilst the cause that effected the former, was certainly more than human, something divine and supernatural. Were men as free from prejudice on the side of the Gospel, as they are with respect to the Mathematics; the Christian religion, I am well persuaded, would meet with the same justice, and among all men be acknowledged a revelation from Heaven, which God hath sent to bless us, in turning away every one of us from our iniquities.

So that, adding this article, *viz.* That the instructions of the Apostles were powerfully seconded by certain supernatural influences on human minds; I say, adding this article to what I have formerly explained, namely, that the first publishers of the Gospel were neither Impostors nor Enthusiasts, and must therefore have been commissioned from Heaven to instruct mankind; may not one hope, that these several articles taken together, will afford conviction to every fair and impartial inquirer, and fully satisfy him, as to the truth and divinity of our holy religion?

May

May thofe influences that attended the firft promulgation of the Gofpel, yet infpire the minds of men, and bring them to fee the things that belong to their peace, *before they be hid from their eyes.*

F I N I S.

Lightning Source UK Ltd.
Milton Keynes UK
UKHW020944281218
334535UK00003B/420/P